CARL HUBBELL

Five Fabulous Seasons that Paved the Way to Cooperstown

Ronald A. Mayer

Mechanicsburg, PA USA

Published by Sunbury Press, Inc.
Mechanicsburg, PA USA

www.sunburypress.com

For information about special discounts for bulk purchases, please contact Sunbury Press Orders Dept. at (855) 338-8359 or orders@sunburypress.com.

To request one of our authors for speaking engagements or book signings, please contact Sunbury Press Publicity Dept. at publicity@sunburypress.com.

FIRST SUNBURY PRESS EDITION: May 2021

Set in Adobe Garamond | Interior design by Crystal Devine | Cover by Lawrence Knorr | Edited by Lawrence Knorr.

Publisher's Cataloging-in-Publication Data
Names: Mayer, Ronald A., author.
Title: Carl Hubbell : five fabulous seasons that paved the way to Cooperstown / Ronald A. Mayer.
Description: What made Carl Hubbell one of the greatest left-handed pitchers ever? It boils down to two things: his remarkable control and one of the best screwballs in baseball history. In Carl Hubbell, baseball historian Ronald Mayer tells the story of how Hubbell's five-year run from 1933 to 1937 cemented his legacy as one of the greatest pitchers of all time.
Identifiers: ISBN : 978-1-62006-481-8 (softcover).
Subjects: BIOGRAPHY & AUTOBIOGRAPHY / Sports | SPORTS & RECREATION / Baseball / General | SPORTS & RECREATION / Baseball / History.

Product of the United States of America
0 1 1 2 3 5 8 13 21 34 55

Continue the Enlightenment!

Also by
Ronald A. Mayer

The 1937 Newark Bears: A Baseball Legend

Perfect! 14 Pitchers of "Perfect" Games

The New Jersey Book of Lists (With Gerald Tomlinson)

Christy Mathewson:
A Game-by-Game Profile of a Legendary Pitcher

The 1923 New York Yankees:
A History of Their First World Championship Season

The 1932 New York Yankees:
The Story of a Legendary Team A Remarkable Season and a
Wild World Series

Baseball Memories . . .
A Collection of 101 Poems Celebrating immortal players, Classic
Games and Wacky Events of The National Pastime

Contents

Acknowledgments

Special thanks to Jacqueline Bacilo, Nancy Mayer, and Glenn Mayer for their timely technical advice; Cassidy Lent, Reference Librarian at A. Bartlett Giamatti Research Center in Cooperstown, New York, for tirelessly providing information about Hubbell and other players; Denis Reagan, Richard Clark, and Joe DeFerrari for their interest and encouragement; Pat Clark, my chief book scout; Debbie DiStasio, Technical Services Specialist at the East Hanover Library for providing critical baseball books. And my wife, Arlene, for her years of patience and understanding.

PREFACE

Carl Owen Hubbell pitched for the New York Giants from 1928 to 1943. During these 16 years, the left-hander won 253 games and lost 154 for a phenomenal .622 winning percentage. He led the Giants to three National League pennants (1933, 1936, and 1937) and one World Championship in 1933. Hubbell was a two-time MVP award winner and a nine-time All-Star. He also led the National League three times in both wins and earned run average. He was called "King Carl" and the "Meal Ticket" for obvious reasons. Carl Hubbell was elected to the Hall of Fame in 1947.

What made Hubbell one of the great left-handers of all time? In the author's opinion, and others, two factors: his remarkable control and his phenomenal screwball. Pitching 3,590.1 innings, he allowed only a mere 1.8 walks per nine innings. That is a lesson in painting the corners. His total mastery of the screwball was the other reason. As is well known, the screwball, thrown by a southpaw, breaks away from right-handed batters but also tends to slow down as it approaches the plate, which acts as an off-speed pitch. It is a double whammy for right-handed hitters. Hubbell, Harry Brecheen, Warren Spahn, Mike Cuellar, Fernando Valenzuela, and Tug McGraw all successfully threw the screwball.

From 1933 to 1937 Carl Hubbell turned in five seasons of masterful baseball. He won 115 and lost 50 for an outstanding .697 winning percentage. During this period, his pitching performance established him as one of the great left-handers of all time, including Sandy Koufax, Warren Spahn, Randy Johnson, Lefty Grove, and Steve Carlton, to name just a few. It catapulted him into the Cooperstown Hall of Fame. Beginning in 1933, Hubbell won 21 or more games each season through 1937.

YEAR	WON	LOST	%	ERA
1933	23	12	.657	1.66
1934	21	12	.636	2.30
1935	23	12	.657	3.27
1936	26	6	.813	2.31
1937	22	8	.733	3.20

In 1933, besides the Giants winning the pennant and World Series, Hubbell managed to record ten shutouts and compile a streak of 45 1/3 scoreless innings. Orel Hershiser holds the record at 59. He also was voted the Most Valuable Player and led the league in victories and earned run average. Moreover, in 1936 and 1937, he won 24 consecutive games, which still stands today. In fact, at the rate baseball is changing, this record, along with Joe DiMaggio's 56-game hitting streak, may never be broken. I say this with extreme caution, recalling the pundits who said, very emphatically, Lou Gehrig's consecutive games played and Babe Ruth's single-season and career home run records would never be broken. Also, in '36, Hubbell took home another MVP award and led the National League in wins, winning percentage, and era. In '37, he once again led the league in total wins, winning percentage, and strikeouts.

I must tell you upfront, so you are not misled; this book is not a biography. It is the story of how an Oklahoma farm boy rose to the major leagues, struggled, and in five years (1933-1937) pitched so brilliantly he was voted into the Hall of Fame. There is some personal information regarding Hubbell's life, but that will be left to his biographers to expand. I focused on the fabulous five seasons and tracked every game Hubbell pitched as a starter or in relief. This book will focus on the seasons and time frame in great detail, both the happy moments and those not so happy.

But there is more to these five seasons at the Polo Grounds than Carl Hubbell. The Giants were led by their great first baseman and future Hall of Famer Bill Terry, who took over the managerial reins from John McGraw, who suddenly resigned in early 1932 due to ill health. Mel Ott, another future Hall of Famer, and Terry were the major offensive threats. Ott's unorthodox left-handed swing was perfectly suited for the short right field (257') wall at the Polo Grounds. He was the first National League player to hit 500 home runs. Ott was aided by Jo-Jo Moore, a left-handed slap hitter who played left field for 12 years with the Giants. Although he was at the top of the batting order, he rarely walked, being a notorious first-ball hitter. He batted over .300 five times and was a solid, dependable player. Gus Mancuso, an outstanding defensive catcher, handled the Giants' exceptional pitching staff. Slow footed, he did manage to bat a respectable .265 for his career. Manager Terry credited the acquisition of Gus as a major factor in the team going from sixth place in 1932 to a pennant and World Series in 1933.

Pitching was the New York Giants' strength during the five fabulous seasons. Hubbell was the ace, but Hal Schumacher joined him for all five seasons, Freddie Fitzsimmons for four, and Roy Parmelee, Slick Castleman, Al Smith, Harry Gumbert, and Cliff Melton at various times. During this period, the Giants' pitching staff led the National League three times and second once.

No doubt, these five fabulous seasons were appreciated by his teammates, Giant fans, the media, and even his peers. "Cubs second baseman Billy Herman said his team's bench emptied when Hubbell was on the mound, as players stood on the dugout steps to watch Hubbell at work, mixing his screwball, curve, change-up, and fastball. He didn't have overpowering stuff, but he was a marvel to watch."[1] You may not be able to stand at the dugout steps like the Chicago Cubs players and watch Hubbell, but you can sit back and read how this left-hander pitched brilliantly during this unprecedented period in his baseball career.

1

A Bumpy Road to the Major Leagues

". . . I WAS LEARNING BY MY OWN EXPERIENCE THAT
THE BEST BALL I HAD WAS THE SCREWBALL."

Carl Owen Hubbell was born on June 22, 1903, to George and Margaret Hubbell. Both parents were also born in the United States. Most, if not all, information has Carl being born in Carthage, Missouri. However, there is one exception. Fritz A. Buckallew notes in his biography Carl's father, George Owen, would tell friends his son was not born in Carthage but rather ". . . in a farmhouse one-half mile north of Red Oak, Missouri, in Lawrence County, twenty miles northeast of Carthage."[1]

Regardless, the date is correct and the fact that Carl was one of seven children, all boys except for Dorothy (in another biography, the sister's name is given as Mildred). Early on, the Hubbell family moved to Meeker, Oklahoma, and a hard life of farming. Years later, in an interview with Rod Roberts, Hubbell was asked what year he moved to Meeker. "Oh, I guess around 1907 or 1908. We moved there when it was Indian Territory. Then it became the 47th state [actually the 46th]. It became a state in 1907."[2] Carl's dad was a tenant farmer who raised cotton and Pecans. The boys all worked long, hard hours on the farm, as most young men did in those days.

It appears the boys all took to sports activities as long as their farm chores were completed, which probably left little time for baseball, which was fast becoming popular around the country. Playing fields and equipment were almost non-existent for the Hubbell boys. It was not uncommon to put together a makeshift ball out of saved twine. Hubbell recalls playing catch with his brothers and one ol' cat, an early form of the game as we know it today. Young Carl also developed strong arms from his daily farm chores, which, no doubt, helped his pitching as he entered high school and beyond.

High school baseball today is well organized, with tryouts for freshman, JV, and varsity teams. Equipment is available whether from the school or owned by the young boy. Leagues are formed among the various high schools, along with schedules for the regular season and state tournaments. It is not uncommon for major league or college scouts to appear at games to keep tabs on potential future major league kids.

When Hubbell went to high school, this situation wasn't even dreamed of. In the *St. Louis Star-Times* sports editor Sid C. Keener interviewed Hubbell in an article entitled, "Carl Hubbell Reveals His Secrets." In it, Hubbell spoke about his early days growing up. "You see, boys around a farm do not have much time for athletics, except baseball. There are no cinder tracks, swimming pools, golf courses, tennis courts, or football gridirons. Only plenty of grass acreage, as it happened that several other boys and myself would get together for some baseball tossing. That was our recreation.

"We made a baseball of yarn, whittled a tree limb for a bat, and used rocks for our bases. We fussed around like that for several years, and finally, at high school, I played on my first regulation team."[3]

The Meeker High School coach, Jeff Hampton, picked Hubbell to be the pitcher because he was the tallest kid who played ball, and he was left-handed. One must believe the coach saw more than those two attributes in the young farm boy, or Hubbell was being modest. This was Hubbell's junior year. "Never did anything but pitch," he says. "Never was interested in anything else."

According to author Buckallew, "Meeker High won the 1922 Class C state tournament in Norman by defeating Lexington 10-1 and Tuttle 5-1 in 17 innings. Hubbell's line at the tournament would become familiar: 2 hits, 17 strikeouts, 1 base on balls."[4] The "C" classification indicated the category of a small town.

Apparently, the baseball bug bit Carl Hubbell for the youngster was "crazy" about playing ball. Like a lot of young kids, he had dreams of playing professional baseball. At this age, it wasn't about money or being a big leaguer. It was about playing every day.

Despite the long hours working the farm, Hubbell found time to play ball on Sunday, pitching for one of the nearby town teams. From all accounts, his first paid game was in Sparks, Oklahoma. As the story goes, he rode his horse nine miles to play the game, which he won 1-0. He was paid $1.00. He also, on occasion, pitched for Meeker's town team.

Hubbell's interest in the game extended to following the events in minor league baseball. He would read the box scores and write-ups of the Western League games and couldn't believe young men played the game every day and didn't have to work a real job. And they got paid to play, which stimulated young Hubbell's thinking. At the time, he was working in the oil fields near Tulsa, according to Hubbell, a dirty and messy job. It didn't take him long to decide to give minor league baseball a try.

"But then you see, there was no farm system, no scout system, no nothing, and all clubs were independent minor league clubs, independent big-league clubs. The big-league clubs bought their players from the minor leagues."[5]

But that was only half the problem. The other half was trying to get a try-out with one of the minor league clubs. So, Hubbell decided to give professional baseball a try. If it didn't work out for him, he could always return to the oil fields, was his thinking. So, Hubbell hopped a train to nearby Cushing. The Cushing Refiners team was a member of the Class D Oklahoma State League. According to Hubbell, he was responsible for getting himself signed by the manager of the Cushing club. First, he pitched batting practice and was impressive enough to have the manager, Ned Pettigrew, sign him to his first contract. In his interview with Roberts, Hubbell does not mention the influence of Ott Reding, a Meeker furniture store manager. Reding knew Pettigrew and convinced him to give Hubbell a look-see. Regardless of the omission, if there was one, Carl Hubbell signed his first professional contract with Cushing in 1923. His salary was $125 a month, which was $5 more than he was making working in the oil fields. He was 20 years old. Hubbell would spend the next five years honing his craft in the minor leagues.

In May 1937, Sid C. Keener of the *St. Louis Star-Times* interviewed Hubbell, who at the time was a star with the New York Giants. They discussed his early days in the minor leagues. "I owe everything I've made in baseball to Ned Pettigrew, manager of the Cushing club," he said. "The team was in first place when I reported. We lost our first five games with me on the squad. The boys held an indignation meeting after the fifth defeat and voted unanimously to have me fired. They said I was a jinx on the bench. Luckily, Pettigrew would have none of that. I won seven of my ten games that year, returned to Cushing in 1924 . . ."[6]

Hubbell's second year in the Oklahoma State League didn't last long. Sometime in July of 1924, the league collapsed, and the franchises were reshaped. Hubbell was transferred to Ardmore, Oklahoma, in the Western Association. With Ardmore, his record was 1-1.

No doubt this was discouraging news to young Hubbell but turned out to be a blessing in disguise. He was notified the Oklahoma Indians of the Western League (Class A) had acquired his contract. He pitched only briefly for the Indians before contracting typhoid fever. Fortunately, Hubbell recovered completely during the offseason and was physically and mentally ready for the 1925 season with his new manager Ned Pettigrew!

It would not be too far an exaggeration to claim 1925 was one of Carl Hubbell's major turning points on his road to Cooperstown. Of course, there would be others, but this was the year the left-hander began tinkering with what would eventually be called his screwball.

Before 1925, Hubbell was experimenting with different pitches. He knew his fast ball and curve would not get him to the major leagues. As far as mechanics and pitching knowledge, Hubbell was a novice. He admitted he had no idea what pitching was all about, that is, until he observed a left-hander by the name of Clarence (Lefty) Thomas. It seems Hubbell was impressed with Thomas. His fast ball would sink and induce ground balls by right-handed batters. In fact, Thomas was performing so well he was called up to the American League pennant-winning Washington Senators on September 26. He pitched in two games, lost both, but turned in a very impressive 2.08 earned run average. The following year Thomas pitched in only 8.2 innings, with no-decisions, before he was sent down to Rochester in the International League (AA), and in 1927 was demoted to Hartford (A) in the Eastern League. Lefty Thomas never returned to the major leagues.

Despite Thomas not teaching Hubbell a particular pitch, he influenced his thinking, which led to his experimentation. Years later, when Hubbell earned his reputation and was now called "King Carl" and the "Meal Ticket," he recalled in a *St. Louis Star-Times* interview his eureka moment. It happened in a game with Oklahoma City. On one delivery, he lost control of the ball as it slipped off his forefinger. "The sphere, moving a bit in the palm, shot off the second finger, took a peculiar drop approaching the plate, and the batter missed it by a foot. I experimented with that thing for the remainder of the game. I noted it became a semi-slow ball, dropped away from right-handed batters, and curved in on the left-handers.

"The batters seemed to have difficulty hitting it solidly. When I used the fast one or the wide curve, they'd whack it high and far. I was learning by my own experience that the best ball I had was the screwball."[7]

Hubbell would continue to perfect the pitch that would eventually become his famous trademark during the 1925 season at Oklahoma City. Actually, the screwball was first made famous by Christy Mathewson back in the early 1900's Deadball Era. At that time, Mathewson called it his fadeaway. Although Mathewson was right-handed, the movement on the ball was similar. To right-handed batters, Matty's ball would move towards them and away from lefties, whereas Hubbell's ball to left-handed batters would move towards them and away from righties.

But the comparison between Hubbell and Mathewson goes beyond the screwball and fadeaway. They were smart, savvy, and crafty pitchers. They used their brain, not just their arms. Also, their personalities were similar. They were quiet, humble, and did not seek celebrity or center stage. They both pitched for the New York Giants and were leaders of their respective pitching staffs. Finally, both had excellent control. One can only imagine what it would have been like if both these giants of the mound were teammates—Matty throwing his fade-away to right-handed batters and Hubbell his screwball to the lefties. An opposing manager would be dizzy trying to settle on a lineup!

Pitching for the Oklahoma City Indians in 1925, Hubbell would throw 285 innings, the most during his entire minor league career. It was quite a workload for a young man, just beginning a professional career in baseball. But Hubbell held up and turned in an eye-opening 17-13 record with a 4.01 earned run average. At this point in his career, Hubbell was still working on his control. He walked 108 batters for an average of four per game. No doubt experimenting with the screwball was a factor. He also was fine-tuning his curve and still developing what eventually would become his outpitch, the screwball.

It wasn't just the Oklahoma fans who recognized a future major leaguer in Carl Hubbell. Some credit must be given to John Holland, the owner of the Oklahoma City Indians, who recognized he had a valuable asset in 22-year-old Carl Hubbell. In his biography of Hubbell, Lowell L. Blaisdell claims, "Holland made his living or at least some of it, by developing promising youthful baseball players, then selling them to higher category minor league teams, or better yet, to major league teams. He acquired the reputation of being an especially shrewd detector of pitching potential."[8]

Holland certainly was on point in Hubbell's case. As Blaisdell points out, he sold his star pitcher to the Detroit Tigers for a reported $20,000. Hubbell, now the property of the Detroit Tigers, reported to spring training camp in 1926. This was when the controversy began as to who let Hubbell get away from the Detroit franchise. Was it Ty Cobb, who was the manager at the time? Was it George McBride, one of the coaches? Or was it someone else or another reason that never surfaced?

Accounts differ, but whatever the answer, this is what happened, according to Hubbell, when asked about throwing the screwball at his first Tiger camp. "Ty Cobb never said one word to me in three years while I was with him. George McBride was the [one], there wasn't but two coaches there, and they were just first and third base. They weren't teachers of no kind or anything," said Hubbell. As the story unfolds, Hubbell was warming up with catcher Johnny Bassler one day and throwing the screwball. "I was throwing it and everything else, and that is when George McBride came up and said, 'what is that?' And I said, 'the screwball.' He said, 'Forget that.' Well, I forgot that, and they forgot Hubbell.

"But the thing I couldn't figure out is why they kept me for three years, and I never pitched one inning of an exhibition game, not even an exhibition game for Detroit."[9]

Interestingly, in the interview, Hubbell did not mention Ty Cobb's name, but in Buckallew's biography, he quotes McBride as saying, "Cobb says to lay off that screwball." The reasoning behind it was that it would eventually ruin your arm as it did to Hub Pruett. But according to Pruett, his "injury was due to overwork, not his fadeaway." In 1922 he pitched in six or seven straight games, and that's when he hurt his arm.

The Pruett story is a fascinating one. The southpaw pitched for four different major league teams during his seven-year career. He was not an effective major league pitcher, finishing his career with a 29-48 record and an inflated 4.63 earned run average. His best year was in 1922, at age 21; he turned in a 7-7 record with a respectable 2.33 earned run average, pitching for the second place St. Louis Browns. So, what was his claim to fame? He owned Babe Ruth! And the fadeaway pitch was the key. And how did Pruett develop the fadeaway? He simply copied Christy Mathewson, his idol, when he was growing up. He reasoned if a right-hander could throw the fadeaway, so could a lefty.

"Pruett spent three seasons in the American League and came in contact with Ruth 30 times. The 'Colossus of Clout' managed only four hits in 21 official at-bats, translating to a microscopic .190 average. Ruth grounded out twice, hit one sacrifice fly, coaxed eight walks, hit one homer, and whiffed 15 times, exactly half the time they battled."[10]

Regardless of Pruett's comment about his injury, Matty knew the screwball put a strain on your arm. So, he used it sparingly during key moments of a tight game. Conversely, Hubbell used his screwball throughout the game, and eventually, he paid the price. In later years his left arm and wrist became deformed.

Although Pruett was out of baseball by 1932, his life was just beginning. He earned his MD degree the same year from St. Louis University and practiced for over 40 years in the St. Louis area. However, there is one final word on this unique story. It occurred about two months before Ruth's death. Pruett met up with the Babe at a baseball dinner held at the Chase Hotel. "I went up and introduced myself and said, 'Thanks Babe, for putting me through medical school. If it hadn't been for you, nobody would have ever heard of me.' The Babe remembered me."

"That's all right, kid," he rasped, stricken with throat cancer. "I'm glad there weren't many more like you, or no one would have heard of me."[11]

In 1926, after a quick look at Hubbell, the young and inexperienced southpaw was sent to the Toronto Maple Leafs in the Class AA International League. It was a promotion for Hubbell and one he deserved based on his performance with Oklahoma City. He was also going to be playing in the brand-new Maple Leaf Stadium. With Toronto, Hubbell won 7 and lost 7 with a 3.77 earned run average. He pitched in 93 innings, mostly in relief, a far cry from the workhorse he was at Oklahoma City. Once again, this time by Toronto manager Dan Howley, Hubbell was told not to throw the screwball. Apparently, word came down from the Tiger's organization.

In hindsight, it appears several factors were hurting Hubbell's chances to be noticed at Toronto, despite the team winning the championship with a sterling 109-57 record. He went unnoticed among an outstanding four-man rotation: Ownie Carroll (21-8), Lefty Stewart (18-9), Jess Doyle (15-7), and Jim Faulkner (15-12). Add Vic Sorrell (8-0), and it is understandable why Hubbell was overlooked at this stage in his development. These five hurlers accounted for over 70% of the 109 victories. Also, Hubbell was still restricted from using his screwball. Finally, issuing free passes to batters at the rate of over four per game was not helping his cause.

Not surprisingly, Toronto manager Howley did not use Hubbell in the Little World Series against Louisville of the American Association. In fact, Hubbell didn't even appear in relief. But Hubbell did have moments when he excelled. In the 1920s, it was the practice of major league clubs to play a minor league team on an off day. Can you imagine that happening today with tight schedules, bloated salaries, and a strong union? It would be highly unlikely. Back then, it was different. Hubbell appeared in three exhibition games.

"Hubbell started for the Leafs against the defending American League Champion Washington Senators on June 3 and pitched a 5-hit shutout, striking out star players Joe Judge, Sam Rice, and Goose Goslin to the thunderous applause of the Toronto fans. On July 7, Hubbell was again given the ball in an exhibition game and threw another complete-game victory, holding the Detroit Tigers to three hits, all of them singles. The *Globe* wrote that "'Carl Hubbell is rapidly forging to the front as a giant-killer,' adding that 'Hubbell's benders made the alleged sluggers wearing Detroit regalia look very ordinary.'"[12]

Either luck or skill ran out on Hubbell late in the season when he faced the New York Yankees in another exhibition game. Despite fanning Babe Ruth in the first inning and carrying a 2-1 lead into the eighth, according to the *Torontoist*, Hubbell was "pounded . . . all over the park." Two out of three victories against major league batters still didn't impress the Tiger brass.

The winter season had barely begun when shock waves reverberated throughout the baseball world. On November 3, 1926, Ty Cobb, one of the Deadball Era's great players, announced his resignation. Cobb had been the player/manager of the Detroit Tigers for the last six years but never winning a pennant. Less than a month later, on November 29, Tris Speaker, another baseball superstar, suddenly stepped down as player/manager of the second-place Cleveland Indians. Speaker fared better at the helm than Cobb, winning the American League pennant and World Series in 1920. Both claimed they were retiring from the game.

The public reaction at first was one of surprise, then suspicion. Questions began to surface. Why was Cobb suddenly unavailable to the press and public? Why did Speaker quit after guiding the Indians to a second-place finish, three games back of the Yankees? Days before Christmas, Commissioner Kenesaw Landis provided the shocking answer. He allowed Cobb and Speaker to resign based on accusations they fixed and bet on the Detroit/Cleveland game on September 25, 1919, seven years prior. This was dynamite news.

However, the evidence consisted of two letters received by pitcher "Dutch" Leonard, a member of the 1919 Tigers but did not play in the questionable game. One letter came from Cobb, the other letter from "Smokey" Joe Wood, a Tiger pitcher/outfielder, who also did not play in the September 25 game.

Landis, with copies of both letters, began his interrogation of Cobb and Wood. Leonard refused to travel to Chicago to meet with Landis for fear of reprisal by Cobb, who was known to be a violent man at times and carried a gun. Oddly, Speaker was never questioned by Landis, according to Cobb's biographer Al Stump. The letters were damaging and indicated betting was discussed along with amounts of money but vague enough to leave doubts of what occurred. Landis, at his office, put the suspects through direct, no-nonsense questioning. Nothing came out of the hearing. After a month's delay, on January 26, 1927, Landis made his decision.

"This is the Cobb-Speaker case," he said. "These players have not been, nor are they now, found guilty of fixing a ball game. By no decent system of justice could such a finding be made." Case closed. Cobb went on to play the next two seasons with the Philadelphia Athletics before retiring. Speaker played one year for the Washington Senators and joined the Athletics the following season, playing alongside Cobb. He, too, retired after the 1928 season.

Human nature being what it is, Hubbell must have been informed about the Cobb-Speaker case. It is also safe to assume he was equally, if not more so, interested in where his career was headed in 1927. The new manager for the Tigers was George Moriarty, who at the time he was named was umpiring in the American League. This was after a 12-year major league career as a third baseman with four different teams, seven of which were the Tigers. Moriarty's downfall as a manager was a lack of experience except for one year managing the Memphis Chicks in the Southern Association. So, it was clear Moriarty had no idea Hubbell was a star in waiting.

Instead of getting invited to the Tigers spring training camp, Hubbell was sent to the Fort Worth Cats in the Texas League. It was a downward move since the Texas League was classified A. Hubbell was not happy with the move. Fortunately for Hubbell, his stay with the Cats was short. He pitched a total of 6.1 innings, starting one game and relieving in three. His record was 0-1 with an elevated 5.68 earned run average, stats that reveal nothing of what Hubbell was capable of performing.

Once again, Hubbell was on the move. This time he was sent to the Decatur Commodores in the Illinois-Indiana-Iowa League, popularly known as the Three-I League. Still the property of the Detroit Tigers, it is difficult to understand the thinking of the men who ran the organization's minor league clubs. The Commodores in 1927 were Classified B. Hubbell was headed in the wrong direction. Despite being discouraged and seriously thinking of another profession, he turned in a fine season with Decatur. He won 14 and lost 7 with a 2.53 ERA. He pitched in 185 innings and started 21 of the 23 games. This performance earned him another invitation to spring training with the Tigers in 1928.

Quoting Yogi, it turned out to be déjà vu all over again. It appeared the Tigers wanted no part of Hubbell, so they sent the 25-year-old southpaw to the Beaumont Exporters in the Class A Texas League. This was the third time Hubbell was "farmed out." The magic number here is three. Major league regulations stated, if a prospect were optioned out for the third time, the club would lose the rights to him. And that was only the beginning of the good news for Hubbell. The manager at Beaumont was former catcher Claude Robertson who gave Hubbell his approval to throw the screwball. A little rusty at first trying to control the pitch, Hubbell began to win with practice and patience. He finished the 1928 season at Beaumont, sometime in the middle of July, with a 12-9 record and an earned run average of 2.97. He would never play in the minor leagues again!

Sometime during the 1928 season, the Detroit Tigers front office must have realized they goofed. Perhaps they received phone calls inquiring about Hubbell's availability by interested major league teams. The Cleveland Indians and New York Yankees were known to be interested in signing Hubbell.

But it appears from all that has been written about the Hubbell signing; the New York Giants had the inside track. With the approval of Giants' manager John McGraw, the man who signed Hubbell was super-scout Dick Kinsella, an interesting character in his own right. However, the circumstances surrounding the signing over the years have become a legend and almost as misleading as Babe Ruth's "called shot" in the 1932 World Series. The important fact remains, Kinsella discovered Hubbell, and the New York Giants signed him for $50,000 with some reports as low as $30,000.

Now back to Kinsella. According to Jim Sandoval in his SABR BioProject, Kinsella was quite a Renaissance man. He was involved in multiple activities throughout his career. At various times he owned a minor league team in the Three-I League. He was a scout for many years, mainly working for John Mc-Graw and the New York Giants. He also helped to organize the 1924 Giants/White Sox European tour. He was involved with the Democratic Party and even owned a painting business. He was an amateur violinist and built the first ballpark in Springfield, Illinois. His crowning achievement was bringing Hubbell to the New York Giants and baseball fans around the country.

So, at age 25, Carl Owen Hubbell, after five bumpy and frustrating years, was now on his way to the New York Giants. He would begin a major league career that will take him to Cooperstown and baseball's Hall of Fame.

2

An Eye-Opening Rookie Season

"I came out of a small town in Oklahoma and
suddenly, I was playing for John McGraw . . ."

In 1928 Carl Hubbell finally made his way out of the minor leagues to the famed
New York Giants, a once powerhouse team managed by the rough-and-tumble
John McGraw. The Giants played their home games at the Polo Grounds, a
ballpark with a long and storied history dating back to 1883 when they were
called the New York Gothams and played their first game. The generic name
Polo Grounds was acquired for apparent reasons; polo was played on the turf.
Two years later, the name Gothams was changed to the Giants. Over the next
several decades, the Giants moved their location and seating capacity to accom-
modate fans as interest in the game grew. "By 1911, the ballpark had a seating
capacity of 31,000 and was the largest stadium in baseball."

The Polo Grounds, built mainly of wood, caught fire and was destroyed.
The fire occurred on April 14, 1911, while the Giants were on the road. A
ballpark of steel and concrete replaced it with a seating capacity of 34,000. "It
was situated in a hollow overlooked by a mini-cliff known as Coogan's Bluff,
the old rectangular-shaped park was located near 155th St. in Manhattan, just
across the Harlem River from the Yankee Stadium."[1]

The proximity to Yankee Stadium in 1928 is fraught with irony. Before
1913, the New York Yankees were a struggling and floundering team playing in a rundown wooden structure called Hilltop Park. They were of little
competition to the mighty Giants. While the Yankee's ownership was deciding
what to do about a new ballpark, they became the tenants of the Polo Grounds
at $65,000 a year. At the time, McGraw and the Giants were the class of the

baseball world and the pride of New York. However, once Babe Ruth became a member of the Yankees in 1920, the situation changed dramatically. With Ruth leading the club, the Yankees' popularity soared, attendance increased, and the Giants found themselves competing for fans. Beginning in 1920, the tenants would outdraw the Giants at the Polo Grounds. This irritated the volatile McGraw, who eventually kicked the Yankees out by raising the rent to $100,000 only to see Yankee ownership in 1923 build a Cathedral-like ballpark almost across the street from McGraw's Polo Grounds, actually a quarter-mile south.

It is doubtful Hubbell knew much, if anything, about the history of the Polo Grounds. It wasn't necessary, anyway. What was critical for Hubbell to know in 1928 was the structure of his new workplace. When Hubbell arrived, the Polo Grounds looked like a bathtub or horseshoe. The left-field foul line was 279 feet from home plate; the right field a mere 258 feet. In addition, the left-field fence was 17 feet high compared to 11 feet in right field. The Polo Grounds was a pull hitter's delight and a dreadful headache for pitchers if they weren't careful. Also, in left field, the upper deck extended about 15 feet over the bottom wall. A high pop fly to left could land in the overhang for a cheap home run. If the overhang were not there, the left fielder would be able to make the catch.

The good news for pitchers was center field. According to the CBS News website, "Just hitting a home run over the center-field fence at the New York Giants' quirky ball ballpark was a Herculean feat. It was 483 feet to dead center, and four people ever did it—Luke Easter in a Negro League game, Hank Aaron, Lou Brock and [Joe] Adcock."[2]

Besides the Polo Grounds odd dimensions, new teammates, and fans, Hubbell had to play for manager John McGraw who already was a living legend by virtue of his winning record. Since 1902 McGraw led the Giants to 10 National League pennants and three World Series Championships. But this was 1928, and McGraw and his Giants hadn't won a pennant since 1924, and it appeared the team would fall short once again. These were not the best of conditions for a rookie to face. Plus, "McGraw was a fiery, driven competitor who did not suffer fools gladly and brawled, verbally and occasionally physically, frequently with the press, opposing managers and players, and even an umpire or two."[3]

One can only imagine what was going through Hubbell's mind as the young southpaw joined the Giants on July 18, 1928, in Chicago. He would be the fifth left-handed pitcher on the club. Ray Foley, an outfielder from Catholic

University, was given his unconditional release to make room for Hubbell. If nothing else, it would make a great trivia question.

Hubbell joined the Giants in Chicago at the Auditorium Hotel after a long train ride from Texas. He was nervous and tired as he entered the lobby and asked to see Jim Tierney, the Giants' road secretary. Several players were hanging around the lobby but paid little attention to the newcomer as he followed Tierney to the manager's suite.

According to writer Ed Fitzgerald, "meeting John McGraw was a momentous occasion in Carl Hubbell's young life. It would have been bad enough for such a shy person to meet the skipper of any major league ball club. But McGraw was the epitome of the rough, tough, dictatorial manager, famous for his rudeness to rookies, and Hubbell was anything but confident as he prepared for their meeting."[4]

Hubbell's anxiety stemmed from the fact he knew McGraw would ask about money. He had been making $400 a month in Beaumont and had made up his mind to ask for $500. But when McGraw asked how much he wanted, Hubbell was taken off guard and began rambling about how it would cost more "to get along up here." Then Hubbell ended by saying, "whatever you say is all right with me." McGraw shocked the young rookie by offering him $750 a month. Hubbell was so surprised all he could do was shake McGraw's hand and seal the deal.

At the time Hubbell joined the Giants, this was the makeup of the team (not the entire roster) for most of the 1928 season:

Catcher Shanty Hogan	Pitchers:
First Base Bill Terry	Left Larry Benton
Second Base Andy Cohen	Lefty Freddie Fitzsimmons
Shortstop Travis Jackson	Lefty Joe Genewich
Third Base Freddie Lindstrom	Lefty Vic Aldridge
Right Field Mel Ott	Lefty Carl Hubbell
Center Field Jimmy Welsh	Righty Jim Faulkner
Left Field Lefty O'Doul	

Before Hubbell's arrival, the Giants' western road trip began in Pittsburgh on July 6, where McGraw hoped to gain ground on the league-leading St. Louis Cardinals. It didn't happen as the Pirates took three of four. The situation worsened when the Giants moved on to St. Louis with the opportunity to move up in the standings facing the front running Cardinals. Once again, the Giants lost three of four as the Western road trip quickly became a disaster. In Cincinnati, hopes were revitalized somewhat when the Giants took three of four from the Reds. Larry Benton (15-4) began the series with a solid game allowing five hits and two runs for the 4-2 win. He was followed by Freddie Fitzsimmons (11-5), who tossed another gem, giving up six hits and one run for the 2-1 victory. Joe Genewich (5-9), who had been struggling, went ten innings for the 3-2 win. The Reds salvaged the last game of the series as the Giants finished the road trip with a miserable 6-10 record and left for the Polo Grounds in fourth place, 7½ games back of the first-place Cards. *The New York Times* greeted McGraw and his beat-up Giants with this headline: Battered Giants Home from West.

Back in the friendly confines of the Polo Grounds, the Giants suddenly did a complete flip flop. During the 19-game home stand, they would win 15 and lose only four but still trailed the Cardinals. Carl Hubbell finally got his chance to pitch in the major leagues. It happened on July 26, the third game into the home stand against the Pittsburgh Pirates. It wasn't pretty! Hubbell didn't make it out of the second inning. His pitching line read: 7 hits and 5 runs, 3 earned. No question, Hubbell was hit hard, but Lindstrom and Cohen's errors exacerbated the situation and led to McGraw pulling the rookie. Hubbell and the Giants lost the game 7-5. Hubbell was depressed and figured he would be back in Texas the next day. Years later, he recalled, "The next day, McGraw called me into his office, and my bags were already packed. Imagine my surprise when he told me not to worry, that he liked the way I challenged the hitters and that if the team had played better in the field, we'd have won."[5]

Perhaps McGraw was trying to build the rookie's confidence or better, yet his good mood might have stemmed from the night before when he had predicted Gene Tunney would defeat Tom Heeney in the World's Heavyweight Championship bout. The fight was held a short distance away at Yankee Stadium (the Bombers were in Detroit). It was Tunney's second defense of his title. The referee stopped the fight in the 11th round, giving Tunney the victory, who retired days later from the ring. It was common knowledge McGraw was known to wager a bet or two over the years.

Carl Hubbell's next appearance was three days later against the Chicago Cubs. The Giants were losing the second game of a doubleheader 3-1 entering the top of the ninth. McGraw sent in Hubbell to hold the Cubs, which he did, but the Giants failed to score in their half of the ninth and lost 3-1.

The Giants won the next two games, with Hubbell picking up his first major league victory in relief. Fitzsimmons started the game and was pounded hard, giving up seven runs on nine hits in eight innings. In the eighth, with the score 3-2, Fitzsimmons allowed four more runs when Kiki Cuyler hit a three-run homer followed by a solo shot off Cliff Heathcote's bat, giving the Cubs a 7-2 lead. The Giants scored in the bottom of the eighth, making the score 7-3. McGraw called on Hubbell once again to mop up, which he did in fine fashion. Little did the 30,000 frantic fans know their Giants would rally for five runs, all with two out, to win the game 8-7 and hand Hubbell his first victory.

In the second game, Bill Walker started and gave up four runs in the fifth, but the Giants fought back with three of their own. McGraw pressing his luck, went to the well once too often, calling on Hubbell. Over the next three innings, Hubbell gave back three runs and was relieved by Chet Nichols. The final score was 10-4 Cubs.

August began with no game scheduled as the Giants awaited Cincinnati's arrival to the Polo Grounds to begin a four-game series. From this point on, the New York Giants dominated the home-stand. They swept the Reds four straight, won two of three from the Cardinals and two from the Cubs to finish out the home-stand. Up and down the lineup, almost everyone contributed, O'Doul, Ott, Lindstrom, Terry, Jackson, Cohen, and Hogan. As evidence, in the last two games of the Cincinnati sweep, the Giants had 38 hits producing 23 runs.

When the St. Louis Cardinals arrived, it couldn't have come at a better time. The Giants were 5½ games back of the league leaders, so the three-game series was important now that the dog days of August had arrived. McGraw chose right-hander Jim Faulkner to start the game but quickly yanked him as the Cards scored three runs in the first and another in the third inning with runners on first and third with one out. Not wanting to let the game get out of hand, McGraw had seen enough. Showing great confidence in his rookie southpaw, he called on Hubbell to stop the bleeding, which he did by inducing a ground ball double play. Then for the next 11 innings, Hubbell blanked the league leaders, allowing a measly three hits. In the meantime, the red-hot Giants managed to tie the game at 4-4 with the help of a two-run homer by Travis Jackson.

In the 15th inning Hubbell finally tired. No doubt the heat and humidity (it was a brutal summer day in New York) and pitch count took their toll. Hubbell allowed two runs while reliever Hal Haid shut the Giants down. The final score was 6-4. The Giants were now 6½ games back. But Hubbell had given his all, lost a heartbreaker, as his record stood at 1-2. A performance like this had to impress the hard-nosed John McGraw. It also taught Hubbell a lesson. Years later, in an interview, he recalled: "I learned that even the best hitters in the major leagues couldn't hit the screwball when it was breaking properly. Right then and there, I decided that it would be my bread-and-butter pitch, regardless of what it would do to my arm."[6]

Despite the 15-inning loss, McGraw had his team still confident and fighting as they whipped the Cardinals the next two games, 10-1 and 10-5. In the 10-1 game, Benton pitched superbly, winning his 18th of the season with Lindstrom driving in half the runs. In the 10-5 win, Genewich picked up his ninth victory with help from Walker and Aldridge. Offensively it was a team effort with 15 hits spread throughout the lineup. The second-place Giants were now only 4½ games back of the Cards.

Four days later, McGraw didn't hesitate to call on Hubbell, who pitched magnificently, blanking the Phillies at Philadelphia on six hits while walking only one batter. It was Hubbell's first shutout of his major league career. He would go on to throw 35 more over 16 years. The final score was 4-0. His record was now 2-2. Shortstop Travis Jackson drove in all four runs with one of his two hits, a three-run blast.

Travis Jackson was born in Waldo, Arkansas, on November 2, 1903, to William and Etta Jackson. He was the only child, and according to Travis, he was spoiled. His dad would play catch with him for hours when he was growing up. These sessions instilled a love of the game in Jackson. He played as often as he could with teams during the summers. "They had an excellent bunch of semipro teams up in Marvell, Holly, Grove, Clarendon, and Marianna, and so I jerked soda there at the drugstore and at night, and on Friday and Saturday we'd play ball games," he recalled years later.[7]

In 1921, Jackson landed a job with the Little Rock Travelers in the Class A Southern Association league managed by Kid Elberfeld. Also, Ouachita Baptist College records indicate Jackson was the freshman class president in the 1921-1922 school year, "but was then bought by the New York Giants and left school." The few mentions of Jackson and college in biographies have him graduating with a BS degree. Ouachita College (now a University) has no record in either school yearbooks or newspapers that Jackson ever graduated or completed a degree.

Over a 14-year major league career, Elberfeld played the infield for six different teams in both leagues. He knew his way around the diamond and was a scout for McGraw. Upon Elberfeld's recommendation, McGraw signed the young shortstop. His first year with Little Rock, Jackson played in only 39 games and batted a weak .200. His second year with the Travelers, Jackson played in 147 games and batted a much improved .280, and showed some speed with 18 doubles, 9 triples. He even hit seven home runs, but the long ball was not his strength. However, one of his eye-opening stats was his whopping 73 errors (.910 fielding %). Eventually, the young and inexperienced shortstop would become one of the best defensively.

Jackson clearly remembered the 73 errors. "I guess I set a world record for errors, at least a league record. I had a pretty good arm, see, but I didn't have much control. And even if I booted a ball, I had to throw it. A lot of those were double errors—two on the same play, a boot, and then a wild throw. The people in the first base and right-field bleachers knew me. When the ball was hit to me, they scattered."[8]

At the tail end of the 1922 season, the Giants, having already clinched the pennant, called up Jackson. He played in three games and went hitless in eight at-bats. The Giants, for the second straight year, beat the Yankees in the World Series. Jackson didn't play, probably because of eligibility rules.

At the beginning of the 1923 season, Dave Bancroft appeared to be the Giants shortstop of the future. But early on in the season, he experienced leg pains. Moreover, by late June, he contracted the flu and was out of the lineup for six weeks. This gave Jackson a golden opportunity to prove to McGraw he could handle the job. The 19-year-old shortstop played the position well and batted .275. No question, McGraw liked what he saw. After the season, Bancroft was traded to the Boston Braves with Casey Stengel for Billy Southworth. The Yankees finally beat the Giants four games to two in the World Series for their first World Championship. Jackson's only appearance was in game two as a pinch hitter. McGraw took the defeat hard but, in the end, before the press, uncharacteristically became the good loser. "The best team won; there's no disputing that," he said.

In 1924 Travis Jackson was now the everyday shortstop for the New York Giants at age 20 as McGraw's men won their fourth consecutive National League pennant, a first in major league baseball. But it was a struggle as they had to beat out the pesky Brooklyn Dodgers by 1½ games. Jackson responded well, playing in 151 games and batting a solid .302. He also demonstrated occasional power and clutch hitting with 11 home runs and 76 RBIs. The Giants' challengers in the World Series were the Washington Senators led by the immortal Walter Johnson. The exciting series went to game seven. After two defeats, Johnson entered the game (on one day's rest) in the top of the ninth with the score tied at 3-3. He blanked the Giants for the next four innings. The Senators scored in the bottom of the 12th to give Washington and Johnson their first World Series Championship. Jackson had a miserable series as he batted .074, going 2 for 27. He would also appear in two more Series in 1933 and 1936, turning in averages of .222 and .190. His four Series totals are ugly—10 for 67 for a .149 average.

From 1925 until his retirement as an active player in 1936, Jackson batted over .300 five times. His best season was in 1930, when he hit .339. The most home runs he hit was 21 in 1929, and late in his career (1934), he drove in 101 runs. Travis Jackson's lifetime batting average was a highly respectable .291. Unquestionably he was a productive hitter. In addition, Casey Stengel once said, "he was the greatest bunter he ever saw." Perhaps the added pressure of the World Series played a role. It's anyone's guess.

But defense was his strength. The 5'10" 160-pound Jackson had a strong arm and could range far and wide, resulting in two interesting career stats. He led the National League in assists four times but also twice in errors. It could be theorized the latter resulted from Jackson getting to balls other shortstops could not reach. He also led the league twice in turning double plays and total chances and fielding percentage three times. His exceptional range earned him the sobriquet "Stonewall." In 1927, 1928, and 1929 *The Sporting News* voted him the most outstanding shortstop.

During his long career, Jackson had his share of injuries. In July 1925, he tore cartilage in his right knee, which reduced his mobility and speed. In April 1927, he underwent an appendectomy. Finally, in 1932 he suffered a chipped bone in his left knee. After the season, he had surgery on both knees, which resulted in him moving from short to third. Injuries or the demands of major league travel didn't interfere with Jackson's private life. In 1928 he married Mary Blackman, a childhood friend from Waldo. They had two children, Dorothy and William.

Travis Jackson retired from major league baseball as an active player after the 1936 season but not from the game. He managed at Jersey City, the Giants farm team in the International League. In a few years, he was back with the parent club coaching for manager Bill Terry. According to SABR author Greg Erion, "Jackson stayed with the Giants as a coach through 1940. He retired after contracting tuberculosis and entered a sanitarium in 1941 to regain his health, a process that took several years. After recovering, he rejoined the Giants as a coach, now under Mel Ott. After Leo Durocher replaced Ott in 1948, Jackson was let go at the end of the season, and his 27-year association with the Giants was severed."[9]

But Jackson was not quite finished with baseball. He joined the Braves organization and managed several minor league teams until 1961, claiming he was tired of the long bus trips. Next, the long wait for the Hall of Fame phone call. It finally came in 1982. Travis Jackson was elected to the Hall of Fame by the Veterans Committee. After his selection, Jackson said, " I was really surprised and happy. Anybody who ever played ball wants to go to the Hall of Fame. Don't let any of them ever kid you."[10]

Five years after the good news from the Hall of Fame, Travis Calvin Jackson died on July 27, 1987. He was 83 years old and was buried in his hometown of Waldo, Arkansas.

After Hubbell shutout the Phillies 4-0, the Giants moved on to Chicago, where they lost two of three to the Cubs. The bright spot of the series was Larry Benton, who chalked up win number 19. Next, the Giants traveled to St. Louis to face the league leaders in a critical three-game set. And here is a baseball oddity. The Giants won all three by an identical score, 3-2.

Hubbell won the second game of the series for his third victory. He made only one costly pitch the entire game. It came in the third inning when Ernie Orsatti hit a two-run homer. Once again, Hubbell's control was impeccable. He didn't walk a batter. Benton won his 20th the next day, completing the sweep of the Cardinals. But the Giants remained in second place three games back.

McGraw's men would continue to chase the Cards deep into September until the Cubs came into the Polo Grounds for a crucial four-game series. The Giants had made up some ground and were now only one game back of the Cardinals as the season quickly drew to a close.

In the meantime, Hubbell was slowly gaining the confidence of McGraw and quietly slipped into the starting rotation despite losing three games in a row. He lost one to Pittsburgh and two to Brooklyn. The lefty was hit hard in the Pirates game, giving up eight hits and five runs in only 4 1/3 innings. It was one of the few times the rookie was off his game. His record was now 3-3. Hubbell was much better three days later but lost a squeaker in extra innings, 4-3 to the Dodgers. With two out in the bottom of the 10th, Del Bissonette hit his

20th homer for the victory. He lost another to Brooklyn 4-2. His record now stood at 3-5. But McGraw, known to be a stubborn man among other things, stuck with Hubbell. McGraw had been around baseball for too many years not to recognize talent and develop it. Christy Mathewson is a perfect example. Now with Hubbell, once again, it paid off.

Hubbell's losing streak ended abruptly! He won the next five in a row bringing his record to a more respectable 8-5. Two of the victories were against the front-running St. Louis Cardinals. On September 20, the rookie beat the great Grover Cleveland Alexander 7-4 in the second game of a doubleheader, putting the Giants only two games back of St. Louis. Benton lost the first game 8-5.

One can only imagine the excitement, the thrill, and the nervous tension the Giants young, inexperienced rookie was going through, facing a living legend in Old Pete, who had won 348 games through 1927. He eventually would end his 20-year career with 373. It is surprising Hubbell lasted the entire game under those conditions. It certainly was a glimpse of the future Hubbell had waiting for him.

So, it was startling *The New York Times* grudgingly gave faint praise to Hubbell's pitching performance. "On the whole, Hubbell pitched well for the Giants in the second game. Being pitted against Alexander might have had its effect on the youngster, but he was cool at the outset and weakened only when he appeared to get tired near the end."[11]

September 21 was a day off for the Giants, but they were back playing the Cardinals the following day. McGraw chose his 20-game winner Freddie Fitzsimmons in the hope of cutting the Card's lead to one game. Facing the Giants was Clarence Mitchell, a left-handed Giant killer who threw the spit ball. A victory by the Cardinals would put them three games ahead with eight remaining, a near-impossible task for New York to overcome.

Beginning at the top of the fifth inning, the score was 3-3, and that's when Fitzsimmons ran into big trouble as 40,000 plus fans were biting their nails. Two walks and a single loaded the bases with no out! McGraw had seen enough as he waved to the bullpen for Hubbell, with only one day's rest. To be sure, it was a confidence builder for Hubbell, and he came through for McGraw. After Jim Bottomley singled, driving in two, making the score 5-3, Hubbell bore down and took charge. He fanned the next batter and then induced a double play.

The Giants came back in the bottom of the fifth to tie the game at 5-5 and scored two more in the seventh. Andy Cohen homered in the eighth to make the final score, Giants 8 Cardinals 5. Hubbell rewarded McGraw for his confidence with four clutch shutout innings. The lefty didn't walk a batter and fanned three. The Giants were now only one game back of the Cardinals, with each club having eight games remaining.

Cincinnati came to the Polo Grounds for a three-game series looking to spoil the Giants' chance for another pennant. But it was not to be. New York won all three by scores of 2-1, 7-4, and 4-3. And wouldn't you know it, the Cardinals, at Ebbets Field in the borough of Brooklyn, won three straight from the Dodgers. However, the next day Brooklyn, behind the strong pitching of Dazzy Vance (22-10), beat St. Louis 6-1 . . . now the Giants were only a half-game back and as close to the Cardinals as two coats of paint.

The Chicago Cubs arrived at the Polo Grounds for a do-or-die four-game series beginning with a twin-bill on September 27. In a heartbreaker, the Giants lost the opener 3-2 behind Hubbell (9-6), who pitched a fine game but not quite as good as veteran Art Nehf (13-7). The over-30,000 crowd was treated to some heated words being exchanged between McGraw and umpire Bill Klem, never a favorite of the Giant manager. It happened in the sixth inning when Giant runner Andy Reese was caught in a rundown between third and home. Cubs catcher Gabby Hartnett stood astride the baseline forcing Reese to slip around Hartnett, forcing him to fall, and finally tagged out. He would have scored if not interfered with by Hartnett. And that was the rationale for the protest. Klem held that a receiver of the ball has the right-of-way. A day later, National League president John A. Heydler, in a long-winded explanation, refused to uphold the protest. It came as no surprise, at least to the Cubs, since Heydler attended the game in question and, in fact, sat "not more than seventy-five feet from the play."

In the meantime, the Cardinals scored six runs in the first inning against the Boston Braves and won the game 8-3, behind the outstanding pitching of Jess Haines. It was his 20th victory, ninth straight, and eighth consecutive complete game. The Giants now trailed the Cardinals by a game and a half.

Not for long, as New York blanked Chicago 2-0 behind the stellar pitching of Joe Genewich. Hogan drove in both runs; one with a home run in the second and the other a sac fly in the fourth. Revenge is sometimes sweet. The victory eliminated the Cubs from the pennant race.

Revenge, however, works both ways, as the Giants would quickly discover. Shockingly, the Cubs won the next two games from the Giants by scores of 7-5 and 6-2. Their two 20-game aces, Larry Benton (25-9) and Freddie Fitzsimmons

(20-9), couldn't get the job done as the Giants and McGraw's hope for pennant number 12 ended on a disappointing note.

The pennant race was over, but the season had one game remaining. Hubbell beat the now pennant-winning St. Louis Cardinals 4-2, bringing his 1928 season record to 10-6, a solid performance by the rookie. His short stat line for the season was quite impressive. In 124 innings, he recorded the second-best ERA at 2.83, right behind Benton at 2.73. Plus, he walked only 21 batters, a future hallmark of what to expect from the 25-year-old southpaw.

Only 8,000 fans showed up for the season's final game, which generally would have been expected considering the pennant race was over. But days before, when it looked like the Giants had a good chance of winning the pennant, it was estimated the club took in between $20,000 and $30,000 in advance ticket sales from the public and speculators. "And there were speculators! They crowded around the entrance to the Polo Grounds yesterday, offering their reserved seat and box seat tickets at bargain rates, but there were few if any takers. Box seats which sell regularly for two dollars were being offered for fifty cents."[12] So in the end, it appeared the Giant fans and the speculators lost the gamble.

The New York Giants finished the season 93-61, two games back of the St. Louis Cardinals. Close, but no cigar. If there was a silver lining, it was the whopping attendance figure of 916,191. Despite losing the pennant, McGraw received outstanding performances from key players. Benton, Fitzsimmons, Genewich, and the surprise rookie Hubbell, all pitched exceptionally well. The team batting average (not including pitchers) was an outstanding .304. Hogan, Terry, Lindstrom, Ott, Welsh, O'Doul, and Reese all batted over .300. Lindstrom led the hitters with a .358 average and 231 hits, including 107 RBIs. Terry drove in 101 runs, and 19-year-old Mel Ott hit 18 home runs, tops on the team.

After 154 games and six months of intense baseball, trying to figure out why you lost a pennant by two measly games is futile. McGraw took the loss the hardest. He hadn't won a pennant since 1924. Next year he would turn 56 and be his 30th year managing the New York Giants. Earlier in the year, he was hit by a cab and broke his leg, but the coup de grace stuck in his craw was the Klem/Heydler decision overturning his protest of the crucial Cub game. It hurt him more than fans knew. McGraw's biographer, Joe Durso, claims McGraw was so enraged with the decision he obtained one of the news photos of the play, framed it, and hung it in his office "as a reminder of man's inhumanity to man." In reality, even if the Giants had won the protested game, all things being equal, they still would have lost the pennant by one game.

3

Eighteen Wins . . . And a No-Hitter

"IF I'M PLAYING CARDS FOR PENNIES, I WANT TO WIN . . ."

Sadly for McGraw and the Giant fans, the 1929 season would be even worse than 1928. It would be the beginning of a long and protracted economic spiral for the entire country, sending Wall Street into a panic and wiping out millions of investors. It would be forever known as the Great Depression. However, one of the bright spots in the baseball world was the pitching of lefty Carl Hubbell, beginning his second season with the New York Giants.

After the heartbreaking defeat in 1928 to the St. Louis Cardinals, McGraw went home to relax and read about the New York Yankees sweeping the Cards in the World Series. Little did he know, or perhaps he did, 1929 would be the beginning of the end for the cocky and feisty, phenomenally successful New York Giants manager. In 1932, after 40 years of managing the Giants, he would finally say farewell. But that poignant moment was in the future.

The man aptly nicknamed "Little Napoleon" had no thoughts of retiring in 1929. He was focused on improving the club, and he didn't waste any time. At the end of October, McGraw traded Lefty O'Doul to the Philadelphia Phillies for Fred Leach and cash. McGraw was looking for more power, and the 30-year-old outfielder looked like the answer. In '28, Leach hit .304 with 13 home runs and 96 RBIs. On the other hand, O'Doul, after spraining his ankle early in '28, batted .319 with 8 homers and 46 runs batted in. On paper, at least, the trade seemed to make sense.

Then on November 12, in another surprise move, the Giants named Ray Schalk to the position of assistant manager under McGraw. Schalk was the former manager of the Chicago White Sox until about halfway through the 1928 season. Schalk had been the White Sox catcher for 18 years and was known for his outstanding defensive skills and handling pitchers. "The undersized backstop was a workhorse for the White Sox clubs of the 1910s and 1920s, and he's regarded as the finest defensive catcher of the Dead Ball Era."[1] He was elected to the Hall of Fame in 1955.

It appears Schalk will be a jack-of-all-trades with the Giants: coaching, handling pitchers and catchers, and assisting McGraw in the "strategical operations."

Moreover, rumors were circulating McGraw was looking to make a deal for either Dolf Luque or Pete Donohue, both Cincinnati right-handers. Nothing came of the rumors as both pitchers stayed with the Reds in 1929. Luque would move to Brooklyn in 1930, and the Giants obtained Donohue the same year.

In early December, McGraw was at it again. This time he sold pitcher Vic Aldridge and utility infielder Russell Wrightstone to the Newark Bears, a minor league club, for a reported $25,000. Aldridge, who came from the Pirates in 1928, was a huge disappointment. His record with the Giants was 4-7 with a bloated 4.83 earned run average. With the Pirates in 1927, Aldridge won 15 games. A better performance by the right-hander and the Giants could have won the '28 pennant, which is a reasonable assumption. Aldridge and Wrightstone never made it back to the major leagues. At the time, the Newark Bears manager was Tris Speaker, and the Aldridge purchase was the first important deal he put together.

Interestingly, the club owners in both leagues unanimously agreed to begin the 1929 season one week later and end a week later due to adverse weather in the spring. But more noteworthy was the announcement at the joint meeting of the National and American leagues. John A. Heydler, president of the senior circuit, offered a revolutionary idea of a ten-man baseball team (in other words, the designated hitter rule). The idea fell flat on its face. Connie Mack, Philadelphia Athletics manager, raised the issue back in 1906, and it went nowhere either. Heydler, however, was not discouraged, as he pointed out to the press. "All I wanted to do was present the idea, no matter if it were tabled. I wanted to go on record. It will give the club owners of both leagues something to think over, and some good may come of it at a future meeting. I still contend the idea has merits. I sincerely hope the club owners of both leagues will give the idea serious consideration."[2] The controversy is still hotly debated today even though the American League adopted the DH rule in 1973. The history of the game is indeed fascinating.

Before spring training began, McGraw and the Giants announced some changes that reflected their frustration of not winning a pennant since 1924. First, the Giants purchased a controlling interest in the Bridgeport club of the Eastern League (Class A). It would serve two purposes: acquiring players at more reasonable prices and a place to park young players who needed more experience. The team would also return to San Antonio, Texas, for spring training, where the Giants won three of the four pennants from 1921 to 1924 and a McGraw favorite site. Finally, it was clearly and emphatically stated McGraw was planning on an intense two-month training period. He wanted his club to be in tip-top condition when the season began. Also, the Giants had scheduled several exhibition games, including those played on their way home to begin the 1929 season.

But in January, it was time for McGraw and Mrs. McGraw to take their annual six-week vacation to Havana, Cuba, aboard the liner *President Roosevelt*. Confident as always, especially after hearing ace pitcher Larry Benton and catcher Shanty Hogan had signed their new contracts, McGraw believed all players would sign with little trouble claiming, "we were quite liberal with the contracts sent out the other day." McGraw continued, "I am thoroughly pleased with our outlook for next season. True, I would have liked to swing one more deal for a pitcher, but I am well enough satisfied with the team as it stands right now. With the material we will take to San Antonio this spring, I am confident the Giants will come North with another colorful, aggressive team that will let the others know there's a race on."[3] McGraw did hire Carl Mays, the highly controversial submarine right-hander. Actually, he was the only manager who offered Mays a contract.

McGraw's upbeat message to Giant fans was reassuring until old rumors surfaced in the press claiming the club was for sale! The rumors named several potential buyers who were interested. In addition, the story had McGraw deeply involved in two different scenarios. First, he was going to head up a syndicate to buy the Giants, and second, he had sold his interest in the club and would resign as manager. It all sounded quite wacky.

The rumors finally ended when the *Times* ran a headline that read: "Bid of $4,000,000 For Giants Denied." And indeed, it was denied, very emphatically, even by the supposed buyers who were identified as vice president William F. Carey and majority stockholder Richard F. Hoyt of the Madison Square Garden Corporation. Before leaving for San Antonio to join his team in spring training, McGraw was even more emphatic, calling it "bunk."

In the meantime, Ray Schalk, McGraw's recently hired assistant, was running a tight ship in San Antonio. He was all over the field with words of advice—batting practice, infield drills, running bases, shagging flies, and working with the pitching staff, imparting knowledge and experience as a former big-league catcher. McGraw was pleased with what he saw. Hubbell was given special attention in fielding his position, especially throwing to second base, which was not emphasized during the heated 1928 pennant race. Also, Hubbell did not receive much training in fielding his position in the minor leagues. Now the focus was on throwing to second and fielding bunts.

The hard work paid off as the exhibition games went well, with the Giants winning 12 of 18 games. While the Giants were beating the Senators 4-0 in their final exhibition game, Schalk found time to obtain President Herbert Hoover's autograph. His signature joined those on a ball previously signed by Presidents William Howard Taft, Warren G. Harding, and Calvin Coolidge.

If predictions have any validity, the New York Giants should win the National League pennant in 1929. More than 60 major league baseball writers and sports editors predicted the Giants to win the pennant. On the other hand, McGraw was cautiously optimistic, saying his club was a "good, well-balanced team." So much for predictions and optimism as the Giants would finish third in the race. However, Carl Hubbell would record an outstanding sophomore year and begin to assert himself as the future ace of the staff.

Rain delayed the Giants' opening game of the 1929 season against the Philadelphia Phillies for two days until April 18. Only 6,000 fans showed up at Baker Bowl, which was no surprise. The weather continued to be lousy— a bitter sunless windy day. Another factor could have been the Phillies' past performance. The last time the team was competitive and in the first division was 1917. During this period, the Phillies spent most of the time living in the basement of the National League. Perhaps with that in mind, McGraw chose Carl Hubbell to start the game rather than ace Larry Benton. It was a good choice as Hubbell allowed seven hits and four runs in seven innings for his first opening day major league victory. Benton pitched two innings of relief and was batted around for five runs, but the Giants managed to score six in the top of the ninth for an unimpressive 11-9 win.

After the opening day win against the Phillies, the Giants made it two in a row behind the stellar pitching of newly acquired Carl Mays. The Giants and Phillies moved on to the Polo Grounds for New York's opener, which was delayed for three days due to continued rain. When the rain finally ended, the

Giants wished it hadn't. Benton lost 3-1 in extra innings. However, the following day, Hubbell went the distance allowing two runs on eight hits for a 9-2 final score. Mel Ott hit his first homer of the season, as did Travis Jackson, while Andy Reese went three for five, driving in two runs.

Hubbell's next two appearances resulted in no-decisions; one was in relief against Boston, the other a start against the Cardinals. On May 8, in the second game against the Pittsburgh Pirates, Carl Hubbell had everything working for him, including his famed screwball. He pitched his first and only no-hitter of his Hall of Fame career. The score was 11-0 as the Giants pounded three Pirate pitches, with Ott hitting two more home runs and driving in four. But after three innings with the Giants leading 6-0, fan interest shifted to the mound. After six innings, the Giants had already scored all 11 runs, and fans were "cheering each putout of a Pirate" during the last three innings. Hubbell was in total command, not needing any sensational defensive plays to keep his no-no alive. But the real test and drama came as so often happens in the ninth inning.

Pinch hitter Harry Riconda led off the ninth by smacking a line drive right at left fielder Chick Fullis who dropped the ball for an error. The next batter Sparky Adams hit a sure double-play ball at shortstop Travis Jackson who fumbled the ball. Two consecutive errors, and now there were two runners on and no out with three future Hall of Famers coming to the plate—brother's Lloyd and Paul Waner and right behind them Pie Traynor. These three Pirates were absolute hitting machines. Lloyd finished the '29 season batting .353, Paul .336, and Pie .356.

Hub, if he didn't know it, was in deep trouble. To his credit, he did not panic. He struck out Lloyd on a curveball for out number one. Older brother Paul was up next. Here's how *Times* reporter Brandt described the crucial moment. "The senior Waner slashed the ball along the ground between the pitcher's box and first base. Like a flash, Hubbell dived for the ball and scooped it cleanly. Whirling, and without waiting to recover balance, he fired the ball to second base."[4] This time, Jackson caught the ball, stepped on second, and fired to Bill Terry at first, completing the double play and preserving the no-hitter.

During the excitement and jubilation of the moment, few fans, if any, realized the significance of the no-hitter. Not so much for the no-hitter but as a preview of what to expect in the future from the lefty when under pressure.

To digress for the moment, as many followers of the game know, Paul and younger brother Lloyd patrolled the Pirates' outfield for 15 years. Paul was known as "Big Poison" and Lloyd as "Little Poison." It is interesting how the nicknames came about.

According to Lloyd, it began in 1927 when the Pirates played the New York Giants at the Polo Grounds. There was a regular fan who would always sit in the center field bleachers. He was loud, and his voice carried all over the ballpark. One day in between games of a doubleheader, the two brothers came out of the clubhouse, and this guy started hollering at the two, nothing malicious or nasty. It sounded like Big and Little Poison but what he was actually saying was Big and Little Person. The brothers got to know the guy and even got him an autographed baseball. With that, he became the biggest rooter of the Waner brothers. Reporters overheard this guy yelling, but they thought he was saying "Poison" instead of "Person." According to Lloyd, no ballplayers ever called them that. And that's how the Waner brothers became "Big Poison" and "Little Poison." As previously mentioned, both were inducted into the Hall of Fame and accounted for a combined 5,611 hits, the most ever by brothers, including the Alou brothers (5,094) and three DiMaggio brothers (4,853).

After Hubbell's no-hitter, the New York Giants' early record was 6-7. They continued to play under .500 ball until May 22, when Fitzsimmons beat Brooklyn 7-3 in 11 innings. It was the beginning of a hot streak in which the club won 15 of 17 games. During this period, Hubbell picked up two victories, putting his record at 6-2. Despite the streak, the Giants were still mired in fourth place behind Pittsburgh, St. Louis, and Chicago in that order.

The Giants would not get that hot again for the remaining 1929 season despite some outstanding individual pitching performances by Hubbell, Bill Walker, and Carl Mays and hitting by Ott, Terry, Lindstrom, and Jackson. McGraw's men finished third with an 84-67 record, a distant 13½ games in back of Joe McCarthy's pennant-winning Chicago Cubs.

Hub led the club in innings pitched with 268; games started 35, strikeouts 106, and victories, 18-11. His earned run average was 3.69, second to Walker's (14-7) 3.09. Mays (6-2) was used by McGraw mainly in relief and did a fine job. At age 37, it was his last major league season. Also, Benton and Fitzsimmons had off years compared to 1928, which badly hurt the club. One of the bright spots was twenty-year-old Mel Ott, who had a remarkable season batting .328 with 42 home runs and 151 RBIs. He also led the league in walks.

"Hub's 18 victories in 1929 earned him a substantial raise, placing him in a bracket comfortable enough to encourage him to get married. On January

26, 1930, at McAlester, Oklahoma, he married a schoolgirl sweetheart named Lucille Harrington."[5]

The man who caught most of those 18 victories was Frank Hogan. He was nicknamed "Shanty" because, so it was said, he resembled a small hut. In other words, "he was a fine broth of a lad." It's been reported he was 6-1, 240 pounds, which probably was his weight in 1925 when he joined the Boston Braves as a 19-year-old catcher. Most of the time, during his 13-year career, he had a weight problem. It went as high as 278. Then again, others claim he made "an excellent target behind the plate."

Shanty's first two seasons in professional baseball were spent between the minor leagues and short stays with the Braves. He played in only 13 games during those two seasons with Boston but batted a solid .286. He was touted to be a fine defensive catcher with a strong arm. In 1927 Shanty was given an opportunity to play regularly. He started in 71 games sharing the catching duties with three others, as the Braves finished in seventh place. He batted a consistent .288.

On January 10, 1928, Hogan and Jimmy Welsh, an undistinguished outfielder, were traded to the New York Giants for Rogers Hornsby. Despite Hornsby turning in an outstanding 1927 season for the Giants with a slash line of .361/.448/.586, it was inevitable the 31-year-old autocratic and outspoken Hornsby would clash with McGraw and owner Stoneham. Hornsby was too difficult to handle and had to go.

Hogan's first season with the Giants was more than what McGraw expected, or maybe not. In 131 games, the durable catcher batted a cool .333 with an OBP of .406. He also showed signs of latent power, hitting 10 home runs and driving in 71. And 1928 was no fluke. For the next three seasons, he hit .300, .339, and .301, respectively, while capably handling the pitching rotation.

After the 1932 season, in late December, Shanty was sold back to the Boston Braves for $25,000. Why? Shanty had a serious problem. Simply put, he loved food and could not stop eating, especially his mother's cooking. He brought her to spring training, rented a cottage for her so she could cook for him. When Hogan reached 250 pounds, McGraw began monitoring Shanty's food intake and frequency. The stories are endless about how Shanty attempted to outwit McGraw in his vigil to contain his catcher's gluttony. Shanty charmed waitresses and even resorted to bribery, it's been reported, all to outsmart his manager.

Food intake wasn't the only problem McGraw had with Hogan. One season he fined him $200 and suspended him from the middle of September to the end of the season. The suspension was brought by a row between Hogan and the Giant trainer. Years later, Hogan confessed during his stay with the Giants, McGraw had fined him a total of $4,000.

Author Noel Hynd relates Shanty's final demise. "Here, the story turns sad. Hogan's production at the other plate fell off in 1932: 8 home runs and a .287 average. Worse, he was so saddled with fat around the shoulders, neck, and arms that throws to second base had to be made sidearm. Larcenous runners were having their way against Hogan. And the Giants, from whom John McGraw retired in midseason for medical reasons, plopped into the second division for the first time since 1915. The new manager, Bill Terry, made changes in the offseason. One of them was to send the popular Hogan back to Boston for $25,000."[6]

Shanty wasn't unhappy with being sent back to the Boston Braves. McGraw was gone, and things were changing at the Polo Grounds, but most importantly, the burly backstop was closer to home. He resided just outside of Boston in Somerville, Massachusetts. No doubt, he had visions of home cooking by his mother, Delia.

Hogan stayed with Boston from 1933 to 1935, doing the bulk of catching, but not distinguishing himself at the plate, home plate that is. To his credit, he did hit .301 in 59 games and made efforts to lose weight but to no avail. It was his swan song. On August 5, he was released by the Braves. A week later, the man with the insatiable appetite was signed by the Cleveland Indians. He never played a game for the Indians in 1935, but in December of the year was sent to the Washington Senators, the details of which are murky.

The Senators signed Shanty towards the end of the 1936 season, and he performed well, batting .323 in only 19 games with an OBP of .421. Equally important, the fans loved him. At the end of the season, owner Clark Griffith suspected Shanty of overindulging and gaining weight. Griffith requested Shanty hop on the scale. It registered a whopping 278 pounds! At that point, Griffith told Shanty to "lose 50 pounds by opening day, or you're off the team."

Realizing this might be the end of his major league career, Shanty went on a strict diet. "He starved himself. He exercised. He starved himself some more. The following spring, he worked out in heavy underwear, three woolen shirts, and a rubber jacket at training camp. He sucked chunks of pineapple for nourishment and refused water until his thirst was unbearable."

"I'm suffering the tortures of the damned," Hogan told writers. "I'd give ten points off my average for an ice-cold bottle of beer."[7]

Opening day finally arrived, and Shanty, much to his delight, weighed in at a slim 228 pounds. That was the good news for all concerned—owner Griffith, manager Bucky Harris, and the fans. The team now had the first-string catcher. The bad news was the Senators got off to a poor start and landed in last place. Adding to their woes, Hogan, after 21 games, was batting a puny .152. The Senators moved quickly. On June 11, they traded for future Hall of Famer Rick Ferrell. Less than two weeks later, the Senators released Hogan, who never played another game in the major leagues.

Shanty died on April 7, 1967, at age 61. However, he did leave somewhat of a legacy, even though few people knew of it at the time or in later years. Whether it is accurate or embellished, it is a fine story authored by Noel Hynd. "For many years, there stood a German restaurant in upper Manhattan, not far from where the Giants played [Polo Grounds]. The restaurant was popular among players and fans. It served steaks of four sizes. The small weighed one pound, the medium was two pounds, and the large weighed three. Finally, the extravaganza, a five-pound he-man sirloin special that could probably have sustained a normal family for a week. It was called simply "The Shanty Hogan."[8]

It is often difficult to determine why a pennant was lost, but McGraw could undoubtedly point fingers at certain individuals . . . and even himself. He was the one who traded Lefty O'Doul to the Phillies for Fred Leach and cash. What kind of a season did Lefty have? He led the National League in batting average (.398), hits (254), plate appearances (732), and on-base percentage (.465). He also chipped in with 32 home runs and 122 RBIs. And Leach? He played in 113 games; batted .290 with eight homers and 47 runs batted in. This is not to say O'Doul would have won the '29 pennant for the Giants or even perform as well for McGraw. It is merely an observation. The '29 season was a disappointment and reflected in the attendance, which dropped from 916,191 in '28 to 868,806 in '29. With the Depression just around the corner, attendance in 1930 would be a challenge, in more ways than one.

4

Almost a Second No-Hitter

"Control is everything. Next comes a knowledge
of each batsman's weak points."

The 1929 World Series between the Philadelphia Athletics and Chicago Cubs, in which Connie Mack's A's, won four games to one, was two weeks old when the New York Exchange crashed! If McGraw and the Giant fans were thinking about the upcoming 1930 season, they now had something more important than baseball to contemplate. Over 16 million shares were traded on that one day. Billions of dollars were lost in an instant. It signaled the beginning of the Great Depression. The economy went into a tailspin, and without warning, millions of people lost jobs and homes. With no jobs, families were forced to join bread and soup lines. The Great Depression lasted about 12 long, miserable years.

Once again, as he did in 1929, John McGraw began making changes to the team in hopes of another National League pennant in 1930. Keep in mind the Giant's last pennant was in 1924. He knew it, and the fans certainly knew it. This drought must have been on his mind. Looking for new pitching, he began in September, before the 1929 season was over, by purchasing left-hander Hub Pruett from the Newark Bears of the International League (AA). Pruett's record with Newark was 16-7 with an excellent 2.43 ERA. McGraw followed up in late 1929 with another purchase, this time Joe Heving from the Memphis Chicks in the Southern Association. His record with the Chicks was 14-10 with a 3.30 earned run average. McGraw would use him almost exclusively in relief.

In addition, McGraw was working on signing his superstars and stars for the coming season. By early February, 30 Giants had signed contracts for the new season. As usual, there were holdouts. Among them were Bill Terry, Freddie Lindstrom, and Ed Roush. Terry and Lindstrom would eventually sign, but Roush was resolute in his demands. The outfielder had a typical season for him in '29, batting .324 in 115 games. Regardless, Roush's holdout reached the point where it infuriated McGraw so much that on March 25, he announced that he was withdrawing his contract offer at spring training in San Antonio. Nothing happened until early May when Commissioner Kenesaw M. Landis entered the impasse and announced that four National League players were now ineligible "for failure to sign contracts." Roush was among the four, and he sat out the entire 1930 season. On March 26, 1931, he was selected off waivers by the Cincinnati Reds.

Shortly after Landis made his announcement, McGraw traded for an outfielder to replace Roush. He acquired Walter Roettger from the St. Louis Cardinals for George Fisher and Eddie Farrell. Roettger's performance for the Cardinals was not impressive. He had a slash line of .253/.287/.349. For the Giants, in 1930, the slash line improved only slightly.

Coming out of spring training and the exhibition games, McGraw was cautiously optimistic. He did make a point that pitching would be a key factor in the Giants' success, despite the showing in exhibition games. Hubbell and Walker, the two southpaws, would be looked upon along with Fitzsimmons to lead the pitching rotation. Without mentioning names, he believed the offense would do a good job. Ott, Terry, Lindstrom, and Jackson, along with Hogan, would be the bats needed to win a pennant.

The Giants began the 1930 season like a team on a mission, winning their first seven games. Hubbell pitched a beauty in the third game, beating the Phillies and 43-year-old Grover Cleveland Alexander 2-1. Hub allowed one run on four hits while striking out seven. By the time the hot streak was over, Hubbell was 2-0, while a four-game losing streak spoiled the encouraging start. McGraw recognized early pitching could be a problem, so he acquired veteran spitball pitcher Clarence Mitchell from the Cardinals for Ralph Judd, a young right-hander who had been with the club for two years and used exclusively in relief. For trivia buffs, Mitchell's name is well known. He is the answer to who is the only player to hit into an unassisted triple play in a World Series? It occurred in the 1920 World Series between Cleveland and Brooklyn. The Robins had men on first and second with no out when Mitchell lined a bullet up the middle and snared by Bill Wambsganss, heading towards second base. Wamby caught the liner for one out, stepped on second for out two, and tagged the runner coming from first, completing the triple play. By the end of May, the Giants were 17-22.

On May 18, Hubbell came close to pitching his second no-hitter in two years. It was the second game of a doubleheader against the Boston Braves before 30,000 at the Polo Grounds. The Giants were leading 2-0, and Hub had a no-hitter going into the eighth when Hank Gowdy singled to spoil the bid. With the no-hitter gone, Boston scored in the eighth and ninth to tie the game. Heving relieved, and the Giants scored in the eleventh. Heving received credit for the victory, adding insult to injury. Hubbell's record remained 4-1.

On May 21, with the Giants in fourth place, McGraw made a blockbuster trade. He sent his former ace pitcher Larry Benton to Cincinnati for star second baseman Hughie Critz. McGraw summed up the rationale behind the trade. "I hate to see Benton go, but somehow he couldn't seem to win for us [at the time Benton was 1-3] anymore, and I think the change will benefit all the parties concerned."[1]

The trade certainly didn't benefit Cincinnati as Benton went 7-12 with an inflated 5.12 ERA. Regarding Critz, he was considered a defensive whiz and was compared to Rogers Hornsby and Frankie Frisch. At the time, McGraw believed Critz was the answer to his second base problems the past two seasons. Perhaps he was, but McGraw had other problems. The most prominent was not winning consistently.

In June, the Giants ran off nine straight victories, with Hubbell picking up two wins during this streak. He beat Cincinnati and his former teammate Benton 9-1 and Pittsburgh 9-2. Against the Pirates, Hub walked five, which was highly unusual for the master of control. His record was now 6-3. After the streak, the Giants were in third place, six games back of first place Brooklyn. But for the rest of June, the Giants were 8-10, still in third place but now 7½ games behind Chicago, who took over first place. By the end of July, New York was treading water, still in third place but now only five games back of Brooklyn. Hubbell's record was a mediocre 9-8.

In early August, the four-way pennant race among the Giants, Robins, Pirates, and Cubs began to heat up as New York visited Ebbets Field to take on Brooklyn, their hated rivals in a four-game series. The two teams split the series, with Hubbell losing the second game 1-0, evening his record to 9-9. It was a shocking loss for a pitcher with pinpoint control. It was a scoreless tie entering the bottom of the ninth. Babe Herman doubled, leading off for the Robins.

Eddie Moore, one of the best bunters in the league, sacrificed Herman to third. McGraw ordered Hubbell to intentionally walk Glenn Wright and Rube Bressler loading the bases. He was looking for the double play as Jake Flowers came to the plate. To the disappointment of the 25,000 fans, Hubbell walked Flowers forcing in Herman with the winning run. As Herman crossed the plate, the hullabaloo began as coaches Dan Bancroft, and Irish Meusel swarmed around umpire Lou Jorda claiming ball four wasn't low. Their violent protesting reached a point where the police were called in to escort Jorda from the field.

After the Brooklyn series, the Giants went on a 16-game road trip to Pittsburgh, Cincinnati, St. Louis, and Chicago without their manager, John McGraw. Bancroft would serve as acting manager. As expected, McGraw's absence during a pennant race late in the season created rumors that spread throughout the baseball community. First, Joseph H. McNally, a wealthy contractor, was to buy a controlling interest in the Giants. Owner Charles A. Stoneham and McGraw quickly squashed it. The other rumor was about McGraw and his contract, which was to expire by year's end. Plus, he was not with the team on the current road trip. Creative minds concluded; the Giants were looking for a new manager. Not true. McGraw's absence was a health issue. He was under doctor's orders not to travel. More specifically, his doctor did not want him sitting on the bench as "the heat and humidity of the bench militated against his recovery."

The Giants road trip was a huge success until the club reached Chicago. The Giants took three of four from Pittsburgh, swept four in Cincinnati, and split four games in St. Louis. Hubbell picked up three victories, one a shutout, as his record stood at 12-9. During these 12 games, Freddie Lindstrom and Bill Terry were almost unstoppable. Lindstrom had at least one hit in every game, going 24 for 54 (.444 average) and driving in 11 runs. Terry was 22 for 51, a torrid .431 pace. The Giants were now only three games back of the league-leading Cubs with a golden opportunity to tighten the gap . . . and even take over first place with a clean sweep.

Freddie Lindstrom was born on the south side of Chicago on November 21, 1905, a short distance from Comiskey Park. He was the youngest of five children. His dad Frederick was a plumbing contractor, his mother Mary, a homemaker. Being so close to the White Sox ballpark made Freddie and the rest of the neighborhood automatic fans. According to Lindstrom, the Cubs were almost nonexistent.

As a loyal White Sox fan, young Freddie had mixed emotions around the time of the First World War. On the one hand, he rooted for their championship teams, but when the scandal broke in 1920 involving eight White Sox players: Arnold "Chick" Gandil, Swede Risberg, Eddie Cicotte, Oscar "Happy" Felsch, "Shoeless" Joe Jackson, Fred McMullin, George "Buck" Weaver and Claude "Lefty" Williams, many of them Freddie's heroes, he was "terribly disappointed." The involvement of his heroes in fixing the 1919 World Series against the Cincinnati Reds "was quite a disillusioning experience," he admitted.

But that bitter pill didn't discourage Freddie, who wanted to be a major league ballplayer early in life. While attending Loyola Academy in Chicago, he was allowed to work out with the Cubs. He believed he did well but never heard from the organization again. Three weeks later, New York Giants scout Dick Kinsella agreed to check out Freddie at a Loyola game arranged by his baseball coach Jake Weiner. "I played a game for Loyola that day, and in the game, I hit four consecutive doubles. I signed a contract with the New York Giants that night, in the Auditorium Hotel. My dad had to come along with me and sign also because I was only sixteen years old."[2]

Freddie never graduated from Loyola. He left in his sophomore year despite his parent's objections, who wanted him to graduate and pursue a law career. But Freddie was in love with the game and had little interest in school, a familiar refrain of young kids with talent in the early days of baseball. In 1985 Frederick C. Lindstrom was inducted into the Loyola Academy Hall of Fame.

In 1922, at age 16, the Giants shipped Freddie off to the Toledo Mud Hens in the American Association (AA). One of his managers at Toledo was the future Hall of Fame catcher, Roger Bresnahan, close friends with John McGraw. It is unknown how much, if any, influence Bresnahan had on young Lindstrom. Bresnahan was known to be fiercely competitive and an "unabashed Irish brawler."

Lindstrom, playing third base, appeared in only 18 games for the Mud Hens and batted .304. One of his teammates was 23-year-old Bill Terry, who was a jack-of-all-trades with the club. He played first, right field, and pitched some relief. The left-handed slugger batted .336 in 88 games with 14 homers. Terry and Lindstrom would return to the Hens in 1923 and turned in solid numbers. Both young prospects gained valuable experience—Lindstrom played in 147 games, but his average dropped to .270 while Terry hit a remarkable .377 in 109 games with 15 home runs. In 1924, it would be goodbye to the Mud Hens as both Lindstrom and Terry were headed for the pennant-winning New York Giants and their manager John McGraw.

In hindsight, Lindstrom admitted the Giants were a close-knit group and rightly so, having won four consecutive pennants, including 1924 when he arrived. He felt he was on the ball club but not part of it. As expected, the regular third baseman for the Giants was Heinie Groh, who in 1924 was entering his 13th year in the major leagues and on two World Champion teams, the 1919 Cincinnati Reds and the 1922 Giants. He was also on the 1923 and 1924 Giant pennant winners. Lindstrom had no chance of replacing Groh at third base. For most of the season, Lindstrom was designated as a utility man. He filled in at third for Groh and at second for Frankie Frisch.

With seven games remaining in the 1924 season, Groh injured his knee and was sidelined. Lindstrom was now the third baseman as the Giants were in a heated pennant race with Brooklyn and Pittsburgh. The Giants took care of the Pirates sweeping them at the end of the season. In the meantime, Brooklyn was playing only .500 ball the last 18 games and was eliminated on the next to last day of the season.

Now it was on to the World Series for Lindstrom and the Giants to face the Washington Senators. It was a classic matchup between two great managers—John McGraw (Little Napoleon) and Bucky Harris (The Boy Wonder). After 17 years pitching for the Senators and at age 36, the great Walter Johnson was finally going to participate in a World Series. Ironically, Lindstrom, in his first year in the major leagues, would play in all seven games. He was 18 years and ten months old, a record that still stands today.

As mentioned previously, it was a wild and unpredictable World Series. Washington won in seven games with Johnson, albeit at the end of his fabulous career, was hit hard in two of his losses. But the "Big Train" redeemed himself in game seven in a four-inning relief appearance, blanking the Giants on three hits and winning the 12-inning game 4-3 for his first-ever World Series victory. Lindstrom had a remarkable series. The third baseman hit .333 with four RBIs, including a four-for-five-game against Johnson.

Sadly, Lindstrom, along with Travis Jackson and Hank Gowdy, will always be remembered for what happened in the 12th inning that allowed Washington and Johnson to win the World Series. With one out in the bottom of the 12th Muddy Ruel hit a high pop up behind the plate. Catcher Gowdy, in pursuit, tripped over his discarded mask and dropped the ball. Still alive at the plate, Ruel promptly doubled. Johnson, batting for himself, hit a routine grounder to Jackson at short, who bobbled the ball. Johnson was safe at first as Ruel held second. Up next, Earl McNealy hit a grounder to Lindstrom, a possible double-play ball. Fate was at work here as the ball hit a pebble and bounced over Lindstrom's head and down the left-field line as Ruel scored the winning run.

Many years later, a humble and joking Lindstrom had this to say about the ignominious ground ball. "It's possible that if it hadn't been for that ball bouncing over my head in the 1924 World Series, a lot of people would have forgotten I ever existed. The association is made so often: Lindstrom, the bad bounce, the World Series. I still hear about it. Some people think I hit the ball; some think I scored the winning run. I have to refresh them on it. 'I didn't do anything but stand there,' I tell them. It was very easy. Anybody could have done it."[3]

In 1925 it was inevitable; Lindstrom would take over the third base position, relegating Groh, with a bum knee, to a part-time player at age 35. Heinie would play one more season with the Giants before he ended up with the Pittsburgh Pirates, ending a 16-year major league career. Meanwhile, Lindstrom, still developing his skills in the field and at the plate, would be McGraw's third baseman for the next seven seasons. He batted a solid .287 in 1925.

For the next six years, Lindstrom would bat over .300. In 1928 he hit .358, while Rogers Hornsby won the batting title with .387. However, Lindstrom did lead the league with 231 hits and was second to Jim Bottomley in the MVP voting. He also hit 14 home runs and drove in 107. It was an impressive year for a 22-year-old. Two years later, Lindstrom recorded an even better slash line: .379/.425/.575. He added 22 homers and 106 RBIs. These stats might be inflated by the fact 1930 was the season of the juiced ball. For example, Hack Wilson hit 56 home runs and drove in 191 runs, a record that still stands today. Bill Terry hit .401, collecting 254 hits—both great players, but neither came close to those numbers again.

By 1931 McGraw's style of managing was no longer effective. The tough, no-nonsense approach with players was passe'. My way or the highway did not sit well with the more modern-day player. You had to be more diplomatic. Times were changing, and McGraw could not adapt. The Giants hadn't won a pennant in eight years. McGraw was 59 years old and in poor health. He had been managing the Giants for 31 years. Perhaps, it was time for a change.

According to Lindstrom, owner Stoneham promised him the managerial job as well as Jim Tierney, club secretary and "right-hand man." He was told by Tierney at the Alamac Hotel in New York with Terry in the room. It was also the season Lindstrom switched from third base to the outfield, a move he was not thrilled about. Ironically, halfway through the season (he only played in 78 games and batted .300), Lindstrom broke his leg and was laid up in St. Francis hospital in Philadelphia. According to Lindstrom, Tierney visited him. "We're making that change we spoke about next year [1932]," he said. "McGraw is going out, and we want to make you manager. We're not doing it this year because of your broken leg. Mr. Stoneham and I have decided to postpone it until next year."[4]

Then in June of 1932, Terry informed Lindstrom that he, Terry, was appointed the New York Giants manager. Lindstrom was "dumbfounded" and disappointed . . . and probably a twinge bitter. Lindstrom finished the season, hitting 15 homers and driving in 92 runs, but for the first time in seven years, his batting average dropped below .300, at a still comfortable .271. It was also the end of his career as a Giant. On December 12, Lindstrom was part of a 3-team trade with Freddie going to the Pittsburgh Pirates after nine years with New York.

When Lindstrom arrived in Pittsburgh, manager George Gibson put him in center field and moved Lloyd Waner to left. Gibson believed Lindstrom would be able to handle covering the wide expanse of center better than Waner. Freddie's first year with the Pirates was a good one, playing between the two Waner brothers in the outfield. He finished the season batting .310 for the seventh and last time in his career. The following season, Lindstrom played in only 97 games and batted .290, an off season for him. For most other major leaguers, however, it would be considered a good performance. He admitted the broken leg suffered in 1931, along with back problems, caused his playing time and performance to suffer. After the 1934 season, Lindstrom and left-hander Larry French were traded to the Chicago Cubs for Guy Bush, Babe Herman, and Jim Weaver.

In 1935 the trade to the Cubs paid off for Lindstrom as well as the team. He helped Chicago win a pennant playing both center field and third base while hitting .275. It was his second World Series, but once again, he was on the losing side. The Detroit Tigers won in six games, despite losing Hank Greenberg in game two when he broke his wrist. Freddie had a miserable series. He played center and third in the first four games and batted an uncharacteristic .200. His stay with the Cubs was short-lived. He was released by the Cubs the following January, but not for long. A week later, he was signed as a free agent by Brooklyn.

During the 1936 season, after 26 games and a .264 batting average, Freddie Lindstrom called it quits. He had been a major league player for 13 seasons, starting at the tender age of 18—nine with the New York Giants, two with the Pittsburgh Pirates, and one each with Chicago and Brooklyn. His lifetime batting average was a worthy .311 with a solid OBP of .351. He batted over .300 seven times and twice collected 231 hits in 1928 when he led the league and again in 1930. His highest batting average was a remarkable .379. He was also one of the great third basemen of his time.

Life after baseball was just as interesting, varied, and successful as his playing days. After leaving Brooklyn, Lindstrom was involved in two business ventures. One was a lake development project in Wisconsin; the other he invested in an "improved light bulb." Neither was as successful as he anticipated.

However, the love of the game was still alive and well when Lindstrom turned his interests to radio. He spent two years as a sports announcer for WLS in Chicago and even managed minor league teams at Fort Smith, Arkansas, and Knoxville, Tennessee.

In 1948 Lindstrom became the baseball coach for Northwestern University in Evanston, Illinois. In 1957 the NU Cats won the Big Ten Championship under coach Lindstrom, the only time in the school's history. The Big Ten title gave the Cats a birth in the NCAA Tournament. Notre Dame eventually eliminated them. Lindstrom's son, Chuck, was the star catcher and joined the Chicago White Sox after college. As the saying goes, "he was up for a cup of coffee." Actually, Chuck caught the last game of the 1958 season for the Sox. His first at-bat, he hit a sacrifice fly. The next two times, he walked and tripled, making him one for one with a batting average of 1.000. Since Chuck never played in another major league game, his lifetime batting average is 1.000. As Casey Stengel would say, "you could look it up."

Freddie Lindstrom resigned as baseball coach at Northwestern in the middle of the 1961 season to become Evanston's postmaster. The reason, according to his son Chuck, was the job gave him long-term benefits. He held that position until 1972, when he retired with his pension. He and his wife, Irene, relocated to New Port Richey in sunny Florida to spend their senior years relaxing and enjoying their 13 grandchildren. They had three sons: Fred Jr., Andy, and Chuck.

While retired and waiting for the call from the Hall of Fame, Freddie, like so many other retired ballplayers, became an avid golfer and a rather good one at that even though he would not admit it. "It's funny, though," Lindstrom said. "All my years of playing baseball, I didn't have any trouble hitting a ball that was thrown every which way at me. Yet the golf ball is just sitting there, waiting to be hit, and I have trouble hitting it."[5]

The call finally came in 1976 from the Veterans Committee. Freddie Lindstrom was now in baseball's coveted Hall of Fame, and rightly so. At the induction in Cooperstown, Freddie, his wife, and three sons were on hand, along with seven of his grandchildren. Six other grandchildren couldn't make it. As tears welled in Freddie's eyes, he said, "this is the greatest thing that has ever happened to me."[6]

Five years later, on October 4, 1981, Freddie Lindstrom died at the age of 75. He and his wife, Irene, are buried in the family plot in the All Saints Cemetery in Des Plaines, Illinois.

The Giants were now headed for Chicago, the last leg of their road trip, only three games behind the league-leading Chicago Cubs. The four-game series was a golden opportunity for the Giants to take over first place. However, they would have to be at the top of their game to sweep the tough Cubs. Forty thousand fans saw the Giants win the first game of the series 13-6, with Wally Roettger leading the offensive assault with a three-run homer in the first inning. New York scored six in the first, two in the fifth, and five in the eighth to nail down the key first game victory. Ott and Jackson contributed three RBIs each as the Giants moved two games back of Chicago. Then the proverbial roof fell in as the Giants lost the next three to the Cubs and two more to Brooklyn before the bleeding stopped. They were now 5½ games back of Chicago. During the five-game disaster, Hubbell lost two as his record was now 12-11.

That was the last hurrah for the New York Giants. They never came as close to the league leaders as August 21, when they were two games back. New York did finish the season strong, winning 10 of the last 12 games, but it was far too late as they finished in third place, five games back of the pennant-winning St. Louis Cardinals.

Surprisingly, in early September, Giants owner Stoneham announced McGraw had signed a new five-year contract, which would not take effect until the present one expired at the end of the season. Stoneham admitted the persistent "foolish rumors" McGraw was leaving for the American League forced him to act quickly.

After all the ups and downs during the season, the Giants finished 87-67, a mere three games better than 1929. Hubbell finished the season with a 17-12 record and a 3.87 ERA, slightly higher than '29. Fitzsimmons was 19-7 with an elevated 4.25 ERA, Walker 17-15, 3.93, and Mitchell 10-3, 3.98. Terry won the batting title with a remarkable .401 average.

Author Leonard Koppett, in his book *Koppett's Concise History of Major League Baseball,* best explains some of the unusual stats in 1930. "This was the season the National League ball was *really* juiced, as never before or since. The whole league hit .303, the Giants leading at .319. The Phillies were second, hitting .315—and finished last. The earned run average was 4.97."[7] He also mentioned Hack Wilson's league record of 56 home runs and 190 RBIs, still a league record. At least 25 regulars hit .333 or better. The fans, however, came out in droves. They loved the excitement and action brought on by the juiced ball and the tight pennant race, which was reflected in the record-setting 5.4 million attendance. The Polo Grounds' attendance was 868,714, only slightly lower than the previous season, despite the third-place finish and early signs of the slowing economy. That would change in the years to come as the Great Depression affected more and more families.

5

Pitched Well but Lacked Support

"ONE OF THE FIRST LESSONS I LEARNED IN THE BIG
LEAGUES WAS NEVER TO SPURN THE WEAKLING."

With a new five-year contract in hand and the disappointing 1930 season in the rear-view mirror, McGraw set his eyes on 1931 and the illusive twelfth pennant. Unlike previous years, McGraw made few significant changes to his everyday lineup. Hogan was behind the plate, Terry at first, Critz at second, and Jackson at short. The big move was the acquisition of Johnny Vergez from the Oakland Oaks of the Pacific Coast League, where in 1929, the right-handed slugger batted .323 and hit 46 home runs. In 1930 his production dropped but was still respectable, hitting .307 with 29 homers. With the acquisition of Vergez, McGraw moved Lindstrom to the outfield along with Ott and Leach. No major pitching changes were made concerning the starting rotation. McGraw was relying heavily on Fitz, Hub, Walker, and Mitchell.

Before discussing the new baseball season and the upcoming spring training, National League president John A. Heydler made an important announcement in early February. The juiced baseball, used in the 1930 season that produced record home runs and batting averages, was no more. No doubt, it came as a great relief to the National League pitches. Heydler made the announcement at the National League's annual meeting. The change to the 1930 ball was quite simple. The outer covering was made much heavier, plus the stitching was raised. Heydler went on to explain, "This heavier covering, it is believed, will slow up the ball to some extent, but the greatest advantage to the pitchers is offered in the raised stitching, which will enable them to get a much firmer grip on the ball."[1]

The Giants' spring training got off to a rocky start in San Antonio, Texas. Four key team members were not at camp and considered holdouts: Bill Terry, Frank Hogan, Freddie Fitzsimmons, and Joe Genewich. Pitcher Hub Pruett was also absent but had an excellent reason. He was a medical student at the time and was studying to become a practicing physician. In fact, Hub never played in 1931 for the Giants or any other major league team. He eventually landed with the Boston Braves in 1932. After a 1-5 record with a bloated 5.14 ERA, Pruett retired to practice medicine.

Concerning the four holdouts, it appeared McGraw was not overly concerned, especially with Genewich. He told the press, "Genewich really hasn't been much help to us for two seasons. And while I would like to see him come on it won't disturb me very much if he chooses to remain in Miami for the balance of the year."[2]

McGraw was certainly correct about Genewich's last two seasons. They were abominable. In 1929 he was 3-7 with a 6.78 ERA; in 1930, 2-5 with a 5.61 ERA. No wonder McGraw was so outspoken. A thorough search of the records shows Genewich never played for the Giants in 1931 or any other major league team. Perhaps Genewich took McGraw's advice and remained in Miami and retired, at least from baseball.

In early March, McGraw made a key move and placed Lindstrom in the outfield to become familiar with the new position. Lindy wasn't overly thrilled with the move but didn't hesitate to make the switch. Also, McGraw took steps to make sure Lindstrom would become proficient in the outfield, so he had coach Chief Bender hit endless fly balls to Freddie. He also received instruction from Mel Ott in the finer points of playing the outfield. It all paid off because, in the end, Lindstrom became equally proficient in the outfield as at third base. After a while, he confessed he enjoyed the outfield better than third and found it easier. He would play mostly center field but felt left was easier than right, mainly because the throw from right to third to cut down a runner was a long one.

McGraw, at the time, commented he was "not definitely committed to the switch." It all depended on Vergez. If he could handle third, as he was led to believe by everyone on the Pacific Coast, then the switch would be permanent. History shows the switch worked out, at least for two seasons, until Lindstrom was traded.

Besides the grind of the daily workouts, some lasting from 10 A.M. to 4 P.M., the holdouts still gained a great deal of attention. Fitzsimmons finally showed up at camp, as did Hogan, but no mention of salaries was forthcoming. That left Terry, who had a magnificent year in 1930 with an outstanding slash line .405/.452/.619 plus 23 home runs and 129 RBIs as the lone holdout. He also led the league with 254 hits. The negotiation battle between Terry and Stoneham became heated as the Giants' first baseman asked for $30,000 and a three-year contract. Apparently realizing $30,000 was a bit too much, Terry lowered his asking price to $25,000 and a one-year contract. He also added, he would agree to be "traded to any club willing to meet his price." Since Stoneham wouldn't budge from his final counteroffer of $22,000, there was a stalemate.

Days later, the negotiations that began in January finally ended. Terry reported to camp two weeks late but in good playing condition. Once again, there was no announcement as to the agreed-upon salary for Terry. Over the years, it was determined Terry signed for $21,500, a princely sum in 1931 during a nasty Depression.

During spring training and the exhibition schedule, both McGraw and Bancroft were emphatic. The key to the Giant fortunes was the pitching staff. Fitzsimmons was entering his seventh season and was a proven winner. Hubbell was entering his fourth and was creeping closer to stardom. Walker was another left-hander McGraw was counting on. Pete Donohue and Clarence Mitchell, two veterans, also showed what they were capable of during the exhibition games. Among the rookies, McGraw touted Hal Schumacher, Jack Berly, and Jim Mooney, two right-handers and a southpaw, who could help in the future.

Of the three, McGraw was on target with Schumacher. Although he didn't contribute much in '31, he did play 13 years with the Giants, ending his career with a 158-121 record and a 3.36 earned run average. He would appear in three World Series with a 2-2 won/lost record and a 4.13 ERA, along with election to two All-Star games.

Conversely, Berly and Mooney had short unimpressive careers. But give Mooney credit for pitching outstanding baseball for the Giants in '31. He finished the season with a 7-1 record and an incredible 2.01 ERA. The following year, Mooney was awful and, at the end of the season, was traded to the St. Louis Cardinals involving six players. The Giants' key acquisition was Gus Mancuso, Hubbell's catcher for his five fabulous seasons.

The Giants opened the 1931 season at Baker Bowl, beating the Phillies 9-5. Freddy Leach was in left field, Ott in center, and Lindstrom in right. The Giants' new outfield went 7 for 14 with three RBIs, undoubtedly pleasing Mc-Graw, as did Vergez at third base—2 for 4 with two RBIs. With his new lineup,

Little Napoleon had a good day as well as Fitzsimmons, who pitched seven innings for the win.

Freddie Fitzsimmons was born July 28, 1901, in Mishawaka, Indiana, to parents Robert and Margaret. Freddie was the second child of five. Despite growing up near Notre Dame in South Bend, Freddie loved the game of baseball. His favorite player at the time was shortstop Honus Wagner. And like so many young boys, he dreamed of becoming a big-league player. Although Freddie idolized Wagner, he decided to become a pitcher and learned to throw the knuckleball from a friend. He didn't play baseball at Mishawaka High School for the simple reason he was too busy playing for the local factory teams.

In 1920, Freddie was invited to a tryout with the Muskegon Muskies of the Class B Central League. He made the club and wound up pitching 100 innings, posting a 3-9 record with a 3.69 ERA. He returned in 1921 and threw over 250 innings while winning 14 and losing 13 games with a slightly improved 3.20 earned run average. Freddie returned for a third season with the Muskies in 1922, this time making an impression, winning 16 games, losing 11 with a 3.34 ERA. At the end of the season, the Indianapolis Indians of the American Association (AA) purchased his contract.

Freddie pitched four seasons for the Indians, winning a total of 40 games and losing 31. The last season was the one that caught the eye of the Giants. The knuckleballer posted a 14-6 record with a 3.77 earned run average. Towards the end of the 1925 season, the Giants bought Freddie's contract from the Indians.

Freddie recalls the moment. "I'll never forget the day I joined the Giants in 1925 after they bought my contract from Indianapolis. We were in Cincinnati, and we got beat a close one. Back in the clubhouse, I undressed and was about to head for the showers when Freddie Lindstrom nudged me."

"Sit still, kid," he told me.

"About then, McGraw stormed into the clubhouse and began ranting. It had been a day game, and there was going to be an outdoor fight at Crosley Field that night, and by the time McGraw finished chewing us out, the fight fans were streaming into the park."[3]

Although the Giants didn't win the pennant in 1925, it certainly wasn't Fitzsimmons' fault. He had an outstanding rookie season. He pitched in a little over 74 innings with a 6-3 record and an impressive 2.65 ERA. The young right-hander brought with him an odd windmill-style delivery. "Fitzsimmons not only would whirl his arms going into his windup but would turn his back on the batter at the last second. Then he'd unleash a pitch with surprising speed and a knuckleball-style flutter."[4]

Fitzsimmons's 1925 debut was the beginning of a 19-year major league career, 13 of which would be on the mound for the New York Giants. His only 20 game season was in 1928, when the Giants finished second with a 93-61 record. Fitz was 20-9 with a 3.68 ERA. He was a workhorse right from the beginning of his career. For example, in 1928, he pitched in over 260 innings, his second-most. In 1934 he threw over 263 innings. Today, only a handful of starting pitchers exceed the 200 threshold. Yes, indeed, Freddie could eat up the innings.

Two years later, in 1930, Freddie led the National League with a winning percentage of .731. His record was 19-7 with a disappointing 4.25 ERA. Perhaps the juiced-up ball that season resulted in high-scoring games, which would elevate the ERA. Once again, McGraw was frustrated, finishing third behind Chicago and pennant-winning St. Louis.

What every major league player dreams of became a reality in 1933 when the Giants won the National League pennant and were headed to the World Series. Sadly, McGraw had retired the year before, turning the reins over to player/manager Bill Terry. Freddie turned in a solid season, helping the Giants win. He won 16, lost 11 with an excellent 2.90 earned run average. The workhorse led the National League with 35 starts.

Now it was on to the World Series to face the heavily favorite Washington Senators, led by player/manager Joe Cronin. After Hubbell and Schumacher beat the Senators in the first two games, Game three was held in Washington D.C. at Griffith Stadium. It rained most of the morning, rendering the game doubtful. But as Franklyn Delano Roosevelt, the newly elected president, entered the stadium, the "skies cleared slightly." "Roosevelt, blessed with his inordinate good fortune, chose that moment to arrive at the game by car. The auto pulled down a Griffith Stadium runway as both teams, and a United States Army band stood in attention. Incredibly, the sun chose that very moment to emerge from the clouds. Surely, if FDR could have that impact on climactic conditions, happy days were here again."[5]

Terry called on Fitz for game number three. He pitched decently but lost 4-0 as Earl Whitehill blanked the Giants on an "artistic" five-hitter. Not surprisingly, Terry came right back with his two winners in games four and five. Both were nail-biters, and both went into extra innings. Hubbell won his game, but Schumacher needed relief help from Dolf Luque, who was credited with the win. Terry had won his first World Series as player/manager, and the New York Giants were once again on top of the National League.

In 1934, at age 32, Fitzsimmons posted his last memorable season with an 18-14 record and an ERA of 3.04. It was the season in which the durable right-hander threw over 263 innings, the most of his remarkable career. Along with others, his performance wasn't quite enough as the Giants were edged out by the St. Louis Cardinals for the pennant, finishing second two games back. This is pure speculation, but perhaps the high number of innings pitched was the cause of Fitz's elbow problem and subsequent poor record the following year.

It was later discovered that his arm had bothered him as early as spring training of 1935 but did nothing about it. By the time July rolled around, Fitz had a record of 4-4 and often didn't make it past the first couple of innings. Then, on July 5, he started against Brooklyn. Fitzsimmons was hit hard and left after four innings, allowing five runs on 11 hits. After the game, Terry had seen enough and sent Fitz to a physician for X-rays of his right elbow, fearing it might be a bone chip. Sure enough, two days later, Fitz underwent surgery to remove a bone chip from his right elbow. He didn't return to the mound until August 26 against Pittsburgh, entering the game in the fifth with the Pirates leading 9-0.

Fitz pitched well, allowing one run on six hits during his five-inning stint. After such a long layoff, it was an impressive return. His fastball, curve, and knuckleball were all on display. However, he didn't get his first start until September 7 and was out of the game in less than two innings, giving up five hits and four runs to Cincinnati. The final score was 4-2 and brought Fitz's record to 4-6.

Eighteen days later, it was an entirely different Freddie Fitzsimmons on the mound against Brooklyn. He hooked up in a pitcher's duel with one of the unique names in baseball—Van Lingle Mungo. He was also an unrivaled character during his playing days on and off the field. The two right-handers battled the entire game, neither allowing a run until Fitz weakened in the bottom of the ninth, giving up the winning run, as his record went to 4-7.

Back in the regular rotation, Freddie pitched the last game of the season, going the distance but losing to the Braves 3-0. His final record was 4-8.

In 1936, Freddie bounced back from his surgery, winning 10 and losing 7 with a 3.32 ERA. He did increase the number of innings pitched to over 141, but a far cry from the 250 plus innings before the surgery. Along with the rest of the pitching staff, led by Hubbell, the Giants won another pennant under the leadership of player/manager Terry. It would be the Giants and Fitz's second World Series in four years. They would meet the New York Yankees without Babe Ruth, who retired from baseball in 1935.

Although the Babe was gone, the Yankees were still a powerful club, featuring rookie Joe DiMaggio and veterans Lou Gehrig and Bill Dickey, among others. The pitching staff was not too shabby either. Red Ruffing, Monte Pearson, and Lefty Gomez led the starting rotation. As predicted, Hubbell started the first game and won. Unlike the '33 Series, Schumacher failed to follow Hub's footsteps and lasted only two innings in an 18-4 drubbing.

Fitz pitched the third game and lost a heartbreaker. The game was tied 1-1, entering the bottom of the eighth. George Selkirk led off for the Yankees with a first-pitch single to right. Jake Powell walked. Next, Tony Lazzeri laid down a perfect sacrifice bunt. With runners on second and third, Red Ruffing pinch-hit for pitcher Bump Hadley and hit back to Fitz, who threw home nailing Selkirk. Powell went to third while Roy Johnson was sent in to run for Ruffing. Up next, Frank Crosetti hit back to the box, the ball deflecting off Fitz, slowing it down. Second baseman Burgess Whitehead changed direction, but the ball lay dead in the inner grass as Powell crossed the plate. Moments later, Red Rolfe grounded out to end the inning. The Giants failed to score in the top of the ninth, losing the game, 2-1. Years later, Fitz contended he should have caught the comebacker off the bat of Crosetti.

Hubbell lost game four. Schumacher redeemed himself and won game five. Terry chose Fitzsimmons, the veteran right-hander, for the crucial game. Clearly, Fitz didn't have much working for him because the Yankees scored five runs in only 3 2/3 innings. The final score was 13-5 as the Yankees won the World Series in six games. It brought Fitz's World Series record to a miserable 0-3, which is not a true reflection of how he pitched. Fitzsimmons was not the only one disappointed. Although saddened, Terry was forthcoming with his praise of the Yankees. "That club," said Bill Terry, shaking his head in the locker room after Game Six, " has everything. They're the toughest club I've ever faced."[6]

There were no significant player changes over the winter as the Giants entered the 1937 season. Terry's club was competitive through April, May, and into June. However, Fitz was struggling with a record of 2-2 with a high 4.61 earned run average. No doubt, he was still recovering from the operation the season before. Then the big news hit the sports pages. Freddie Fitzsimmons was traded to rival Brooklyn for 22-year-old right-hander Tom Baker. Looking back, the Dodgers certainly got the better of the deal. In the two seasons with the Giants, Baker pitched a total of 35 innings and racked up one victory . . . and was out of baseball for good.

Fitz was with Brooklyn for seven years with a record of 47-32 and an ERA of 3.41. By far, his best season with the Dodgers was 1940. Freddie had a phenomenal year, leading all National League pitchers with a .889 winning percentage. His record was a brilliant 16-2 with a 2.81 ERA. He was 38 years old.

Fitz even had the good fortune to participate in his third and final World Series when Brooklyn won the National League pennant in 1941. They faced the powerful Yankees, with Fitz starting game three. He pitched excellent baseball, blanking the Yankees for seven innings on four hits. Hugh Casey relieved in the eighth and gave up two runs. Brooklyn came back with a run in their half, but that's the way the game ended, 2-1 Yanks. Fitz didn't pitch again in the Series as the Bronx Bombers won the next two games to clinch the Championship.

After the '41 Series, Fitz won only three games for Brooklyn during the next two seasons. The Dodgers released him in July of 1943. Shortly after that, Fitz signed a two-year contract to manage the Phillies, replacing Bucky Harris, once The Boy Wonder. Harris was canned by Philadelphia president William Cox after more than half the season was completed, with a miserable 39-53 mark. The Phillies under Fitz finished seventh. The following year, 1944, the Phillies finished last (61-92). By 1945, with an 18-51 record and mired in last place, Fitz was let go as the Phillies manager. As to managerial success, Fitz was a flop, but he still had a lot to offer as a coach. The knuckleballer was tagged with the irreverent sobriquet "Fat Freddie," coached for the Braves, Giants, Cubs, and Kansas City Athletics in the American League. Although Fitzsimmons hurled some hard luck games during his career, his nickname might have been the most unjust, at least, according to renowned sports announcer and writer Red Barber. Years later, Red recalled, "Fred always looked fat. That's how he got his nickname. However, Fred was built like a bear, and he was just as quick as a disturbed bear, just as strong and, when aroused, just as mean. When you saw Fred stripped, you realized he wasn't fat."[7]

Fitzsimmons pitched in the National League for 19 years, 13 with New York and seven with Brooklyn. He compiled a record of 217-146 with a 3.51 ERA. He appeared in three World Series with a mark of 0-3 and an earned run average of 3.86. Freddie Fitzsimmons died on November 18, 1979. He was 78.

New York jumped off to a good start in 1931 with a 5-1 record. However, Hubbell didn't get his first start of the season until game seven against Boston at Braves Field. He pitched a dandy of a game but lost 1-0 with the Braves scoring in the bottom of the ninth. Socks Seibold pitched one of the season's best games, holding the Giant's middle of the order—Lindstrom, Terry, and Ott, hitless.

On May 9, against the Cubs, Hubbell lasted only three innings before Mc-Graw pulled him, trailing 4-1. Hub wound up with a -decision as the Giants came back with a run in the fourth on a Jackson homer and three in the eighth, led by Ott'stwo-run blast. A week later, Hub was hammered once more, this time by the Cardinals, for five runs (three earned) on five hits as McGraw gave him the hook after three innings. Again, the Giants fought back and won the game 7-5, another no-decision for Hubbell. Both Ott and Terry got off to slow starts but would pick up the pace as the season progressed.

Ten days later, Hubbell was tapped to start again against the Boston Braves. He pitched a magnificent two-hit shutout, walking one batter and striking out seven. The final score was 3-0, evening his record at 2-2. In the second game of the doubleheader, another southpaw, Bill Walker, continued to throw up goose eggs, blanking Boston on eight scattered hits.

The two shutouts were only part of the enjoyment for the 20,000 New York fans. It was Bill Terry Day. Between games, the president of the New York chapter of the Baseball Writers Association presented Terry with a plaque, naming him "Player of the Year" for his remarkable 1930 season. To show the writers they made the correct decision, Terry went 3 for 4 in the second game.

On May 30, in the first game of a doubleheader, Hub was back in the four-day rotation as he lost to the Brooklyn Robins 5-2. All it took was one bad pitch in the 10th inning to Del Bissonette, who homered with two on to break the 2-2 tie. By the end of May, the Giants were 23-13, in second place, one game back of the St. Louis Cardinals with a record of 23-11.

During June, the Giants remained in second place but lost ground to the Cardinals. They now trailed St. Louis by 3½ games. Hubbell was far from dominating during the month, winning two and losing two, and even picked up a save in a relief role (MLB adopted the save stat in 1969 and amended it for the 1974 and 1975 seasons). But again and again, he would show flashes of the talent that would earn him the nickname the " Meal Ticket." It was on June 24 against the Chicago Cubs. He pitched another two-hit shutout, fanning nine and issuing only one walk for a sparkling 2-0 victory.

Then came July! The Giants record for the month was a poor 13-16. In their defense, the club did lose quite a few one-run games. While this was happening, the Cardinals played .617 baseball for the month and for the season, .630. So, it was no surprise the Giants were nine games back of the surging Cardinals at the end of July.

Hubbell won three and lost two games during the month, bringing his record to 7-7. One of the losses was to the Cardinals, a 2-1 squeaker, in the first game of a doubleheader. Hub pitched a solid eight innings, allowing four hits and two runs. Unfortunately for Hubbell, the Cards bunched three of the four hits in the fourth inning, and that's all they needed. Sylvester Johnson held the Giants to one run, Mel Ott's 17th homer of the season. The Giants lost the second game by the same score, dropping them to third place, 6 1/2 games back of the Redbirds.

Right from the get-go, the day had started badly when National League president Heydler slapped a three-day suspension on McGraw for the previous day's actions. Umpire Bob Clarke ejected McGraw for his "vigorous protest" over a decision the ump had made. When McGraw received word of the suspension, he went ballistic and tracked down Heydler before game one and denounced his actions in "strident tones." Yes, it was a bad day for the New York Giants and their fans. It would only get worse.

Hubbell finished the month by beating Cincinnati 4-2 and Pittsburgh 6-2. In between those two victories, Freddie Fitzsimmons continued to pitch well, building towards a solid season. On July 25, he threw a dazzling four-hit shutout defeating Cincinnati 5-0, bringing his record to 12-7.

Hubbell and the Giants jumped off to a fast start in August, winning their first five games, reviving the pennant hopes of their loyal fans. Hub began the mini streak with a 2-0 victory over the Boston Braves. It was his third shutout of the season. Bancroft was managing the club as McGraw continued to fight an ever-increasing illness. Sitting in the stands was Braves owner Judge Emil Fuchs, who in four short years would hire Babe Ruth under the pretense he would manage his club, a position the Yankees would not offer the Babe. As it turned out, Ruth never managed the Braves and retired after 28 games in the 1935 season.

Surprisingly, the Giants played well in August, winning 22 and losing 11 games. But it did little to change the standings, as the St. Louis Cardinals played even better baseball with a 20-8 record, a .714 winning percentage compared to the Giants .666. Regardless, the Giants were a frustrating ten games back of the runaway Cardinals at the end of the month.

Hubbell finished August with an 11-10 record, winning four games and losing three. In addition to opening the month with a superb shutout, he also beat Cincinnati. He didn't walk a batter the entire game, which helped his cause and the 3-1 victory. Eventually, Hub would become a master at putting the baseball where he wanted, especially the screwball. One of his three losses was a real bummer. He did a masterful pitching job for seven innings against the first-place Cardinals and left the game behind 1-0. Jack Berly pitched the eighth and gave up two runs. The Giants came back in the bottom of the eighth to score two but lost 3-2.

Hubbell opened September with a flurry, winning his first three starts. He beat Boston 9-2, picked up a save against Brooklyn (his third), and beat the Phillies and Pittsburgh in that order. The game against the Phillies was exceptional. The crafty left-hander spun a nifty three-hit shutout, winning 6-0 as Ott belted home run number 28. It was Hub's fourth shutout of the season. He walked one and fanned nine. His victory over the Pirates broke their eight-game winning streak and brought Hubbell's record to 14-10. *New York Times* writer John Drebinger described Hubbell's pitching as "a thing of beauty." The victory barely kept the Giants' pennant hopes alive as they trailed St. Louis by seven games with 13 remaining.

But those slim hopes were quickly dashed when the Giants lost nine of the 13 games while the Cardinals finished the season, winning 12 of 17, including seven games in a row. The season ended with the Giants in second place, a distant 13 games behind the pennant-winning Cardinals.

No excuses should be given for the Giants' awful second-place finish. The offense led by Terry and Ott did their job. According to *Baseball-Reference*, seven of the ten everyday players hit over .300 and as a team were ranked number one in batting average. The pitching staff was also ranked number one with regard to earned run average with a 3.30 mark. Walker (16-9, 2.26 ERA) and Fitzsimmons (18-11, 3.05 ERA) led the club in pitching. Hubbell's 14-12 record was not impressive, but his earned run average of 2.65, second to Walker, who led the National League, indicates he could have used more run support. In addition, Hubbell struck out 155 batters, second to the Cardinals Bill Hallahan who had 159.

However, Hub was inconsistent during the season, one game looking unhittable, the next not making it out of the first inning. Here's a perfect example. In the first three games Hubbell won in September, he allowed a total of three runs. In the last two games he pitched, he lost to Cincinnati 7-3 and Chicago 16-6. In the Reds game, he allowed 13 hits. The Cubs game was even more embarrassing. Before a crowd of 47,000, Hub lasted 1/3 of an inning! He retired the first batter, but the next four hit him solidly. Coupled by Lindstrom and Ethan Allen miscues, Hubbell was chased from the game. Not a good way to end the season.

The 1931 season for the New York Giants and Carl Hubbell was at best perplexing. In particular, McGraw's continued absence from the dugout, due to ill health, must have been disturbing to the club, with all due respect to Dave Bancroft. Age and illness would finally catch up to McGraw in 1932, leaving the leadership and club in a state of flux. Despite the changes and the team's poor showing, Carl Hubbell would have a breakout year in 1932. It would open the door to his five fabulous seasons.

6

Becoming the Ace

"I THINK A FELLOW PITCHES WITH HIS LEGS AND
WIND AS MUCH AS WITH HIS ARM."

In 1932 John McGraw was entering his 31st season as manager of the New York Giants. It would turn out to be an unexpected and shocking season for loyal Giant fans. Author Leonard Koppett described it as a "topsy-turvey" season for the entire league. The previous year the St. Louis Cardinals ran away with the league. In '32, they would sink to sixth place, a distant 18 games back of Chicago. In early August, the Cubs fired Rogers Hornsby and replaced him with their popular first baseman Charlie Grimm, who was given the nickname "Jolly Cholly" for the obvious reason he was always in good cheer. He was never or rarely in a bad mood. When Grimm took over the managerial reins, the Cubs were five games back of the league-leading Pittsburgh Pirates. Aided by a 14-game winning streak, Grimm brought the pennant to the Windy City as Pittsburgh finished second, four games back, under new manager George Gibson. Brooklyn also had a new manager, Max Carey, who replaced Wilbert Robinson, who ran the Robins (beginning in '32, called the Dodgers) for 18 seasons and was known affectionately by all as Uncle Robbie. The best Carey could do was third place, nine games back of the Cubs. The odd season continued as the Giants finished in sixth place, tied with the Cardinals. It was a position the McGraw Giants hadn't been in since their last-place finish in 1915!

McGraw began 1932 with only minor changes to the previous season's everyday lineup. Hogan caught, Terry was at first, Critz at second, and Vergez at third base. Doc Marshall and Travis Jackson shared the shortstop position. In the outfield, Freddy Leach was sold to the Boston Braves in March for $10,000.

That left Ott, Lindstrom, and Moore in the outfield, with Ethan Allen and Len Koenecke (an Indianapolis recruit) replacing the regulars when needed.

Also, there were not many pitching staff changes, just disappointments, except for Hubbell, who became the new ace of the rotation. Fitzsimmons, Walker, Mitchell, and Mooney all had off years compared to '31. Fitz went from 18-11 to 11-11, Walker from 16-9 to 8-12, Mitchell 13-11 to 1-3, and Mooney 7-1 to 6-10. Looking at it from a winning percentage point of view, it is even more revealing. Those four pitchers went from a .627 winning percentage to a miserable .419. And it wasn't for lack of support. The earned run averages reflected their poor pitching. Fitz finished with an ERA of 4.43, Walker 4.14, Mitchell 4.15, and Mooney 5.05.

The 1932 New York Giants spring training lasted almost eight weeks and was one of the longest ever by the McGrawmen. It was an excellent camp. The Giants record was 23-9 and against the Cubs was 5-3, the Pirates 2-0, and the Tigers 6-2. You would think such a record, even considering spring training games that don't count, McGraw would be his usual brash, optimistic self. *Times* sportswriter Drebinger diplomatically blamed McGraw's lack of enthusiasm on superstition. Filling the McGraw void, the writer pointed out the superb infield of Terry, Critz, Jackson, and Vergez with one caveat, Critz's arm that could hurt the completion of a double play. Terry came to Critz's defense rather emphatically. "Hughie is the greatest fielding second baseman in the game today, and I wouldn't care if he never completed a double play. He makes enough simple outs; no other player could make to more than offset any double plays he may miss."[1]

The outfield of Ott and Lindstrom with Koenecke and Allen, the former playing against right-handers and the latter against southpaws, was the original plan. It didn't work out, so Jo-Jo Moore and Chick Fullis played most of the games in left.

The Giants got off to a poor start beginning with the opening day game at the Polo Grounds. After all the usual fanfare and mayor Jimmy Walker throwing out the first ball, the Phillies blasted Walker for seven hits and seven runs and was showering after one inning.

Hubbell fell right in line as he lost his first two starts. The first loss was to the same Phillies 7-6 and the second to Boston. Walker started against Boston and pitched better than his first game. He pitched seven innings and gave up five runs. Luque relieved him and pitched two innings. He left with the score tied at 6-6. McGraw then called on Hub, who pitched three innings of shutout ball. But the Giants couldn't score either, so entering the 13th inning, the game was still tied at 6-6. Hub faltered and gave up two runs. The Giants came back with one run but fell short as the Braves won 8-7. Hubbell recorded his second loss, and the Giants were 1-5.

Author Fred Stein in *Under Coogan's Bluff* points out that McGraw in '32 was a disturbed man. No doubt, McGraw's age and years of pressure managing, along with his recent lack of success and health, finally caught up with him. "For the last few years, managing had become more and more of a strain on the high-strung little Irishman. He suffered from a number of physical ailments, and his normal irascibility had intensified and led him into uncontrolled outbursts at anyone—the fans, other baseball officials, and his own players."[2]

On April 24, Hubbell finally won his first game of the 1932 season. He scattered five hits and allowed two runs in a complete game, beating the Brooklyn Dodgers 7-2 before a paid crowd of 32,000. Hub's control was almost perfect as he allowed only two free passes. The Giants' offense woke up with a 16-hit barrage, led by Critz and Fullis with three hits each.

By the end of May, it was clear that even to die-hard Giant fans, it would be a long, frustrating season. The team was struggling to reach .500. Their record was 17-22 after a loss to the Braves on May 31. It would take them until June 15 and a six-game winning streak to reach .500 at 25-25. Two days later, they were at 26-26, but that was their last hurrah. They would come close but always fall back to below .500. It was like watching Sisyphus, the Greek King, endlessly roll a boulder up a hill only to see it roll back down.

Considering the lack of support from his teammates, May was a good month for Hubbell. He was 4-1. It could have been 5-1 considering, early in the month, he pitched seven innings against Brooklyn, allowing only one run but came away with a no-decision as Dolf Luque failed in relief and took the 3-1 loss. The only game Hubbell lost in May was to the Dodgers, and it was a heartbreaker.

It turned out to be an old-fashioned pitcher's duel between Hubbell and Watty Clark (a 20-game winner), two tough southpaws. After nine innings, the game was tied at 2-2. Both Brooklyn runs came on homers, one by Lefty O'Doul, the other by High Pockets Kelley who received his nickname because of his gangly 6' 4" frame. Ironically, both were former Giant players. In the top of the 12th, Brooklyn scored. Al Lopez singled, was sacrificed to second, and scampered home on a single by Johnny Frederick, off of Terry's shinbone. It would have been a tough loss for either pitcher but going somewhat unnoticed was Hubbell's 15 strikeouts, a record for the season in a single game.

He beat St. Louis 4-1, scattering six hits and only walking one; he beat Cincinnati 9-1 on six hits and no walks, with Terry and Hogan driving in two runs each. But it wasn't Hubbell's steady pitching or the Giants' outburst of hitting that aroused the 25,000 Cincinnati fans in the eighth inning. It was a decision by umpire Bill Klem. The fans in right field were so incensed they began heaving pop bottles onto the field. It lasted for ten minutes before special police entered the scene and restored order.

Hubbell beat Brooklyn 9-4 and Boston 6-2. Against the Robins, he walked two and gave up one to the Braves. Hubbell was establishing himself as a master of pinpoint control and the ace of the staff. Through May, Hub pitched a total of 77 plus innings and allowed a mere 13 walks. The great Satchel Paige has been given credit for many famous quotes. Whether he said them or not is irrelevant. When the discussion centers on a pitcher's control, Satchel's comments are interesting, if not meaningful. For example, "Just take the ball and throw it where you want. Throw strikes. Home plate doesn't move." And if all fails, "If a man can beat you, walk him."

Then came June, and all hell broke loose. But first, let author Noel Hynd give you his assessment of McGraw's distress and health at the time. ". . . McGraw found himself in a strange position. His players were in active rebellion against him, resenting his old-fashioned Napoleonic ways and the 'company spies' he hired as coaches. His pitchers, even the great Hubbell, resented his insistence at calling every pitch from the bench. The team was in and out of last place, and the fits of rage and frustration only increased in intensity." Hynd continues, "McGraw had suffered from sinus trouble most of his life and ptomaine poisoning within the last year. But now there were kidney problems that were accelerating, plus a general wearing down of energy and health."[3]

On June 3, John McGraw, the living legend, dramatically and unexpectedly announced his resignation after 30 years guiding the Giants to 10 pennants (including four in a row) and three World Championships. It was a shocker to many in the baseball world.

In a formal typewritten statement to the press, McGraw said, in part, "For over two years due to ill health, I have been contemplating the necessity of turning over the management of the Giants to someone else.

"My doctor advises me, because of my sinus condition, that it would be inadvisable to attempt any road trips with the club this season, so I suggested to

Mr. Stoneham that another manager be appointed, inasmuch as it is impossible for me to manage the club unless I accompany it, to which Mr. Stoneham agreed."[4]

Tributes to McGraw kept pouring in, hailing the veteran manager as having a great influence in developing the game of baseball. Kenesaw M. Landis, Commissioner of Baseball; John A. Heydler, president of the National League; Emil Fuchs, president of the Braves; William E. Benswanger, president of the Pirates; and Clark Griffith, president of the Senators praised McGraw as did the following managers: Joe McCarthy (Yankees), Max Carey (Dodgers), Bill McKechnie (Braves), Burt Shotton (Phillies), Gabby Street (Cardinals), George Gibson (Pirates), Rogers Hornsby (Cubs), and Connie Mack (A's).

At the same time, McGraw was making his announcement, Stoneham named Giants star first baseman, Bill Terry, as the new manager. It is an amusing story of how Terry became the new manager, which began months before in spring training. McGraw became angry with Terry during spring training when the first baseman was a holdout and refused to sign his contract. Eventually, he did sign for $18,000, a cut of $5,000. When the season began, McGraw was still sizzling over the holdout incident.

Then one day, the Giants lost a game to the Dodgers after leading by four runs. First, Val Picinich of the Dodgers homered off Larry Benton. Also, Terry booted a scorching grounder off his chest. After the game, McGraw and Terry argued vehemently, blaming each other for the loss. Terry said, "Don't blame me. Anyone could have seen that Benton didn't have it today. If you'd done what you should have done, you'd have yanked him. I didn't lose the game. You did."

After that blowup, McGraw didn't speak to Terry for weeks. "It was a funny feeling to go through spring training without ever talking to your manager. Then the next conversation I had with him was in June when I was told he wanted to see me in his office," said Terry. Entering McGraw's office, Terry was told to sit down with his back to the door. McGraw offered the job to Terry, who was shocked but immediately accepted without even thinking about it.[5]

Going almost unnoticed on June 3 were offensive explosions by two popular New York Yankee players as they walloped Connie Mack's Philadelphia Athletics 20-13. First, Lou Gehrig smashed four home runs in consecutive at-bats. The feat tied the all-time record by Bobby Lowe in 1894 and Ed Delahanty in 1896! (It is interesting to note from 1893 to 1895, Lowe hit a total of 38 homers. In the other 15 years of his career, he hit a mere 33.) With two more at-bats remaining, the Philadelphia crowd encouraged Gehrig to hit number five. But it was not to be. He grounded out in the eighth and came to bat again in the ninth. From the dugout, Bill Dickey viewed the scene. "I'll never forget the day Gehrig hit four home runs in a game in Philadelphia—one in left field, one in left-center, one in right-center, and one in right—and in that order. All well-hit balls. Just went around the horn with it. That day made me very happy. We did have a disappointing moment in that game because the fifth ball he hit looked like it was going into the lower left-field seats, and Al Simmons boosted himself up on the left-field fence and made the greatest one-handed catch you ever saw on it. Lou very easily could've had five homers in one game."[6]

Second was Tony Lazzeri's record-setting afternoon. Poosh `Em Up hit for the natural cycle (single, double, triple, home run in that order). He became one of 14 major league players to accomplish the feat. However, Lazzeri became the only player to finish off the cycle with a grand slam.

Considering the change in managers and the ensuing turmoil that was expected, the Giants had a surprising month of June, going 13-11. But the club was still stuck in sixth place, four games back of front running Pittsburgh.

One of Terry's early moves as the new manager was his handling of Len Koenecke. He was not a big fan of the outfielder who hit .353 in the American Association. So, on June 9, after going hitless in a 7-0 loss to the Cardinals, Terry optioned him to the Jersey City Skeeters of the International League (AA).

But the Koenecke story doesn't end in Jersey City. He also played for Brooklyn in 1934 and batted .320. He returned in 1935, but his performance slipped as drinking became a serious problem. The Dodgers cut him on September 16. According to *The Sporting News,* "Koenecke had been paid off for the season earlier in the day in St. Louis and boarded an airline for Detroit. In the latter city, he chartered another plane and was nearing Toronto when the broad-shouldered outfielder became engaged in a fight with the ship's pilot and co-pilot.

"High above New Toronto, Ont., Koenecke is alleged to have thrown the co-pilot to the floor of the plane and was beating him when Pilot William J. Mulqueeney of Detroit pulled a small fire extinguisher from the wall and struck the player on the head. He then landed the plane in a field, where it was found Koenecke was dead.

"Mulqueeney claimed his plane was almost out of control, and he had lost his sense of direction. "I had to make a quick decision," the pilot continued in his statement to authorities in New Toronto. "It was either a case of the three of us crashing or me quieting Koenecke. I waited my chance and struck him with the extinguisher. Then I landed as quickly as possible, not knowing, of course, that he was dead."[7]

Hubbell, now pitching for new manager Bill Terry, went 2-2 in June with three no-decisions and one save. The loss against the Chicago Cubs at the Polo Grounds was a particularly tough one to swallow. Hub allowed two runs in the first inning, not all his fault. Woody English led off for the Cubs with a single that hit the third-base bag. Billy Herman sacrificed him to second. Kiki Cuyler then tripled off the left-field wall scoring English. When Lindstrom's relay sailed past third, Cuyler continued on home. In the meantime, Burleigh Grimes, the veteran spitballer, handcuffed the Giant batters. For seven innings, Grimes was almost invincible, allowing three singles and a walk. No runner reached second. Sam Leslie pinch hit for Hubbell and homered in the eighth, making the score 2-1. Sam Gibson shut down the Cubs in the ninth, but the Giants failed to score in their half. It certainly was a game Hub could have won with more support. The loss also snapped the Giants' six-game winning streak.

One of Hubbell's two victories was against the St. Louis Cardinals. This was a game he did get a lot of support, as the Giants pounded out 13 hits and nine runs for an easy 9-1 victory. Hubbell was brilliant. The lefty was in total command from start to finish. He allowed two hits, one a home run by Ernie Orsatti in the eighth inning to spoil the shutout, the other a single by his mound opponent Bill Hallahan. Hub's masterpiece included no walks and six strikeouts, bringing his record to 7-4. It also broke a three-game losing streak. Terry led the offense with a 4-for-5 day, driving in two and scoring three runs.

At the end of June, the Giants were still stuck in seventh place, but there was hope, as thin as it might be, since they were only four games back of the current league-leading Pirates. With a hot winning streak, the gap could easily disappear. Hubbell did all he could in July to help the club with a 5-1 record. The Giants, particularly the pitching (minus Hubbell), did not hold up as the team record was 15-20. By the end of the month, the Giants were a whopping 13 1/2 games back of the Pirates.

During July, Hubbell won five games in a row interspersed with two no-decisions. On July 3, he beat Boston 5-2. Once again, Hub's control was perfect, not allowing a free pass. The screwball and pinpoint control would define Hubbell during his upcoming fabulous five seasons.

Hubbell's next victory came on July 12 when he beat the Cincinnati Reds 4-3 and, as he did in June, was the stopper, breaking the Giants' four-game losing streak. Hub scattered six hits and helped his cause by not walking a batter. Even with the victory, the Giants remained in seventh place, a whopping ten games back of the Pirates. Hub's record was 9-5.

Four days later, Hubbell beat St. Louis 4-1 for his 10th victory. He allowed five hits but was wild by his standard, giving up two walks. He compensated somewhat by fanning nine. On July 20, he handcuffed Chicago 9-1 improving his record to 11-5. Yes, he didn't walk a batter. On July 24, in the first game of a doubleheader with the Braves, Fitzsimmons was pitching a solid game entering the bottom of the eighth tied at 3-3. Pinky Hargrave and Tom Zachary singled with one out. Fitz then walked Rabbit Maranville to load the bases. Terry quickly called for Hubbell to put out the fire. It was not to be this afternoon. Hub threw one pitch to pinch hitter Wes Schulmerich, who singled to center, scoring Hargrave with the winning run.

Next, Hub beat the Pirates 7-3 for his 12th victory and fifth in a row. It wasn't one of his better-pitched games. He gave up a homer to Adam Comorosky in the third, but the Giants came right back with four runs of their own. The four spot was led by Terry's 16th homer, a three-run blast to right. That's all Hubbell needed. He scattered 11 hits and kept league-leading Pittsburgh from big innings as the Giants tacked on more runs.

Hubbell ended the month with a loss to Cincinnati 3-1, although he didn't pitch badly. With any kind of support, he could have had another victory. He only allowed three runs and walked none in eight innings. But the Giants couldn't touch Ownie Carroll, or at least put more pressure on the right-hander, when those few opportunities appeared. For example, in the fifth, Terry opened with a double but did not score. In the seventh, with runners on first and second and one out, Gil English hit into a double play. The Giants finally reached Carroll for a run in the ninth, but it was too little too late

The Giants finished July on a high note, taking both ends of a double-header from last place Cincinnati (hey, a win is a win), 4-3 and 6-4. They were now 13½ games back of the Pittsburgh Pirates as the season quickly drew to a close. One of the big contributors for the month was 23-year-old Mel Ott. For July, the young right fielder batted a cool .330, including six home runs and 28 RBIs while scoring 30 runs.

Melvin Thomas Ott was born March 2, 1909, in Gretna, Louisiana, located across the Mississippi River from downtown New Orleans. His parents, Charles and Carrie, were of Danish descent. He was one of three children. Mel's father worked for an oil company for years, but baseball was in the family bloodline. Mel's father was a catcher, and his uncle Miller was a pitcher. Both played semi-pro ball. It was no surprise then; young Mel loved the game and excelled at an early age. When Mel was 11 years old and big for his age, he played baseball almost every day. He played basketball and football too. He played baseball in grammar school and high school as a catcher. According to sports columnist Jimmy Powers, writing for the *Daily News* in his column *Powerhouse*, Mel quit high school two months before graduation but later was given his diploma.

Years later, Mel recalled, "I have been playing baseball as far back as I can remember. My father and uncle were good semi-pro players. As a matter of fact, my uncle beat the Cleveland Indians in an exhibition game 1-0. They took me out to the ballpark before I could walk. I was only 15-years-old when the backer of the semi-pro team I was catching for took me to Mr. McGraw for a look."[8]

What Ott was referring to was an incident in 1924. He was given a tryout with the New Orleans Pelicans of the Southern Association (A). The team was no slouch as they won the pennant the year before. It was determined Mel was too young, so arrangements were made for him to play with a lumber mill team in Patterson, Louisiana, a town approximately 90 miles above New Orleans. It just so happened that the team owner was Harry Williams, a millionaire and friend of McGraw.

Mel played well at Patterson and became the regular catcher. Williams paid him $150 a month plus expenses. He also was quick to recognize the young kid had talent and, no doubt, immediately thought of his friend McGraw. "Later in the summer, Williams left for a trip to Europe. He stopped in New York City to see his friend John McGraw and told him about the wonderful catcher and hitter he had on his team out in Patterson."[9]

Since Williams had recommended players to McGraw before, the Giant manager readily accepted his advice and sent Mel a contract. He was told to report to the Polo Grounds for a tryout in the fall of 1925. At the workout, Mel impressed both Frankie Frisch and McGraw with his solid hitting. So, in 1926 16-year-old Melvin Thomas Ott was given a contract to play for the New York Giants and legendary manager John McGraw. But according to Ott, "even making good for McGraw" wasn't his biggest problem. It was getting his mother's permission to leave home for New York City. Mel had no trouble with getting his dad's okay, being a ballplayer himself. Eventually, Mel's mother came around and gave him her blessing. It is interesting to speculate what effect it would have had on the New York Giants and even baseball if Mel's mom prevailed.

Right from the start, McGraw took a fatherly interest in Mel. Some even say it was the son McGraw never had. Of course, that is pure speculation. What McGraw did do was immediately convert Mel to an outfielder. He was not going to be a catcher. His stocky legs were not designed to do a lot of crouching, besides the everyday beating a catcher endures. Keep in mind; this was 1926, catching equipment was nowhere near the sophistication of today. Young Mel would not have lasted 22 years, except in the outfield. McGraw made a great call.

McGraw was also fiercely determined no minor league manager would tinker with his young, future superstar's development. So, for the first full season, 1925, Mel sat on the bench alongside McGraw. One final critical demand McGraw insisted would not change, and that was Mel's batting stance.

"Master Melvin," as one scribe labeled him early in his career, had a highly unorthodox stance. Over the years, Ott's batting style has been described by many as strange, to say the least. As a left-handed batter, he would lift his right leg in the air and drop his bat low while the pitch was delivered. It helped generate power from his 5'9" 170-pound frame. The first time New York Yankee outfielder Tommy Henrich saw Ott, he claimed he would be a sucker for a changeup. Henrich changed his mind quickly when he saw Cleveland's great Mel Harder, in an exhibition game, throw the changeup to Ott, who promptly smacked it out of the ballpark.

So, it was no surprise when McGraw watched the 16-year-old taking batting practice at the Polo Grounds. Weird stance and all, he was pounding the ball all over the field as McGraw stood in amazement. "That kid has the finest natural batting form I've ever seen. But don't tell him. It will make him feel self-conscious and spoil everything."[10] This coming from the man who wasted few superlatives when evaluating baseball talent.

For the next two years, 1926-27, McGraw brought his teenage phenom along slowly. He was used mostly as a pinch hitter and played in the outfield. Ott led the National League with "46 pinch-hit at-bats in 1927." McGraw was so protective of his future star he didn't even want him to hang around with veteran players who might steer him in the wrong direction. When Hubbell arrived in 1928, he and Ott became roommates and eventually longtime friends.

In 1928 Mel became the starting right fielder for the Giants, and what a season it was, considering his age and inexperience. He played in 124 games, batted .322 with 18 home runs and 77 RBIs. It was just a hint of what Giant fans could expect in the future . . . and he didn't disappoint. For the next 17 years, Mel would put up numbers that would send him straight to the Hall of Fame. Here's what he accomplished in his 22-year career, all with the New York Giants.

In 1929 a career-high of 42 home runs plus driving in 151. He led the league with 113 walks

In 1930 led the league with a .458 OBP while hitting .349 and driving in 119 with 25 homers

In 1931 he led the league with 80 walks

In 1932 he led the league with 39 home runs, 100 walks, and a .424 on-base percentage

In 1933 he led the league with 75 walks

In 1934 he led the league with 35 homers and 135 RBIs

In 1936 he led the league with 33 homers

In 1937 he led the league with 31 home runs and 102 walks

In 1938 he led the league with 36 home runs, 116 runs scored, and a .442 OBP

In 1939 he led the league with a .449 OBP

In 1942 he led the league with 118 runs, 30 homers, and 109 walks

In 1945 he was the first player in the National League to hit 500 home runs

(Source: Baseball-Reference.com)

Mel Ott also played in three World Series, 1933, 1936, and 1937. In 1933 the Giants, led by Bill Terry, beat the Washington Senators in five games. The fifth and deciding game was won dramatically by Ott, with his second homer of the Series, in the 10th inning. It was hit off Jack Russell. The other two Series were played against the New York Yankees, and the Giants lost both. In '36, the Yankees were without Ruth, who had retired. But they still beat the Giants in six games. Then in '37, in a classic rematch, the Yankees once again beat the Giants, led by Joe DiMaggio, Lou Gehrig, Bill Dickey, Tony Lazzeri, and the pitching of Lefty Gomez. Mel was also chosen for 12 All-Star Games beginning in 1934 through 1945. Master Melvin, in late 1937, was named by manager Terry as the new captain of the Giants.

To sum up Mel's stats, he was an active player for the Giants for 22 years, appearing in 2,730 games, collecting 2,876 hits for a batting average of .304 and an OBP of .414. He also hit 511 home runs and drove in 1,860 runners. Not too shabby for a 16-year-old coming out of the small town of Gretna, Louisiana.

Six days before the infamous Japanese attack on Pearl Harbor, Mel Ott, at the age of 32, was named the New York Giants manager. According to Horace Stoneham, Ott's appointment came as a complete surprise to the mild-mannered, soft-spoken, and shy home run king. Also, Terry had high praise for his successor. "I believe Ott will make an ideal manager. I don't think there is anyone in the world who doesn't wish him well, and, while some may feel that perhaps he is too quiet and retiring to make a strong leader, let me tell you that in his own way, he can be mighty aggressive if the situation demands it."[11]

Agreeing with Terry that Ott would make an ideal manager were some of the well-known major league sportswriters. They included Jimmy Powers, *New York Daily News*; Harold Parrott, *Brooklyn Eagle*; Joe Williams, *New York World-Telegram*; Stanley Frank, *New York Post*; Bill Corum, *New York Journal American*; and John P. Carmichael, *Chicago Dailey News*.

Initially, Mel proved the scribes correct as he led the Giants to a third-place finish in 1942 with a respectable record of 85-67, a solid improvement over the previous year's fifth-place (74-79) under Terry. As history will show, 1942 was Ott's finest year as a manager. The best Ott could do during the next five years was finish fourth with an 81-73 record. In 1948, after a slow start (37-38), Ott was replaced by the highly controversial Brooklyn Dodger manager Leo Durocher.

In hindsight, Ott, the manager, took on a whole new persona. He wasn't the reserved, quiet, nice guy fans, reporters, and others knew as a ballplayer. "Normally mild-mannered, he suffered the Giants' poor play with outbursts stemming from frustration. He levied numerous player fines and made public criticisms of the team's performance. It is said he acted out of character those first few years, trying to explode his 'shy and retiring image."[12]

After Ott was relieved of his managerial duties, he worked with his former roommate, Carl Hubbell, to run the Giants farm system. He did this until his contract expired in 1950. However, Ott continued to stay active by landing a job in the Pacific Coast League managing the Oakland Oaks. In 1951, the Oaks finished fifth in an eight-team league, 19½ games in back of the Seattle

Rainiers. The following year, Ott did an outstanding job guiding Oakland to a second-place finish, with a mark of 104-76, five games back of the Hollywood Stars.

Out of baseball for the next two years and still a young man, Mel realized he missed the game. In 1955, he landed a job with Mutual Network's "Game of the Day," broadcasting games on the radio. The following year he found himself in the broadcast booth with Van Patrick, announcing the Detroit Tiger games. In 1958, after the baseball season was finished and Mel's duties were over, tragedy struck him and his wife, Mildred. They were driving home to Metairie, Louisiana, on November 14, after having dinner at a restaurant. Back on the highway, a heavy fog had settled in. Mel's station wagon collided head-on with another car driven by a 50-year-old carpenter, Leslie S. Curry, who was killed instantly. Mel and his wife suffered multiple injuries. Both were taken to a hospital in Gulfport, Mississippi. On November 20, Mel was taken to a New Orleans hospital and underwent kidney surgery but died the next day. He was 49 years old. Mildred died in 1999 at age 90.

Although August began on a high note with the Giants extending their July winning streak to six, the month had a terrible ending. Terry found his club losing their last six games. August was almost a repeat of July. The club still floundered with a losing record of 14-17.

Hubbell also had a frustrating month, posting a losing record of 2-4. Three of the four losses were by one run. Hub began the month winning his 13th game by beating the Cardinals 4-1. He spread eight hits, walked one, and whiffed six. Ott's triple accounted for two of the four Giant runs. His other victory was against the Pirates, where he was the beneficiary of a six-run, first-inning explosion. In this game, Terry went 3 for 5. One of the hits was his 33rd double of the season. At first glance, 33 doubles with half a month of baseball remaining seems commendable. It paled, however, compared to the year Pittsburgh's Paul Waner was having. For example, on May 20, in a game against the Cardinals, he smacked four doubles in five at-bats. For the year, Waner would break Chuck Klein's National League record for the most doubles in a season with an eye-opening 62! No wonder he was given the nickname "Big Poison."

The three games Hub lost were: 4-3 to Chicago, 2-1 to Brooklyn in 10 innings, and 4-3 to Pittsburgh. Hubbell lasted only two innings in the latter game, a rare poor performance by the star southpaw. His record entering September was 14-10, and New York was a discouraging 59-70, putting the Giants a hefty 17½ games behind the now red hot first-place Chicago Cubs. Although not mathematically eliminated from the pennant race, realistically, it had been over for the Giants for some time. Moreover, the schedule was a serious hurdle. They were faced with seven doubleheaders in September, putting an unbearable strain on the already underperforming pitching staff.

To Terry's and the Giants' credit, they never gave up in September, even though it was a hopeless task. The team finished the month 18-11 with Hubbell winning four and losing one. The loss came on September 5, in relief of Schumacher, who relieved Mooney. Terry called on Hubbell in the bottom of the eighth to save the day. With runners on first and second, Hub allowed a single, making the score 4-3 Giants. But in the bottom of the ninth, he allowed two runs on a single, a sacrifice, and two doubles—final score Phillies 5 Giants 4.

After the poor relief outing, Hubbell didn't pitch again for six days. The rest probably helped, for he won his last four starts of the season and finished with an outstanding record of 18-11 and an impressive 2.50 earned run average in 284 innings, the most of his career to date. It is not unreasonable to conjecture; Hubbell could have easily been a 20-game winner in 1932. He lost seven one-run games. With a tad more offense, from his teammates, in only two of the seven, his record could have been 20-9.

The Giants' season was a calamity. First, a slow start from which the team never recovered. Second, the sudden retiring of John McGraw had to cause confusion and uncertainty among the players. Third, Terry was thrust into a managerial position with zero experience, not an ideal situation, plus he had to contend with the added burden of being a player/manager. Fourth, the pitching rotation was a huge disappointment. Only two pitchers on the entire staff could boast of winning records—Hi Bell (8-4 with a 3.68 ERA) at age 34, would be out of baseball after two more seasons and Hubbell. Although Schumacher, at 21, showed promise and would become a star in 1933 and beyond.

The Giants' dismal performance clearly showed up in attendance at the Polo Grounds. It was a pathetic 484,868, a far cry from the 916,191 in 1928. Granted, the Depression had some effect but certainly not all. In fact, for the next five years, when the Giants fielded competitive teams, and Hubbell dominated the National League, attendance rose steadily to 926,887 by 1937. It's axiomatic, regardless of the product—car, dishwasher, TV—if it's good and reliable and the customer is satisfied, it will sell. It applies to baseball as well, even though it's a game. It is also a product (entertainment) to be sold. Simply put, if the team is no good, it will be reflected in attendance.

It is safe to say that the New York Giants front office, Bill Terry, sports media, and fans didn't know what the next five seasons would be like in the city of New York. Or how Carl Hubbell and his unhittable screwball would dominate the National League and pave the way for him to enter Cooperstown.

7

Most Wins, Lowest ERA, MVP

"I LEARNED THAT EVEN THE BEST HITTERS IN THE MAJOR LEAGUES COULDN'T HIT THE SCREWBALL."

Bill Terry took over the Giants' managerial job about halfway through the 1932 season, improving slightly on McGraw's record but still could only finish sixth. Memphis Bill, as he was called by the press, didn't let the poor showing of the Giants affect his play. The star first baseman owned a slash line of .350/.382/.580, including 28 home runs and 117 RBIs.

Now Terry would have the opportunity to manage the Giants for a full season in 1933. He didn't waste much time either after the conclusion of the '32 season. He sent outfielder Ethan Allen, backup catcher Bob O'Farrell, and two pitchers, Bill Walker and Jim Mooney, to the St. Louis Cardinals for catcher Gus Mancuso and pitcher Ray Starr. The gem of the trade was Mancuso, buried in the Cardinals farm system until Landis stepped in and forced St. Louis to put him on the major league roster or lose him. Mancuso was not much of a hitter but was a fine catcher who would handle the Giants pitching staff skillfully. Hubbell had high praise for the agile Mancuso, who caught Hub during his five fabulous seasons of pitching domination. The acquisition of Mancuso made the slow-footed and heavy Shanty Hogan expendable. By the end of December, Terry had sold Hogan to the Boston Braves for a reported $25,000.

Freddie Lindstrom was still upset over not being made the Giants manager when, according to him, he was promised the job. So, Freddie requested he be traded. Terry obliged, and Freddie became part of a three-team deal involving the Pirates and Phillies, with Lindstrom going to Pittsburgh and Chick Fullis to Philadelphia. Also, the Giants received Kiddo Davis from the Phillies and Glenn Spencer from the Pirates. The Pirates sent Gus Dugas to Philadelphia.

For the Giants, the trade meant Davis would replace Lindstrom in the outfield. Then, in the middle of June, the Giants picked up veteran outfielder Lefty O'Doul (age 36) from Brooklyn for first baseman Sam Leslie. O'Doul would play in 78 games and bat .306.

There was one other position Terry had to deal with, and that was at shortstop. Travis Jackson had been the regular shortstop since 1923, but in '32, he injured his knee and was still not fully recovered. Terry chose John Blondy Ryan, a brash young (27) graduate from Holy Cross, to replace Jackson, who still played a part-time role.

Terry's trades and maneuvering resulted in an experienced (except for Ryan) lineup of Mancuso behind the plate, Terry at first, Hughie Critz at second, and Johnny Vergez at third. The outfield consisted of Mel Ott, Jo-Jo Moore, two proven players, and new addition Davis. Based on the results from the 1932 season, the pitching staff could be a problem, except for Hubbell. Keep in mind, Fitzsimmons, Walker, Mooney, Hoyt, Mitchell, Parmelee, and Schumacher were all disappointments. None had a winning record. On the bright side, Terry was particularly high on 21-year-old Schumacher and his devastating sinker.

In his book Under Coogan's Bluff, author Fred Stein offered this assessment of the Giants' pennant chances in 1933. "On paper, the Giant club which began spring training at Los Angeles was not a pennant contender. The consensus of players, managers, and sports writers throughout the league was that the Giants were facing a long season with only four proven stars, a prayer, and a string of nameless faces in Giant uniforms."[1]

It was a frank and harsh statement that was validated, again on paper, when the Associated Press annual sports writers' poll ranked the Giants sixth! Forty-two favored the Pirates for first place, while only 18 picked the Giants for the first division. It became quite comical when, before opening day, sports writers asked Terry how the Giants would fare this year.

"I think we'll do third or better," answered Terry.

The writers began to chuckle. Chalk it up to overconfidence in a manager beginning his first full year. Terry continued, "I'm telling you guys, we're a cinch for the first division if Parmelee and Schumacher come through. Of course, I'm taking Fitz and Hubbell for granted. If any of you think I'm kidding, put your money where your mouth is."[2] By the end of the season, Terry had the last laugh and might have been a few dollars richer, courtesy of the doubting sportswriters.

The Giants were to open the 1933 season at Boston, but rain, snow, and a mixture of both postponed the entire series, one day after another. On the last day, Braves Field was declared unfit to play. In the meantime, while other teams around both leagues were enjoying opening day festivities, John A. Heydler, president of the National League, warned all the players, "the championship season ahead may see the popularity of baseball put to the acid test and urging upon all to bend every effort to retain the public interest in the game."[3]

Heydler's major concern was the Depression, although he didn't mention the word but danced around it using the term "more stringent money conditions." He also emphasized competition from other sports and amusements that could affect the popularity of the game. More to the point, Heydler laid down practices for the players to keep in mind during the long season:

1. Do not mingle with other players on the field.
2. Do not enter the clubhouse or dressing rooms of the other team.
3. Do not take it easy with a lopsided score against you.
4. More action and hustle are needed.
5. Be alert and interested during the entire game.

Heydler ended his pep talk by quoting President Roosevelt, "Major League Baseball has done as much as any one thing in this country to keep up the spirit of the people."[4]

Jumping on the rah-rah bandwagon was the president of the American League, Will Harridge. He also warned the players that fraternizing with the opposition was not good for the game, especially on the field. He added one other warning; any assault of one player to another would result in a 30-day suspension without pay.

The New York Giants 1933 season finally got underway on April 16 against the Brooklyn Dodgers at Ebbets Field. And what a game it was! It pitted two southpaws against each other, the Giant's ace Hubbell and Brooklyn's Joe Shaute. After the Giants went through repeated postponements in Boston, the game, would you believe, lasted 14 innings and ended in a 1-1 tie. One reporter described the game as a "breathless pitching duel."

The Giants struck first, in the second inning, with an unearned run. The Dodgers came back in the seventh on a Hack Wilson triple and scored on Tony

Cuccinello's single. Both Hubbell and Shaute went 11 innings and matched each other pitch for pitch. Their stat line was almost identical. Shaute allowed eight hits and one run but walked two and struck out one. Hub also gave up eight hits and one run but fanned seven and walked none; the latter, along with his nasty screwball, would be his trademark for the next five years.

Terry was eager to begin the season with a victory, so he called on Hubbell, on one day's rest, to stop Philadelphia's rally in the bottom of the ninth. The Giants were leading 3-2 when Fitzsimmons wilted in the eighth. Adolfo Luque, the Cuban-born right-hander, came in and held the Phillies at 3-2. But in the bottom of the ninth, he walked the leadoff batter who was sacrificed to second. Terry had seen enough. Hubbell entered the ninth and struck out pinch hitter Al Todd for the second out and enticed another pinch hitter, Eddie Delker, to tap back to the box for the third out and the Giants' first victory of the new season. Fitz was credited with the win and Hub the save.

Opening day at the Polo Grounds finally arrived as 10,000 fans suffered cold, frigid weather, many wearing coats and wrapped in blankets. Promptly at 3 P.M. New York City mayor John P. O'Brien and his entourage opened the ceremonies by raising the flag and playing the "Star-Spangled Banner," by the Manhattan College band. With the Giants and the Boston Braves lined up, O'Brien led a parade of dignitaries, including McGraw, Stoneham, Secretary Jim Tierney, Police Commissioner James S. Bolan, and Gerard O'Brien, son of the mayor. It was McGraw's first opening day as a spectator and not the Giants manager since 1903. He graciously shook Terry's hand and wished him well during the season.

Then Hubbell took over and dominated the game. He allowed four hits, walked two but struck out 13. His screwball worked to perfection as he monopolized the game for a 1-0 victory. It was his first shutout as he would register nine more during the season.

Four days later, Hubbell pitched another gem. Somewhat out of character, he walked three batters. It was his second consecutive shutout, whipping the Dodgers at the Polo Grounds 4-0, before a thrilled crowd of 15,000. But it was a costly victory for the Giants. In the fifth inning, Brooklyn starter Shaute's erratic pitch hit Terry, breaking his right wrist and sidelining the Giants manager and star first baseman for an estimated three to four weeks. Sam Leslie replaced Terry, who would manage from the dugout with a cast on his wrist. Ironically, Leslie drove in two of the four Giant runs.

Meanwhile, Hubbell continued to hold the Dodgers spellbound, scattering four measly singles while chalking up another win. Since the April 16 tie game, Hub has pitched 22 2/3 innings without yielding a run. It was a preview of the greatness to come. Hubbell's record was now 2-0.

Terry wasn't giving Hubbell much rest, using him both as a starter and reliever, at least in the early stages of the season. Such was the case when Hub came on in relief against the Phillies, in the seventh inning, with the score tied 2-2. While Hubbell was baffling the Phillies for three innings with his screwball, the Giants scored three runs in the bottom of the eighth to win their fifth straight game 5-2. Mancuso, Ryan, and Hubbell accounted for the three runs. The victory put the Giants in first place by a half-game over the Pirates. Hubbell ran his scoreless inning streak to 25 2/3. His record was now 3-0.

The inevitable had to happen, and it did, which was a huge disappointment to the loyal New York Giant fans. Boston beat the Giants in a doubleheader 3-0 and 8-4, before 35,000 at Braves Field. Hubbell took his first loss of the season in the opener, plus ending his scoreless innings streak at 27 2/3. Adding insult to injury, the Giants were toppled from first place as the Pirates beat Cincinnati. Hubbell's record was now 3-1.

Hubbell began the month of May on a positive note. He picked up a save, his second on May 4, against the Chicago Cubs. Parmelee started the game and "acquitted himself nobly," as one writer noted. He left after eight innings leading 5-4. Terry was taking no chances with a one-run lead and Chicago's heavy hitters coming up. He quickly called on Hub to protect the lead and win. Hub responded, retiring the side in one-two-three order. Terry, Fitzsimmons, and others knew of Parmelee's tendency to fold under pressure. Fitz, in an article for the *Saturday Evening Post*, wrote, "The worst or most pitiful example I ever knew of a fellow who went to pieces under pressure was Roy Parmelee, a big, strong right-hander who had all the earmarks of a twenty-game winner when he broke in with the Giants in 1933." Fitz added, "Bill Terry, the Giant manager, never gave Parmelee any advance notice when he was due to pitch. If Roy knew he was working the next day, he couldn't sleep."[5] Clearly, Terry wasn't going to gamble on Roy when he knew Hubbell was available in the bullpen. It was Hubbell's second save.

Three days later, on May 7, Hubbell beat Cincinnati 1-0 for his third shutout of the early season. It was the first game of a doubleheader, which saw an estimated 40,000 fans jam into the Polo Grounds. It was a typical dominating pitching performance from the left-handed screwball artist. He scattered five singles, walked one, and fanned five. Believe it or not, Hub was outpitched by the Red's Bob Smith, who allowed only two hits. Sadly, one was a home run by Terry's replacement, Leslie. The Giants were now 1½ games back of Pittsburgh, and Hubbell's record stood at 4-1. (Note: for all current baseball fans, the game was played in one hour and 27 minutes. Wow!)

From this point on, it was mostly downhill for Hub. He lost to the tough Pittsburgh club 7-6. Hubbell's screwball was not working on this gloomy day at the Polo Grounds. He allowed 12 hits and all seven runs while the Giants tried to play catch-up all game. For what it was worth, the Giants outhit the Pirates but just couldn't bunch them together. A rare home run by Hubbell, in the third inning, brought little satisfaction to the Giants' cause. As the *Times* reported, the Pirates "had the added distinction of humbling the great Carl Hubbell."

Hubbell beat Chicago 4-1, then lost two in a row. St. Louis beat him 2-1 and Brooklyn 5-4, two close games that could have gone either way. The St. Louis loss was the first of a twin bill. The Giants lost the nightcap, also by a score of 8-4, as Fitz was pounded for eight hits and six runs in five innings. The Cards have won the first five games against the Terrymen so far this season. It was no surprise then when Jo-Jo Moore said, "I consider the St. Louis team the strongest visiting team at the Polo Grounds this spring. With four good starting pitchers and an alert, hustling team, the Giants have a fine chance to fool pre-season prophets who counted them a long way out of the pennant race."[6]

Terry continued to show great confidence in Hubbell, as he repeatedly called upon him in relief. Such was the case in one of the five losses to St. Louis. Hub relieved Parmelee but wound up with a no-decision. Years later, when Rod Roberts interviewed Hubbell, relief pitching was discussed. "We got to going good in '33 in the middle of the season we were right up there," said Hubbell. "I started relieving quite a bit. We pitched every fourth day, and the day after I had a day's rest, we'd have to pitch fifteen minutes batting practice. Bill [Terry] told me, 'You won't have to pitch batting practice if you go down to the bull pen. I might need you to pitch an inning or two.' If there was a chance we could stay up there, I would go down. I started something, though, because I did a lot of relieving."[7]

By the beginning of June, the Giants were in the thick of a three-way pennant race with Pittsburgh and St. Louis. Hubbell's record at the beginning of the new month was 5-4. By the end of June, his record would be 10-5, including two more relief appearances and shutout number four. Equally important, the Giants took over first place, 2½ games ahead of the Cardinals.

Standings as of June 30, 1933			
TEAM	W	L	GB
New York	40	25	–
St. Louis	39	29	2.5
Pittsburgh	36	33	6

Hubbell began the month of June, beating the Phillies 11-3. It was not one of his better-pitched games, but the Giants unleashed their bats on four Phillies pitchers, collecting 19 hits. The Giants' scoring came in two innings, the fifth (six runs) and sixth (five runs). Blondy Ryan and Kiddo Davis drove in three runs each.

Hubbell went on to beat Brooklyn 7-2, dropping the Dodgers to seventh place, much to the joy of the Giant faithful. It was a typical Hubbell game. He dominated from the start, allowing eight hits, two runs, and walking none. Two days later, Terry called on Hub to save a game once again. Parmelee started against the Phillies and didn't last two innings, giving up six runs. Hi Bell entered the game and held Philadelphia scoreless until Hub arrived in the sixth inning. By that time, the Giants had captured the lead, 7-6. The Giants pounded out three homers. Ott hit number seven, Terry his third, and the big blow, a grand slam from Homer (no pun intended) Peel. It would be Peel's only home run of the season; an outfielder picked up from the St. Louis Cardinals in 1932. Terry was back on first base after a short stay as a pinch hitter, beginning in late May, which means Leslie was now expendable. Sure enough, about a week later, Terry sent Sam Leslie to Brooklyn for left-hander Watty Clark and veteran outfielder Lefty O'Doul. Hubbell's excellent four-inning relief appearance, one hit, one walk, and four strikeouts brought his record to 8-4.

According to most accounts, the nickname "the Meal Ticket" was given by the media. As author Nathan Salent stated, "It was not until 1933 that Hubbell became an overpowering pitcher, and earned the nickname the Meal Ticket because of his ability to win crucial games and prevent losing streaks."[8] His ability to win was based on his devastating screwball and pin point control, which allowed him to dominate the opposition and control the game. During his fabulous five seasons, it was a rare occasion when he was hit hard.

After the 7-6 victory over Philadelphia, a clutch relief effort, Hubbell went on to win two more games before ending the month with a loss. His first victory was over Boston 6-3, despite the Giants making seven errors. Hub was in trouble in the third inning but escaped without being scored upon and finished allowing only six hits for his ninth win. Hubbell's next two games ended in no-decisions. He started against his nemesis, the Brooklyn Dodgers, but left after 6 2/3 innings as the Giants eventually won the game in the seventh inning. Lefty O'Doul, who was recently acquired from the Dodgers, made Terry look like a managerial genius. With the bases loaded, O'Doul singled in two runs giving the Giants an 8-7 lead, which they held on to for the victory.

The other no-decision came three days later when Terry, for the sixth time, called on his ace with Chicago leading 5-3. Hub did his job for two innings, but the Giants failed to score. The loss and a St. Louis victory narrowed the Giants' lead to 1½ games.

The Meal Ticket's final victory of the month was a 4-0 masterpiece over Cincinnati as *Times* reporter Drebinger commented, "The southpaw master of the screwball happened to be about at his best, and though he allowed five hits, even giving up three in one inning before retiring a man, he exercised his famous twister so adroitly that the Giants scored a comparatively easy 4-0 shutout victory."[9]

It was Hubbell's fourth shutout of the season, but he ended the month by losing to Pittsburgh 5-2. It was the first game of a doubleheader at the Polo Grounds. However, the exciting second game once again made Terry look like he could do no wrong. Parmelee started the game and left after seven innings, trailing the Pirates 4-2. He was relieved by Dolf Luque, who blanked the Pirates for two innings as the Giants tied the game in the bottom of the ninth 4-4. George Uhle held Pittsburgh at bay in the tenth and made Terry smile, recalling the trade he made for Mancuso. Here's what happened in the bottom of the tenth. With runners on first and third, one out, right-hander Bill Swift was rushed into the game. He threw one pitch, and Mancuso, not known as a power hitter, blasted the ball into the right-field stands, and the game was over. The Giants win 7-4.

Terry didn't obtain Mancuso for his bat and certainly not his power. In a 17-year major league career, he hit .265 with 53 home runs. What Terry wanted was his glove and the way Gus handled the pitching staff. Author Peter Williams in his wonderful book, "*When the Giants Were Giants,*" writes about the Mancuso acquisition. "Although Mancuso had been only a bullpen catcher for the Cardinals, Terry felt this was the best trade he ever made. He knew Mancuso was particularly good at blocking the wayward pitch, and he wanted this skill because of Schumacher's sinker and, of course, Hubbell's screwball."[10]

No doubt Terry rejoiced in the victory over the Pirates, but he was looking ahead to the critical five-game series with the tough St. Louis Cardinals, a team that had beaten the Giants all five games they played. The Cards trailed New York by 4½ games. A sweep of the series by St. Louis would knock the Terrymen out of first place and, in all probability, shatter the confidence of the Giants.

Based on previous meetings, it was not impossible, as the Cardinals had the talent led by manager Gabby Street, quite a character in his own right. A "loquacious Southerner," he became famous for catching a baseball dropped from the top of the Washington Monument. He also caught Walter Johnson for four seasons and managed the Cardinals to a pennant in 1930 and a World Series in 1931. However, he would soon be replaced by Frankie Frisch over his differences with the young and brash Dizzy Dean, who, along with Tex Carlton and Bill Hallahan, would lead the pitching staff. The Cards were a scrappy bunch with veteran Frisch and Pepper Martin along with Leo Durocher at shortstop. Joe "Ducky" Medwick, at 21, was their power guy. But this colorful bunch would have to wait until 1934, when known as the Gashouse Gang, to become an American legend.

So, the Terrymen had their hands full when the Cardinals won the first two games of the series, narrowing the Giants' first-place lead to a mere 2½ games. Carlton beat Watty Clark, who lasted less than three innings, 7-3. The next day Dean bested Schumacher in a heartbreaker 1-0. Young Hal made a bad pitch to Ducky Medwick in the top of the ninth for his sixth homer of the season and the only run of the game.

The Cardinals had now beaten the Giants seven in a row as the third game of the important series began. It pitted Bill Walker, who was part of the trade bringing Mancuso to the Giants, against veteran Fitzsimmons. As the game developed, it didn't matter who was pitching for the Giants, as the Terrymen finally woke up. They bludgeoned Walker and his replacement, Syl Johnson, for 17 hits and 11 runs. The final score was 11-1, and the Giants' lead increased to 3½.

The series ended the next day, July 2, with a doubleheader. Hubbell faced Carlton, and the Meal Ticket pitched one of the greatest games in major league baseball history. Perhaps more accurately, Hubbell pitched two of the greatest games in the history of major league baseball. The duel between Hub and

Carlton lasted an incredible 18 innings! Both starters matched each other, pitch for pitch while recording zeroes inning after inning until Jesse Haines, a "sly thirty-nine-year old veteran," relieved a tired Carlton in the bottom of the 17th inning. Haines retired the Giants in the bottom of the inning. Hubbell retired the Cardinals in the top of the 18th and was due to bat in the bottom half.

The inning began with a walk to Moore, who was sacrificed to second by Mancuso. With the winning run at second, Terry sent Jackson to pinch-hit for Ryan. Manager Street had Jackson intentionally walked, setting up a possible double play and forcing Terry to make a decision to let Hubbell hit or not. Terry let Hub bat as the 50,000 fans pleaded for their star pitcher Hubbell to produce a classic story book ending to an unbelievable game. But it was not to be, as Hubbell forced Jackson at second for out number two. With Hub at first and Moore on third, Critz stepped to the plate as the Polo Grounds crowd erupted.

Author Noel Hynd described the final minutes. "It had now been four hours since the game began. A sunny warm day was now overcast, and a cool wind was whipping in off the Harlem River. Critz, as was his habit, stuffed tobacco in his mouth, took a few practice swings, and stepped into the batter's box. Haines worked the count to two, and one before Critz slapped the ball past Haines's ear out into center field. For a moment, the park was stunned, then a roar went up that probably could have been heard at Yankee Stadium across the river. Moore came home, and Hubbell stood on second as his Giant teammates mobbed him."[11]

The game was finally over after four hours and three minutes. Carl Hubbell had pitched himself into major league history books with an unprecedented performance. He allowed six hits, no walks, and struck out 12. In addition, 12 of the innings were perfect. Frankie Frisch would hit .303 for the season and Pepper Martin .316. They each went 0-7 against Hubbell, and this was only the beginning of July for Hub, who would continue to pitch brilliantly.

The exhausted and emotionally drained fans now awaited the second game, not knowing what to expect. It matched the Cardinals' young and eccentric Dizzy Dean against Roy Parmelee, an erratic right-hander who had one of the best seasons of his 10-year career. As the stunned crowd would witness, Parmelee pitched the best game of his career, a 1-0 shutout. His stat line was incredibly impressive. He allowed four hits, struck out 13 . . . and walked none! This from a pitcher who had trouble locating the plate and was given the nickname "Tarzan" by *New York Daily News* writer Jimmy Powers because of his wildness.

To sum up, for 27 unbelievable innings Hubbell and Parmelee held the Cardinals to a total of 10 hits, no runs, and no walks! More importantly, the Giants' lead was now 5½ games over the Cards. Hubbell wouldn't pitch again for the Giants until July 9, but in the meantime, baseball fans were being treated to the first All-Star Game between the best players from both leagues, competing against each other.

The birth of the All-Star Game has an interesting history. In 1933, the city of Chicago hosted a World's Fair known as the Century of Progress International Exposition. The event was created to celebrate the city's Centennial. It had a second purpose, and that was to lessen the effects of the Depression that had been dragging the country down since 1929. Perhaps it would bring renewed hope to the country.

Newly elected Mayor Edward Kelly had an idea of holding a major athletic event along with the Exposition. He approached Colonel Robert McCormick, the publisher of the *Chicago Tribune*, with his idea. McCormick turned the project over to his sports editor, Arch Ward. Immediately Ward knew what he wanted to do, a one-time game between the best players in the American and National leagues. It was to be called the "Game of the Century." It would be played at Comiskey Park in Chicago. In addition, the players would be selected by the fans. Ward sold the idea to the presidents of both leagues and various team owners. Keep in mind, attendance since 1930 had been plummeting precipitously, and the future did not look bright. Ward was successful. Commissioner Kenesaw Mountain Landis approved, and the game was scheduled for July 6.

In the meantime, ballots were printed in newspapers across the country for fans to cast their votes. It was a star-studded list of future Hall of Famers—Ruth, Gehrig, Gehringer, Grove, Frisch, Klein, Terry, Hubbell, and Foxx, to name a few. Two titans of baseball were chosen to manage. Connie Mack was selected to manage the American League and John McGraw, coming out of retirement, the National League. Assisting Mack, at his request, was the Yankee manager Joe McCarthy while Max Carey, manager of the Dodgers, would help McGraw.

The historic game was a huge success, both with the fans and at the turnstiles. Over 49,000 attended the first major league All-Star Game at Comiskey Park in Chicago. The Cardinals Bill Hallahan started for the NL while the Yankees Lefty Gomez took the hill for the AL. Gomez, General Crowder, and Lefty Grove each pitched three innings for the AL. In the NL, Hallahan pitched two innings, Lon Warneke four, and Hubbell two. The AL scored first with a run in the second inning when Gomez singled in Jimmy Dykes from second. The next inning, Ruth delighted the huge crowd by blasting a home run into the right-field bleachers with Charlie Gehringer on base. The NL finally got to Crowder in the top of the sixth when the gang from St. Louis took over. Pepper Martin singled in a run, and later with the bases empty, Frankie Frisch homered to right to make the score 3-2. But not for long, as Warneke gave up a single to Earl Averill, scoring Joe Cronin and increasing the AL lead to 4-2. And that's the way the game ended. Winning pitcher: Gomez, losing pitcher: Hallahan.

Hubbell pitched two innings, which raises a question: what happened to the promise McGraw made to Terry of not using Hub after his 18-inning marathon? Could the stormy relationship between McGraw and Terry be the reason, or was it something else? Little, if anything, was reported in the press. Coincidence or not, the next game Hubbell pitched, he was hit hard. It was against the Chicago Cubs on July 9. He gave up six hits, four runs in only 4 2/3 innings, very unlike Hubbell. His record was now 11-6.

Four days later, Hubbell began a five-game winning streak in which he pitched 45 1/3 scoreless innings (see Appendix A). It began at Sportsman's Park against the Cardinals, who in 1934 were tagged with the sobriquet "The Gashouse Gang." Hub won the game 3-2, allowing two runs on seven hits and, in typical fashion, didn't walk a batter. Vergez won the game in the ninth with a clutch home run off Tex Carlton. Hubbell blanked the Cards in the last three innings to begin the streak and drop St. Louis to fourth place. In the meantime, the Cubs, playing well, managed to take over second place, three games back of the Giants.

On three days' rest, the Meal Ticket pitched his sixth shutout of the season. It was the second game of a doubleheader against Cincinnati at Redland Field. The final score was 1-0 thanks to Terry, who doubled and scored on a clutch single by Vergez in the fourth inning. Hubbell's record was now 13-6, and his scoreless innings streak was at a modest 12. Oh yes, Hub scattered eight hits . . . and you guessed it, didn't walk a batter.

While many baseball fans were following the exciting race in the National League, among the Giants, Cubs, Pirates, and Cardinals, over in the American League, the race couldn't be any tighter. The Yankees and Senators were tied for first place with identical won/lost records of 54-31. The Philadelphia Athletics were struggling mightily to keep pace. This was a team that finished first or second in the standings the past six years. Connie Mack, manager and part-owner of the Philadelphia Athletics, like many of the major league clubs during the Depression, was having financial difficulties. Mack needed money, to put it bluntly. Thus, he began selling off star players. The first to go in September 1932 were Al Simmons, Jimmy Dykes, and Mule Haas to the White Sox for $100,000. The effects surfaced in '33 and weakened the club despite Grove's 24-8 season and Foxx whacking 48 home runs, driving in 163 runs, and hitting .356. It takes more than two players to win a pennant. At this point, the A's were a distant 10½ games back and would finish 19½ off the pace.

By August, the Senators, led by player/manager Joe Cronin, began pulling away from the Yankees. The Senators had an excellent infield with Joe Kuhel on first, batting .322 with 11 homers and 117 RBIs, Buddy Myer at second batting .302, and shortstop Cronin at .309 with 118 runs batted in. Ossie Bluege at third had a lifetime batting average of .272. In the outfield for Washington were three solid hitters, Heinie Manush .336, Fred Schute .295, and Goose Goslin .297. The pitching staff was led by two 20-game winners, General Crowder 24-15 and Earl Whitehill 22-8.

In 1933 the Yankees problem was not offense, despite Ruth "slowing down." Out of eight everyday players, five hit .300 or better, and the sixth, Tony Lazzeri, hit .294. The problem was pitching. It appeared the staff of the '32 World Champion Yankees all had off years—Red Ruffing, George Pipgras, Johnny Allen, Herb Pennock, and even Lefty Gomez, who went from 24-7 to 16-10. The team ERA ranked number one in '32, dropped to five in '33. In hindsight, it was obvious why Washington won the pennant.

Back in the National League, Terry wasn't paying too much attention to the A's and Yankees' problems. He had his hands full fighting off his pesky rivals every day. Hubbell was certainly doing his part as he once again answered the call in relief. It was the second game of a doubleheader against the Pirates and the beginning of a long six-game series. Pittsburgh won the first game 4-1. In game two, left-hander Bill Clark started for the Giants and, after being handed a 4-0 lead in the first inning, couldn't handle the prosperity. Pittsburgh scored three in their half but not before Terry called on Hubbell to end the inning. Hub pitched 8 1/3 innings of scoreless baseball, but he did allow a run in the first, charged to Clark, keeping his streak alive at 20 1/3 innings. The Giants tacked on three more runs as Hub was credited with the victory. His record was now 14-6.

Three days later, on two days' rest, Hubbell (move over "Iron Man" McGinnity) tossed his seventh shutout of the season. He beat Pittsburgh 1-0, giving up six singles, fanned four, and issued no walks. The only run of the game came in the first inning when Ott drove in Critz from third. Hubbell's record was now 15-6, and his scoreless streak at 29 1/3 innings and counting. The victory maintained the Giants' narrow 2½ game lead over Chicago.

Next, the Giants faced Brooklyn in a four-game series. The first three, the Giants won, and then Terry called on Hubbell, his ace of the staff. "King Carl," another one of his nicknames, faced the Dodgers Van Lingle Mungo. Here were two of the most diametrically opposite personalities in all of baseball.

Carl Hubbell was a shy, modest man who was liked and admired by many. He was quiet and rarely boasted about his numerous accomplishments. He was respected and cherished by his teammates. He was a family man who married his high school sweetheart and had two sons. On the field, he never complained about errors or engaged in a fight. Now, here's how Mungo was described in *The Ballplayers,* edited by Mike Shatzkin. "Mungo was wild and mean, a high-kicking fireballer with a fierce temper. He was known as a drinker and was involved in some bizarre off-the-field incidents. He once had to be smuggled out of Cuba to escape the machete-wielding husband of a nightclub dancer with whom he had been caught in bed."[12]

Despite their differences in personalities, lifestyle, and pitching techniques, the July 27 game at the Polo Grounds was a thing of beauty to watch. Mungo held the Giants scoreless for six innings, but he weakened in the bottom of the seventh. With two out, Blondy Ryan tripled to right-center, and Hubbell, if his pitching wasn't enough, singled for the only run he needed. The Giants tacked on another run in the seventh when O'Doul doubled, scoring Critz. King Carl registered his eighth shutout, allowing four hits, but oddly walked three. However, only twice during the game did Brooklyn have a runner reach second base; that's how dominating he was. Even *The Sporting News* commented on Hubbell's performance. "Hubbell's pitching this season has been the most sensational since the ball was 'hopped' up to meet the demand for home runs. He has hurled eight shutouts, a feat that has not been equaled since 1920 when Babe Adams turned in that number."[13] His record was now 16-6, and his scoreless streak reached 38 1/3 innings. The victory concluded the four-game sweep of the rival Dodgers and increased the Giants' lead over the Chicago Cubs to five games.

The Boston Braves, managed by future Hall of Famer Bill McKechnie, arrived next at the Polo Grounds and surprisingly took two of three games from the Giants. In one of the losses, Terry had to call on Hubbell to relieve

Schumacher in the eighth with Boston in front 5-3. As expected, Hubbell did his job not allowing further damage, but the Giants couldn't touch Ben Cantwell, as the Braves went on to win 5-3. Schumacher was tagged with the loss as Hubbell extended his scoreless innings to 40 1/3. If it was any consolation to Terry, not many teams hit Cantwell in '33. He finished the season 20-10 with a 2.62 earned run average. Two years later, Cantwell led the league with an unbelievable 25 losses. At one point, he lost 13 straight. In fairness to Cantwell, many of the losses were due to a lack of support. In nine of the losses, the Braves scored only 13 runs. There is more to the Cantwell story. In 1934 he developed bone spurs in his right elbow, causing pain and affecting his delivery. He chose not to have surgery and pitched the remaining two years of his career in pain.

The loss to the Braves, coupled with the Pirates winning a doubleheader from Cincinnati, and the Cubs losing a twin-bill to St. Louis, tightened up the race. It also dropped Chicago to fourth place as Pittsburgh took over second, only 3½ games back of the Giants.

After a great July, Hubbell stumbled slightly in August, posting a 3-3 record. Perhaps he was tiring from pitching with inadequate rest between starts or frequent relief appearances. It could also have been simply he was human and experienced off days.

On August 1, Hub lost to the pesky Boston Braves 3-1. He gave up two runs in the sixth inning and left the game trailing 2-1. Dolf Luque, in relief, didn't help the situation when the former Giant catcher, Shanty Hogan, took the Cuban-born right-hander deep in the seventh inning. The loss ended the scoreless innings streak for Hubbell at 45 1/3. At the time, King Carl fell short of the record held by Walter Johnson of the Washington Senators at 55 2/3 innings, set in 1913, and Jack Coombs of the Philadelphia A's at 53 in 1910. The all-time record is held by Orel Hershiser of the Los Angeles Dodgers at 59. Hubbell is ranked seventh.

Returning to the 3-1 loss, by today's forgiving standards, Hubbell's performance would be considered a "quality start," defined as pitching at least six innings and allowing three earned runs or less. However, it is highly unlikely Hubbell would have been proud of his six-inning performance or any other starter in major league baseball in 1933. Times indeed have changed. Hubbell's record was now 16-7.

Two days later, Terry inexplicably called on his Meal Ticket to relieve Clark in a game against the Phillies. There were two outs and runners on first and third in the bottom of the sixth inning, with the Giants holding a comfortable

7-1 lead! Hubbell shut the Phillies down for 2 1/3 innings while the Giants scored nine more runs in the eighth and two in the ninth for good measure. The final score was Giants 18, Phillies 1. In hindsight, it is impossible to explain Bill Terry's thinking. Granted, he did not know his club would tack on 11 more runs after Hubbell entered the game. But why not use the half dozen other relief pitchers. Also, the Phillies were a perennial second division club for years and not known for late-game rallies.

Before 22,000 fans at Brooklyn, with one day's rest, Hubbell was pounded by the Dodgers for 10 hits and six runs, handing him his eighth loss of the season. Hub's poor performance raises the question once again: was Hub being overworked? The final score was Brooklyn 6 New York 3. Happily, the Giants won the second game of the doubleheader to stay 3½ games ahead of the Pirates. Hubbell's record was now 16-8.

Now with six days rest, Hubbell lost his third straight game in August. The dreadful Phillies eked out a 2-1 victory behind the outstanding pitching of Phil Collins and the hitting of one player, their big first baseman, Don Hurst. The left-handed swinger connected twice off Hubbell. In the second inning, he belted a homer into the upper right field with two out. The second homer came in the seventh, again with two out, but this time he sent a line drive into the lower right-field stands. Aside from Hurst, Hubbell pitched his customary fine game. In addition to the home runs, he allowed only five singles while issuing one pass. A tad more offense by the Terrymen, and the outcome would have been different. Hubbell's record was now 16-9. But here's the good news, the Giants were still 3½ games ahead of Pittsburgh, and Hubbell would begin a four-game winning streak.

The first of the four games was against Chicago and their 24-year-old phenom, Lon Warneke nicknamed, "The Arkansas Humming Bird." The previous year, Warneke led the league in victories (22-6) and ERA (2.37). So, the 20,000 fans were expecting a low-scoring pitcher's duel but were surprised when the Giants teed off on the Cubs right-hander. The bombardment began in the second inning when Mel Ott smacked home run number seventeen. The Giants scored two more runs in each of the fourth and fifth innings, staking Hubbell to a 5-0 lead after six. In the top of the seventh, Kiki Cuyler homered off Hub spoiling his potential shutout. The Giants answered Cuyler with three runs of their own in the seventh, making the score 8-1. However, in the eighth, Terry had to pull his ace left-hander when he loaded the bases with no out. Terry called on Hi Bell to stop Chicago. He did, but not before three Cubs had crossed the plate, making the score 8-4, and that's how the game ended as Bell shut the door on the Cubs in the ninth. Although it wasn't one of Hubbell's finest moments, he was still credited with the win, his 17th of the season against nine losses.

With Hubbell's 17th victory, coupled with the Braves beating Pittsburgh, the Giants now led by six games. The Terrymen beat the Cubs the following day for their fifth straight win. It was a key victory prior to Pittsburgh arriving at the Polo Grounds for an important four-game series, consisting of two twin-bills. The Giants won the first doubleheader. In the first game, Luque picked up the win, in relief, of Fitzsimmons 8-5. Parmelee (12-5) pitched a fine game in the nightcap, winning 6-2, extending the Giants' winning streak to seven games.

The following day King Carl, before 42,000 spectators, prevailed once again over the Pirates 2-1. He allowed five hits while walking one batter. His record was now 18-9 and nearing a 20-game season. The Giants streak climbed to eight straight. But in the second and final game with the Pirates, what began as a pitching duel with a 1-1 game through five innings, ended up a 7-2 Pittsburgh victory. Clark, Luque, and Spencer pitched for the Giants, with the first two giving up seven runs. Home runs by Ott, his 20th, and Mancuso his fifth accounted for the two Giant runs. Although Ott was ranked number three among the National League home run leaders, two of his teammates were also given recognition. Vergez had 14 and O'Doul 12. A comparison between the two leagues, at season's end, clearly shows the AL was a powerhouse with a total of 607 home runs compared to the NL with 460. It could be a significant factor come the World Series. Despite the split, which ended the Giants' winning streak at eight, the Terrymen still had a comfortable lead, as shown below.

TEAM	W	L	GB
New York	71	44	–
Chicago	66	55	8
Pittsburgh	63	56	10
St. Louis	64	57	10

After the Pittsburgh Pirates, the wild bunch from St. Louis visited the Polo Grounds for a whopping six-game series, in which the Giants could only manage to win two games and tie one. Hubbell pitched one of the two victories. It was yet another brilliant performance by the Meal Ticket. He was in total control allowing five singles, one walk, and no runs for his ninth shutout of the season. His record was now 19-9, ever closer to the magical 20.

Next, the Giants moved on to Boston for six games which began on a sour note but ended upbeat. The Terrymen lost the first game of the series 7-3 along with Johnny Vergez. After going 2 for 4, including his 16th home run, the third baseman was rushed to St. Elizabeth's Hospital, where he underwent an operation for acute appendicitis. It was expected he would remain in the hospital for a week to ten days. It was also reported, "There is, of course, no chance whatever that Johnny will be able to play another game for the Giants this year."[14] Terry immediately replaced Vergez with the hobbled Travis Jackson, who was still convalescing from off-season surgery on his left knee.

In game two of the Boston series, Terry called on Hubbell with only two days' rest. King Carl turned in a masterpiece to win 2-0 in 10 innings. In his book *Under Coogan's Bluff,* author Fred Stein said, "Reformed baseball writer Heywood Broun, looking on from the press box, marveled at Hubbell's control as the great left-hander pitched his tenth shutout of the season. Hubbell not only did not walk a batter but never was behind a hitter at any time in the ten innings, or even went to a three and two count in the game." Commented Brown, "Such control in a left-hander is incredible."[15] However accurate or embellished Brown's comments are; there is no question, Hubbell pitched a magnificent game for his 20th victory.

After taking the next three games from the Braves, plus a tie game, the Giants lost three of five to Pittsburgh. Hubbell was trounced in the first game and lasted 3 1/3 innings, giving up eight hits and four runs before he was rescued. The final score was 6-1. Hub's record was now 20-10. But before the Terrymen left Pittsburgh, the Meal Ticket got his revenge and 21st victory by whipping the Pirates 2-1. The "master manipulator of the screwball," as *New York Times* reporter Drebinger called Hubbell, allowed six hits and walked one batter. The victory was also important for the Giants, as it restored their lead over third-place Pittsburgh to 6½ games.

The next stop for the Giants was Cincinnati before they took on Chicago in a six-game series, the most critical of the season. But first, the Terrymen vanquished Cincinnati four straight. Regrettably, Terry had to use the "over-taxed" Hubbell in relief twice. In the second game of the series, he relieved Fitzsimmons, who left Hubbell with a 3-1 lead, and the bases loaded and no out in the seventh. Hubbell retired the next three batters without allowing a run and repeated his domination in the eighth and ninth innings. In a brilliant three-inning stint, Hubbell retired nine straight batters. The Giants scored three times before the game ended 6-1, as Fitz won his 15th and Hub his fourth save. In the second game of the doubleheader, young Hal Schumacher pitched a dandy of a game-winning 2-1 in 11 innings for his 18th victory.

The next day Terry called on Hi Bell, who was primarily a reliever, to start the game. The reason was to give his starting rotation a well-deserved rest. But when the Giants scored two runs in the top of the seventh for a 3-1 lead, Terry took no chances of possibly losing the game. There was no question Terry wanted to win the National League pennant badly. So, guess who he called upon to preserve the lead? Not a difficult question. Of course, it was the Meal Ticket and the man, among the entire rotation, who most needed a well-deserved rest.

Once again, Hubbell untiringly answered the call and delivered exactly what Terry expected. He pitched three scoreless innings and allowed one hit and no walks for his fifth and final save of the season. The victory put the Terrymen eight games ahead of the second-place Cubs as the Giants headed for Chicago and the crucial six-game series.

The Chicago series began with a doubleheader in rain and gale-like winds. The Cubs won the first game 2-0 behind the outstanding pitching of Guy Bush (18-11). Equally important was how quickly the Cubs pounced on Hubbell (21-11) for two runs in the first inning, helped by Terry's error. After two innings, with the score still 2-0, the rain came down in buckets, delaying the game for two hours. By the time it stopped and the field cleared, Terry was reluctant to bring back the overworked Hubbell. He sent in Bill Shores, who pitched extremely well, blanking the Cubs over the next six innings, but it was too late. The Cubs' victory narrowed the Giants' lead to 6½ games. It became 5½ the following day, when the Cubs won 4-3, behind the pitching of Charlie Root and Pat Malone.

Due to the nasty weather and a postponed game, the next four games were played as two twin-bills, taxing both pitching rotations to the max. But the Terrymen rose to the occasion, winning both ends of the first doubleheader, 5-1 behind Schumacher's (19-10) outstanding pitching and 4-0 as Parmelee and Bell teamed up to allow only two hits.

Then before 30,000 partisan fans, the final blow came the following day when the Giants swept the second doubleheader from the Cubs. In the opener, Hubbell gave up 12 hits (no walks) but still managed to hold Chicago to one run and a 2-1 victory. It was the 29th time this season the Giants' pitching staff held the opposition to one run in addition to the 23 shutouts. Hubbell's record was now 22-11. The Giants beat Chicago 6-3 in the second game and dropped them to third place, a distant 9½ games back, as the Pirates took over second 8½ behind.

Although "games back" was a meaningful number, in reality, it was just a matter of time before the Giants would mathematically clinch the National League pennant. But first, the Giant fans had to suffer some anxious moments as the team traveled to St. Louis, the last series, before heading home to the friendly confines of the Polo Grounds. In the first game of the series, Parmelee and Luque (8-2) combined to beat the great Dizzy Dean 4-3, inching ever closer to the pennant.

The following day, September 18, tragedy almost struck when Fitz was hit in the neck by a line drive in the second inning. He had to leave the game and was replaced by Bell, who eventually gave way to Hubbell, with the Giants barely leading 3-2. Unlike Hub, he gave up a run in the sixth to tie the game. Nothing to worry about, King Carl dominated all season, and he could do it again. Looking back, the scene was now set for a Hollywood ending and a rewarding season for new manager Bill Terry. The Giants had their ace and stopper on the mound . . . and all could see, via the scoreboard, the Pirates had lost the second game of their doubleheader 6-0. All Hubbell had to do was shut down the Cards while his teammates provided the winning run, and the pennant was theirs.

Sadly, it didn't happen. The Giants failed to score over the last five innings off of Carleton (16-10), and Hubbell proved he was human. In the Cards eighth, a triple by light-hitting Leo Durocher followed by Carleton's single gave St. Louis a 4-3 victory. The welcome news was Fitz was not seriously injured, and the Giant's celebration would have to wait another day. And that's exactly what occurred on September 19 as author Williams wrote, "At exactly 3:15 P.M., one of the writers in the press box at Sportsman's Park waved down to Terry and shouted that the second-place Pirates had lost the second game of their doubleheader with the Phils. It no longer mattered what happened in the game the Giants were playing with the Cards. They had won the pennant. Players in the dugout stood up, and when the scoreboard verified the report, several tossed their caps and waved their arms. Terry said this was his biggest thrill in baseball, and he told reporters twice that the team had done it because of its remarkable 'spirit' and 'fight.'"[16]

For the record, the Giants lost the game that "no longer mattered" as the Cards clobbered them 12-3, with Schumacher (19-11) taking the loss. For most of the remaining games, Terry rested his everyday players and his remarkable starting rotation. But towards the season's end, he gave Parmelee, Hubbell, Schumacher, and Fitzsimmons; a warmup start in preparation for the upcoming World Series. Hubbell, in his warmup outing, dominated, as he had done all season long. He beat Philadelphia 3-1, scattering eight hits and allowing one walk. He finished the season leading the National League in wins (23-12), ERA (1.66), shutouts (10), and innings pitched (338.2).

In the meantime, over in the American League, the battle between the New York Yankees and Washington Senators continued until September 21, when Joe Cronin's club beat the St. Louis Browns 2-1 to clinch the AL pennant. It was the first flag the Senators won since 1925.

Interestingly, it was the Giants' first pennant since 1924, a long stretch for New York fans accustomed to winning under John McGraw. It is also informative to note the correlation between winning baseball and attendance at the games. The Giants' attendance climbed from 484,868 in 1932 to 604,471 in 1933, a remarkable increase under any economic conditions, but during the Depression, simply an amazing accomplishment. Clearly, the idiom, "Build a better mousetrap, and the world will beat a path to your door," has some merit.

Washington Senators manager Joe Cronin wasted no time in preparing his club for the World Series. After Washington clinched the pennant and before the regular season ended, Cronin persuaded St. Louis Browns' left-hander Garland Braxton, formerly of the Senators, to play the role of Carl Hubbell. Braxton was a screwball pitcher and had modest success playing for four AL teams. Pitching for Washington in 1928, he led the league with a 2.51 earned run average. According to Cronin, Braxton's screwball "looks very much like Hubbell's except that he hasn't got quite as much speed." During the practice session, the Washington batters were hitting his screwball but with little authority. Based on Hubbell's World Series performance, Cronin's experiment with Braxton turned out to be a bust.

The matchup between the Senators and Giants was an interesting study in contrasts, resulting in the oddsmakers favoring Washington and their productive batting order. The Senators topped the American League in hitting. Left fielder Heine Manush led the club with a .336 average. He also drove in 95 runs. First baseman Joe Kuhel followed with a .322 average and had 107 RBIs. Two other infielders, player/manager Joe Cronin at short hit .309 and led the team with 118 RBIs while Buddy Myer at second batted .302. If you could call them that, the two weak links were catcher Luke Sewell (.264) and Ossie Bluege (.261) at third. The other two outfielders supporting Manush were Goose Goslin (.297) in right and Fred Schulte (.295) in center.

There was, however, more to this team than just hitting. The Senators pitching staff was far from shabby. Washington boasted two 20-game winners. Here are the six hurlers who logged the most innings, with Russell used mainly in relief.

PITCHER	W	L	ERA
General Crowder	24	15	3.97
Earl Whitehill	22	8	3.33
Lefty Stewart	15	6	3.82
Monte Weaver	10	5	3.25
Jack Russell	12	6	2.69
Tommy Holmes	7	7	4.80

There was a striking difference between the Senators' offensive prowess and that of the Giants. New York had one .300 hitter, their manager Bill Terry at .322. But the average is misleading, considering he lost playing time early in the season with a broken wrist. He was a much better hitter, as his .341 lifetime average proves. The club's big bopper was right fielder Mel Ott who batted .283 with 23 home runs and 103 RBIs. Rounding out the rest of the outfield was Jo-Jo Moore (.292) in left and Kiddo Davis (.258) in center. Along with Terry in the infield was Hughie Critz (.246) at second, Blondy Ryan (.238) at short, and Travis Jackson in place of Johnny Vergez at third. Vergez would be missed. He had a fine season before the appendicitis operation, hitting .271 with 16 home runs and 72 RBIs, the second most behind Ott. The catcher Gus Mancuso, not known for his bat, hit a respectable .264. But when Terry traded for him in the fall of 1932, the new manager mainly looked for a catcher who could handle a pitching staff, and Mancuso fit the bill.

The Sporting News praised Terry's judgment in trading for Mancuso. "It can readily be observed that when one member of a pitching staff shows a big improvement over his previous year's work, this can be credited to natural development. But when an entire staff, including a couple of doubtful winners, steps out on a victorious march, there must be some other influence. In the case of the New York Giants, little Gus Mancuso is being given a great deal of credit for the improvement in Bill Terry's staff, which has been carrying on so effectively since the opening of the season. The pitchers themselves say 'FuMancuso' is the real reason."[17]

Most experts believed the Giant pitching staff had the edge over the Senators, despite having only one 20-game winner. The Meal Ticket (23-12) and a 1.66 ERA was more than a 20-game winner. He and his almost unhittable screwball, plus pinpoint control, was a dominating combination and an inspiration all its own. Plus, Hubbell was used in critical situations as a spot reliever, and he was an indefatigable workhorse. Add Hal Schumacher (19-12) with a 2.16 ERA, veteran Freddie Fitzsimmons (16-11) 2.90 ERA, and Roy Parmelee (13-8) 3.17 ERA, and it's no surprise they were the number one pitching staff in the National League. Let's not forget Dolf Luque (8-2) with an earned run average of 2.69 with four saves and Hi Bell (6-5) with an ERA of 2.05 with five saves.

Those were the matchups on paper, but the game is played on grass and so much depends on who is hot or who is not . . . and so many other factors, for example, errors, bad calls, timely hits, poor base running, etc.

With the World Series only days away, the enthusiasm and excitement in New York were running high for Terry and the Giants. At the beginning of the season, this was a team that was scoffed at, and a manager laughed at when he claimed the Giants would finish "third or better." Terry and his hustling and talented bunch ignited the Giant fans as advanced World Series ticket sales were being gobbled up. Interestingly, box seats were selling at $6.60 and, in the lower grandstand, $5.50!

As expected, both managers expressed confidence in their clubs. It appeared Terry was more cautious. "I think in a short series pitching counts, and this will be a short series. We have the pitching staff both for starting and relief if that is necessary. We're looking for a tough series. We're prepared. You can't say who will win. I have never made a practice of predicting and don't intend to start now. We are ready."[18]

Cronin seemed bolder in assessing the series. "We are taking the field confident of victory. We wouldn't go out there if we didn't think we could win. I won't say how long the series will be. You can't very well dope that. It depends on the breaks. But we have the hitting and the better ball club all-around."[19]

Game 1, October 3, 1933, at Polo Grounds

Over 46,000 fans roared when the New York Giants and Carl Hubbell took the field. The decibel level even increased when the Meal Ticket struck out the first three Senators—Buddy Myer, Goose Goslin, and Heinie Manush. The surprise of the afternoon was Cronin's selection of Lefty Stewart, his number three hurler, to start for Washington. Many expected Crowder, their ace who won 24 games during the season. No doubt Cronin regretted the choice when Ott lined a 400-foot homer into the right-field seats with Moore on in the first for a quick 2-0 lead. Two innings later, Stewart was gone as the Giants scored another pair of runs and led 4-0. In the top of the fourth, the Senators scored an unearned run when Critz booted a grounder, and Jackson fumbled a ball long enough to eliminate the double play as Washington scored. Rarely ruffled in a close game, Hubbell took control and calmly blanked Washington until the ninth. Once again, Hubbell was the victim of poor defense, as the Senators scored another unearned run, but he got out of the jam with relative ease. The final score was New York 4 Washington 2. After the game, Terry gave Hubbell the ball as they both left the field for the clubhouse and the victory celebration. It was Hubbell's first World Series victory, and it was a dandy. He allowed five hits, two runs (both unearned), two walks, and struck out 10. It was vintage Hubbell.

Game 2, October 4, 1933, at Polo Grounds

Another raucous crowd of near 36,000 went away delighted as their New York Giants whipped the Washington Senators 6-1, behind the outstanding pitching of Hal Schumacher. The right-hander allowed one run in the third inning when Goslin took him deep into the right-field stands. But the Giants entered the sixth inning with a vengeance, scoring six runs off the Senators ace, General Crowder. The uprising began when Moore singled, was forced at second by Critz, who went to third on Terry's double. With first base open, Cronin elected to intentionally walk Ott, as the crowd booed, loading the bases with one out. Terry counted by sending O'Doul to pinch hit for Davis. O'Doul singled up the middle, scoring Critz and Terry and sending Ott to second as the crowd roared. Jackson, up next, singled to right, scoring Ott and sending O'Doul to third. Mancuso surprised everyone. With a 1-1 count, he dropped a bunt down third, scoring O'Doul. Mancuso was safe at first as Jackson ambled into second. Ryan whiffed for the second out. Schumacher helped his cause with a single to left scoring Jackson as Mancuso stopped at second. Moore, the guy who started the Merry Go Round, singled again, scoring Mancuso for the final run of the inning. At that point, Cronin removed Crowder, but the damage was done.

Embolden by the five-run lead, Schumacher shutout the Senators for the last three innings. Overall, he allowed five hits, one of them Goslin's homer. With a two-game lead, the Giants now headed for Griffith Stadium in Washington, D. C.

Game 3, October 5, 1933, at Griffith Stadium

President Roosevelt threw out the first ball as he tried valiantly to remain impartial, being a current resident in Washington and a former New Yorker with the Giants, his "home team." In addition to the president, a "large part of Washington officialdom" was present with foreign diplomats. And like the postman who goes for a walk on his day off, the enormously popular Babe Ruth was in the press box.

On the mound were two veteran pitchers, Freddy Fitzsimmons for the Giants and left-hander Earl Whitehill for the Senators. The lefty blanked the Giants 4-0 on five hits. Although Fitz pitched a decent game with some offensive support, the outcome might have been different. But credit must be given to Whitehill, who pitched a marvelous game under a great deal of pressure, not just the more than 26,000 fans in the stands and the famous names, but most importantly, the Senators were down two games to none. Another loss, and it would have put Washington in an almost impossible position—to win four straight.

Author Williams penned a clever and perceptive comment. "It looked to Cronin as though the momentum might have shifted to his club. It looked to Terry as though he'd pitch Hubbell the next day."[20]

Game 4, October 6, 1933, at Griffith Stadium

Terry's pitching choice for game four was either Hubbell or Parmelee. He chose Hub, who had been his Meal Ticket all season and game one of the series. Cronin chose Monte Weaver, a fine young hurler who won 22 games for the Senators the previous year. But the tall right-hander was up against one of the great pitchers of his time.

The Giants drew first blood in the fourth inning when Terry hit a monster home run into the center-field bleachers. In the meantime, Hubbell, as he had done all season, was pitching shutout ball until the seventh inning. With one out, Kuhel reached first when Hubbell juggled his bunt for an error. Bluege sacrificed Kuhel to second. Sewell then smashed Hubbell's first pitch for a single to center, scoring Kuhel and tying the game as more than 27,000 fans came alive.

The score remained 1-1 until the top of the 11th inning. In quick fashion, the hobbled Jackson surprised everyone at Griffith Stadium when he bunted down the third baseline for a single. Mancuso sacrificed Jackson to second. With a 1-0 count, Ryan singled to left, scoring Jackson, and like a blink of the eye, the Giants took a 2-1 lead.

One of the great traits Hubbell possessed was his calm and cool demeanor when the pressure of the game was at its peak. Just such a situation occurred in the bottom of the 11th. Hubbell managed to get himself into a bases-loaded one-out situation with pinch hitter Cliff Bolton coming to bat. A left-handed batter, Bolton was mostly a backup player but not an automatic out. For the '33 season, he hit .410, but it was a small sample size, 16 for 39. Regardless, Hub had to be incredibly careful with such a hitter. Any number of situations could tie or win the game for the Senators. With the boisterous crowd on their feet, King Carl lived up to his name as he induced Bolton to hit into a 6-4-3 double play to end the game. Again, Hubbell pitched brilliantly. Author Williams adds an interesting revelation about the double play. "Terry told me [Williams] that Ryan and Hughie Critz talked him into letting them play deep in the infield, to set up the double play, and he added that he was happy they had done so."[21] Now Terry and the Giants needed one more game to take home a World Championship.

Game 5, October 7, 1933, at Griffith Stadium

Terry selected Schumacher to pitch, which was a no-brainer after his magnificent game two performance. Cronin, as he did in game two, called on his ace Crowder. Again, Crowder couldn't get past the sixth inning. In the second, Jackson singled, Mancuso walked, Ryan sacrificed the runners to second and third. In a surprise at-bat, Schumacher singled to center, and the Giants were ahead 2-0. In the sixth, the Giants tacked on another run and chased Crowder, who was replaced by Jack Russell, who retired the side with no further damage.

Give the Senators credit; the club was not giving up even with two quick outs in the bottom of the sixth. Manush and Cronin singled, setting up a first and third situation for Schulte. The center fielder, a consistent hitter but not known for the long ball, launched Schumacher's first pitch "high and far" into the left-field bleachers to tie the game 3-3. Giant fans, back in New York, listening on the radio, must have felt depressed as the inning continued. Kuhel singled to right. Bluege followed with a vicious liner inside the third baseline, knocked down by Jackson but his throw to Terry was late, putting runners on first and third. Terry had seen enough as he called on Luque, who induced Sewell to ground to Critz at second for the final out of the inning.

Luque and Russell pitched shutout ball until the top of the 10th. Critz flied out. Terry grounded out. Ott ran the count to two, and two then blasted the next pitch into the center field bleachers off Schulte's glove, who toppled into the stands. It was first ruled a double but reversed as Ott trotted around the bases, giving the Giants a 4-3 lead.

Luque closed out the victory in the bottom of the 10th but not before Giant fans went through some anxious moments. With runners on first and second, two out, Luque struck out Kuhel on three pitches. The New York Giants were the 1933 World Champions.

After all the celebrations plus the lavish praise bestowed on Terry and before the players headed for their respective homes, Hubbell was singled out for his contribution. He was voted the Most Valuable Player of the World Series by the 17 writers chosen from rival clubs. It would not be the last award Hubbell received for his astonishing 1933 season. He was also voted the Most Valuable Player in the National League by the Baseball Writers' Association of America committee. The last pitcher to be awarded this honor was Dazzy Vance with Brooklyn in 1924.

The ultimate award came last when Hubbell was named the Outstanding Individual Performer of 1933. This award was so prestigious because the competition involved all sports, amateur or professional, covering many talented athletes. It was conducted by *The Associated Press,* polling sports editors, and writers from across the nation.

Hubbell was often described as a modest, shy individual but supremely proud yet humble. Based on his personality, it would not be surprising he enjoyed his homecoming as much as the awards previously mentioned. "Meeker, Oklahoma, may have been a small town, but because it had the biggest hero, Carl Hubbell, it went all out, setting up a full day's celebration with bands, parades, a baseball game, and a dinner. Meeker had a population of only seven hundred and fifty, but the crowd topped ten thousand."[22]

Unquestionably, Carl Hubbell put together one incredible season in 1933. But it was only the beginning of his five fabulous seasons which would pave the way, years later, for his entrance into the Hall of Fame. The next season, 1934, would be just as memorable and personally rewarding for the man from Meeker, master of the screwball.

8

Lowest ERA, Most Saves

". . . THANKS TO THAT ALL-STAR GAME [1934], PEOPLE
THINK ABOUT ME AT LEAST ONCE A YEAR."

Fresh from gardening praise and adulation for his team's marvelous World Series triumph, Bill Terry signed a four-year contract worth $27,500. Hubbell also received a well-deserved raise to $17,500. Compared to today's astronomical contracts, it is a joke. In 1934, however, with the Depression taking its toll on millions of people, these were enviable salaries.

Unlike the previous off-season, Terry made only minor acquisitions. He was content with the club that won the National League pennant and beat the favored Washington Senators in five games in the World Series. And why shouldn't he be? He did, however, make some minor trades and additions to the club. In November, he traded pitcher Glenn Spencer to Cincinnati for utility infielder George Grantham. In December, Terry obtained pitcher Joe Bowman from Portland of the Pacific Coast League for third baseman Gil English. In addition, the Giants added left-hander Al Smith and righty Slick Castleman. Neither one would contribute much in 1934 but did so during the pennant-winning years of 1936 and 1937.

Terry was content with not making drastic changes to a club that most knowledgeable baseball people picked to win again. The Associated Press polled 97 writers, and 40 (41%) selected the Giants to repeat, and why not. Vergez was back at third after a bout with appendicitis, causing him to miss the last part of the '33 season and all of the World Series. The rejuvenated Jackson appeared healthy again and back at short. Terry would show no ill effects from the broken wrist by playing in 153 games. The outfield was strengthened in March when

Terry traded light-hitting Kiddo Davis to the St. Louis Cardinals for George Watkins. He would patrol center field between Ott and Moore, two solid and consistent players. There was one problem. Gus Mancuso was stricken with typhoid fever in February. According to the attending physician, "The disease appeared to be of a mild form and that Mancuso should be able to report for training sometime next month unless complications developed."[1]

Finally, Terry had to like his four-man rotation of Hubbell, Fitzsimmons, Schumacher, and Parmelee, especially the latter two with one more season of experience. Add the ageless Luque in relief, and Terry can be forgiven for his cockiness or joking manner, however you want to characterize it, when he was being interviewed by a group of sportswriters in January. Joke or not, Terry and others would pay for it down to the last day of the season.

Here's how the interview went during the major leagues' annual business meeting in New York. Terry was high on his club and singled out the Giants competition that could give them trouble, namely Pittsburgh, Chicago, St. Louis, and Boston. At this point, *The New York Times* reporter Roscoe McGowen, who covered the Brooklyn Dodgers, asked the logical question, what about Brooklyn? Terry answered with a smile and the now-famous lines, "Brooklyn, I haven't heard anything from them. Are they still in the league?"[2]

No doubt, it was an innocent comment meant to be lighthearted. Well, the next day, in print, it didn't read quite so funny. "Thousands of letters poured into the Giants' office, all of them from irate Dodger rooters. The Dodgers had left their fans cold since falling , deep into the second division. But Terry's offhand comment had fired them up. Wait until the season started. Their team would show Terry whether or not Brooklyn was still in the league!"[3]

In addition to the firestorm Terry's comment made with the Dodger faithful, it didn't sit well with Brooklyn's front office, particularly new business manager Bob Quinn. Quinn took umbrage at Terry's comments fearing it would affect gate receipts. Others believed Quinn was faking anger to build the rivalry between the two clubs to increase gate receipts. He also went after Max Carey, the Dodger manager, for not responding to Terry's remark. Quinn felt so strongly about it he fired Carey. Then again, it could have been a convenient excuse to rid the club of a manager who finished sixth after third place the year before. At any rate, Quinn went ahead and hired the ever-popular, loquacious, and press-friendly Casey Stengel. It was Casey's first major league managerial position. Casey, on his own or encouraged by Quinn, when asked by the press for a statement, said, "The first thing I want to say is that the Dodgers are still in the league." It was red meat for Dodger fans. Casey would do no better than Carey. During the three years (1934, 1935, and 1936), he managed Brooklyn, the club finished sixth, fifth, and seventh, respectively. Casey was gone after the '36 season but would return to manage the Boston club of the National League for six seasons, also with very little success.

But "The Ol' Perfessor" finally hit pay dirt in 1949 when the New York Yankees hired him and then, after 12 years, unceremoniously fired him after winning ten pennants and seven World Series. When the Yankees told him his services were no longer needed because they wanted a youth program, Casey made the now-famous quip, "I'll never make the mistake of being seventy again."

On February 26, *The New York Times* ran this shocking headline on their front page, "John J. McGraw is dead at 60; called baseball's greatest figure." And he certainly was whether you liked him or not. The name John McGraw was synonymous with baseball. The man nicknamed "Little Napoleon" and "Mugsy" enjoyed a 17-year major league career finishing with a lifetime batting average of .334 and an OBP of .466. Despite these phenomenal numbers, he achieved his fame for his "great baseball mind" and managerial skills, especially at the helm of the New York Giants from 1902 to 1932, a 31-year span where the Giants won 2,583 games, ten pennants, and three World Series.

McGraw was a tough, no-nonsense leader who would frequently administer tongue-lashings to his ballplayers. He was a tyrant, and winning was everything. He berated umpires unmercifully and held the record for ejections with 132 (this number varies with the source) until Bobby Cox of the Atlanta Braves broke it with 161.

Condolences from the baseball and sporting world came pouring in, expressing their sorrow that a great leader had passed. Among those that expressed their sympathies in telegrams or to the press were: James A. Farley, Postmaster General; Joseph McCarthy, New York Yankee manager; John F. Curry, leader of Tammany Hall; Judge Emil Fuchs, president of the Boston Braves; John A. Heydler, president of the National League; Eddie Collins, manager of the Boston Red Sox; Charles A. Stoneham, president of the New York Giants; Edward Burke, part-owner of the Havre de Grace race track in Maryland; James Tierney, secretary of the Giants; Kenesaw Mountain Landis, commissioner of Major League Baseball; William Harridge, president of the American League; William M. Walker, president of the Chicago Cubs; Connie Mack, manager/part-owner of the Philadelphia Athletics to name a few.

In addition, hundreds of ballplayers praised the great leader while Carl Hubbell "attributed all his success as a pitcher to the teachings of McGraw." Bill Terry probably expressed the sentiments of many, even though he and McGraw fought for years, when he said, "He was by far and away the greatest baseball manager of all time, and I doubt whether his records, achievements, and personality ever can be equaled by any other. I always considered him the foremost authority on the game. His many triumphs lay chiefly in the fact that he always kept himself abreast of the times and usually was several jumps ahead. I attribute much of my success last year to the solid groundwork of baseball, which I learned under him. Baseball will never know another John McGraw."[4]

As cold as it may seem, life and baseball go on as the Giants training camp began in their new location at Flamingo Field, Miami Beach, Florida. Spring training was nothing special, just business as usual. Although Terry did announce there would be two drills a day, but shorter rather than one long one due to the hot weather. After closely checking the new training field, Terry claimed, "This promises to be the finest camp I ever was in."

After the Giants broke training camp, they hooked up with the Cleveland Indians, playing their way north until opening day. "The Giants-Indians tour took them through several southern cities in which major league baseball was rarely ever seen—New Orleans, Baton Rouge, Meridian, Montgomery, Atlanta, Charlotte, Asheville, Nashville, and Louisville."[5]

Fans hungry for baseball and eager to watch some of the most talented players in the game were filling the stadiums with large crowds, but it was a tiresome journey for the players. The 14-game schedule finally ended in Cleveland for the last two games. The first was canceled due to "a baby blizzard and a biting gale." The following day with the Giants president, Charles A. Stoneham, at the game, Cleveland won 5-4, taking the series nine games to three with one tie.

With his club's dominance over the Giants, Cleveland manager Walter Johnson, in his first full year leading the club, was poised for a successful season. The future Hall of Famer took over the reins in 1933 and brought the club to a fourth-place finish. In 1934, the Indians would improve to third behind Johnson's leadership, but it was not without harsh criticism from the fans and press. Despite the Cleveland players public support of Johnson, the fans wanted him gone . . . and gone he was before the season was over, replaced by Coach Steve O'Neill. Walter Johnson never managed in the major leagues again.

So as not to mislead, Johnson did have some success as a manager before arriving at Cleveland. In 1929, "The Big Train" began a four-year stint as skipper of the Washington Senators, a club he was somewhat familiar with since he pitched for them for 21 years, posting a phenomenal record of 417-279 with a 2.17 ERA. Johnson managed the Senators from 1929 to 1932. In the last three seasons, his club won over 92 games each year. However, the highest the Senators could finish was in 1930, ending in second place (94-60) behind the great Philadelphia Athletics club (102-52), the eventual winners of the World Series over the St. Louis Cardinals. But in the end, Johnson was fired after the 1932 season. The reasons for Johnson's firing range from poor handling of the pitching staff (hard to believe) to being too much of a gentleman. Perhaps Durocher was correct when he said, "nice guys finish last."

Over 40,000 baseball fans packed the Polo Grounds on opening day, April 17, to witness the beginning of the 1934 season and hopefully another National League pennant. Despite the usual opening day festivities, marching band, hoisting of the American flag, and dozens of politicians and celebrities, there was a mood of sadness. A bugler played taps near the dugout where the late John McGraw stood for three decades. It was a beautiful and moving tribute to the departed Little Napoleon, which, no doubt, caused many a tear.

This done, the Giants went on to thrash the Philadelphia Phillies 6-1, behind the outstanding pitching of screwball artist Carl Hubbell. The left-hander gave up four hits and walked two batters. The only tally allowed was a home run by catcher Jimmy Wilson in the seventh inning. Equally important, the victory was the start of a five-game winning streak by the Giants.

Four days later, Hubbell tossed his first shutout of the season, beating the Boston Braves 2-0. It was another gem as the lefty scattered six singles and did not walk a batter. Twenty-five-year-old Paul Richards was behind the plate for both of Hubbell's early victories, with Mancuso still recovering from a bout with typhoid.

Richards had a long and varied career in professional baseball. As a young reserve catcher, he played for eight years with four different teams, finishing with a meager .227 batting average. His strength was defense and a strong arm. Richards is credited with inventing the oversize catcher's mitt to handle knuckleball pitchers. But it was as a field and general manager where he built his reputation, despite ever winning a pennant. He managed the Baltimore Orioles for eight years and the Chicago White Sox for five. His best showing was in 1960 when the Orioles finished second, behind the New York Yankees. As a general manager, he was instrumental in forming the Houston Colt 45s and making them competitive. He also was the man behind rejuvenating the

Milwaukee club when they moved to Atlanta. He eventually became Atlanta's vice-president in charge of all player personnel. The book *The Ballplayers* sums up Paul Richards' well-earned reputation. "He often got a team ready to win, only to move to another franchise before success was realized. He was considered among baseball's most brilliant and innovative strategists, an astute judge of pitching talent, and a skilled teacher."[6]

With their 5-1 record, the Giants traveled to Philadelphia to open the season for the Phillies at Baker Bowl. Schumacher started for the Giants and, in an odd turn of events, wound up hitting better than he pitched. After giving up seven runs, he was chased in the eighth but was still leading when Terry had to call on Hubbell to shut down the Phillies and preserve the 11-7 victory. Surprisingly, Schumacher hit two home runs and drove in five. He was credited with the W as Hubbell earned a save. Not to be outdone, Ott blasted two home runs giving him three early in the season.

Taking his regular four-day rotation turn, Hubbell nearly pitched another shutout beating Boston 4-1 at Braves Field. Boston scored their lone run in the ninth as the Giants were turning a double play. "The famed left-handed screwball master," as the *Times* called him, is now 3-0. Once again, Ott homered, his fourth to go along with his .385 batting average. Jo-Jo Moore was also off to a great start batting .389.

The Giants were also off to an encouraging start (7-3) before hosting their bitter rivals, the Brooklyn Dodgers, in a three-game series at the Polo Grounds. The Terrymen swept the series 5-0, 10-9, and 6-5. Perhaps Terry knew something when, before the season began, he quipped about the Dodgers still being in the league.

In the second game of the Brooklyn series in which the Giants won 10-9, Hubbell had to be called upon again in relief. Rookie Joe Bowman, making his major league debut, pitched decently and was replaced after six innings with a comfortable 10-2 lead. Terry didn't want to press his luck with the youngster and brought in Luque to wrap up the game. The Cuban veteran didn't get a batter out as Brooklyn scored two. Hubbell was immediately rushed into the game, but he allowed two more runs charged to Luque, making the score 10-7. Brooklyn scored two runs in the ninth before Hubbell mercifully got the final out. Bowman was credited with the win; Hubbell a save and Terry with a nerve-wracking afternoon.

In Pittsburgh for a three-game series, Hubbell proved he had bad days. The Pirates racked up 12 hits off the usually stingy left-hander, winning the game 4-3. They also won the series, taking two of three, as the Giants were eager to move on to Cincinnati for another three-game series. Hubbell's record was now 3-1.

The Giants and Hubbell bounced back in Cincinnati, winning two out of three, thanks to "Master Melvin." It was in the second game with Hub on the brink of losing. The Reds were ahead 2-1 in the top of the ninth. A walk, a hit by Terry, and Ott's rare double to left field scored both runners for the lead. Hubbell, in short order, took care of the Reds' in the ninth. His record was now 4-1.

The next stop for the Giants was in St. Louis for four games. The Cardinals won the first three. Dizzy tossed a five-hit shutout in the first game, and brother Paul beat Hubbell in game three in 10 innings, 3-2. It was quite a duel between Paul and Hub. Dean allowed nine hits and two runs while fanning six. Hub allowed nine hits, three runs in 9 1/3 innings while striking out seven. Hubbell's record was now 4-2 as the Giants dropped to fourth place.

The final stop on the current western trip was in Chicago. The Giants lost the first two games, and it took Hubbell and Ott to salvage one game to end this "disastrous" trip at 5-8. Before 10,000 shivering Chicago fans, from a gale-like wind blowing off Lake Michigan, Hubbell beat Charlie Root 10-3. The screwball master had it working today, as he gave up only seven hits, no walks, and whiffed five. Hub's record was now 5-2. Ott, who had been on fire since opening day, went 2 for 5 with four RBIs, including a three-run homer. It was number seven for Ott and put him two back of Chuck Klein of the Cubs. Master Melvin was also hitting .368, fourth-best in the league at the time. Interestingly, this was Mancuso's first starting assignment catching Hubbell since game four of the 1933 World Series. Gus won his battle with typhoid fever and was now back behind the plate.

Gus Mancuso was born in Galveston, Texas, on December 5, 1905, to Franco and Heppie Mancuso (nee Lindermann). Franco was of Sicilian heritage, and Heppie, the daughter of a German father and Cherokee mother. Including Gus, Franco and Heppie had seven children. Early on, the Mancusos moved to Houston to build a life. Sadly, Franco died in his forties, which meant Heppie was left to support and care for her large family, which she did as a midwife and nurse.

Baseball attracted Gus at a young age as he recalls, "I began as a pitcher in grammar school and, later, pitched for three years in high school. Then because we had no catcher, I went behind the bat. At the age of 17, I graduated from high and got a job as a printer's devil in the multigraph department of the Texas Oil Company."[7]

Never one to be idle, Gus decided to organize a baseball team. He knew some good players he could recruit. The only problem was his team had no equipment and no uniforms. No problem. Gus went house to house with a sales pitch asking for a donation, so he could form a team to represent the community. According to Gus' recollection, he received only $35 from visiting homes but fortunately, an unnamed benefactor contributed another $30. In those days, that was enough to get started.

"We entered our team in the intermediate department of the Houston City League, and I was both a pitcher and catcher. My ability to play ball caught the eye of a chap on the First National Bank, and I was given a job in the transient department of the bank, specializing in rubber checks and the position of catcher on the bank team."[8] Apparently in demand, Gus also played for several other local clubs. It was inevitable his talent would be recognized, and it was, by Fred Ankenman, president of the Houston Buffaloes of the Texas League. Gus was 19 years old.

"Houston offered him $125 a month and started him at Mount Pleasant in the Class D East Texas League, the bottom rung of professional baseball. The young and inexperienced Gus went to spring training with the parent St. Louis Cardinals in 1926 but returned to the minors. After the season, he married Lorena Carolyn Sue Dill. They would have two children, Emma Jean and August Jr."[9]

In 1927 Gus played for the Syracuse Stars, an affiliate of the St. Louis Cardinals of the International League (AA). The team finished second behind the Buffalo Bisons. The manager at the time was Burt Shotton, who became famous when Branch Rickey hired him to take over in 1947 to replace Leo Durocher as skipper of the Brooklyn Dodgers. Commissioner Happy Chandler had suspended Durocher for "conduct detrimental to baseball." Mancuso played in 82 games and batted .372.

The following year Mancuso was the victim of a glut of catchers for the Cardinals. Their starting backstop was the newly acquired Jimmy Wilson. So, Mancuso was sent to the Minneapolis Millers (AA), where he batted .295 in 48 games. But there is more to the story. It was in July when Mancuso was sent to the Millers. It looked like the Cardinals were going to win the pennant when Gus was called into vice president Branch Rickey's office for a chat. After greeting Gus, he said, " I've bad news for you. I must send you to Minneapolis. I know it is heartbreaking. Once upon a time, I was a young ballplayer, and I know exactly how you feel." Rickey sympathized with young Gus, explaining he knew how he felt, but this wouldn't be the last chance to play for a pennant winner and in a World Series. He also told Mancuso he wasn't ready for "the big show." He needed more seasoning in the minors.

Mancuso was devastated. "I was heartbroken. I could not keep the tears back. But Branch Rickey was right. I needed the additional schooling, and I wasn't ready for the majors. I played my best for Minneapolis and gave them everything I had."[10]

Still not ready for the parent club in 1929, Mancuso split the season catching for the Houston Buffaloes (A) and the Rochester Redwings (AA). When the 1930 season rolled around, the Cardinals catcher, Jimmy Wilson, was coming off a great season. The veteran backstop had caught 120 games in '29 and batted .325 plus driving in 71 runs. Mancuso's chance of getting any significant playing time was slim to none. Supposedly, St. Louis offered him additional compensation for returning to Rochester. Gus agreed, and that's when Commissioner Landis stepped in. He ruled the Cardinals had run out of options and had to "keep him or sell him."

In 1930 Gus Mancuso finally arrived as a 24-year-old rookie major league catcher for the St. Louis Cardinals. He had an outstanding season as a backup to Wilson. His slash line was .366/.415/.551 and an on-base-plus-slugging (OPS) of .965 in 76 games. More importantly, in mid-September, Wilson sprained his ankle and was out for the rest of the season as Mancuso became the full-time catcher and helped lead the Cardinals to the pennant. Their opponent was Connie Mack's Philadelphia Athletics, an elite powerhouse, with Lefty Grove, George Earnshaw, Al Simmons, Jimmy Foxx, and Mickey Cochrane, to name a few.

Mancuso caught the first two games of the Series and performed well. By the time the Series shifted to Sportsman's Park in St. Louis, Wilson had returned to the lineup. He caught the last four games as the A's won the World Series in six.

In 1931, a healthy Wilson was back behind the plate, as Mancuso was again relegated to being a backup catcher. However, there was one saving grace, the Cardinals won the pennant and returned to the World Series facing the Philadelphia Athletics one more time. It took the Cardinals, led by Pepper Martin, to become the new World Champions. Mancuso played little. In game one, he pinch-hit. In game six, he caught in the late innings. On the positive side, few ballplayers can say they played in two World Series in their first two full seasons in the major leagues. It was a valuable experience that would serve Mancuso in the future.

The following year was Mancuso's last with the St. Louis Cardinals, even though he split the catching duties with Wilson. He had a fine season, batting .284 in 103 games. Back in New York, the legendary John McGraw called it quits as manager of the Giants. The great Bill Terry replaced him. Memphis Bill, shortly after the '32 season was over, traded for Mancuso. The new manager wanted a young, durable, and talented backstop to handle his elite pitching rotation, led by Carl Hubbell, the emerging superstar and future Hall of Famer.

Mancuso would remain with the New York Giants for six years and was a key factor in Hubbell's success, along with Schumacher, Fitzsimmons, Parmelee, and reliever Luque. During his stay with the Giants, the team won three pennants and one World Series. He was an absolute workhorse behind the plate. During his first four years with the Giants, he caught 533 games, an average of over 133 per season.

In 1933, his first year with the Giants, the team won the pennant and World Series. Mancuso caught 144 games and batted a steady .264. More importantly, he was a major factor in Hubbell winning 23 games, the first of his five consecutive 20-plus seasons. The Giants won the World Series beating the Washington Senators in five games. Gus caught every game but offensively had a miserable Series, batting an anemic .118. The Giants' pitching stymied the Senators' powerful lineup, guided by Mancuso's defense and game-calling behind the plate. During the season, Terry said it best. "Gus is a pitcher's catcher. He's smart. All the pitchers like to work with him; that's why he's in there all the time. Richards is a fine young catcher, but why break up our battery system while Gus is getting so much out of the boys."[11]

In the next two years, 1934 and 1935, Gus continued to take on the role of iron man. In '34, the Giants narrowly lost the pennant to Gus' former team, the Cardinals. Mancuso caught 122 games and did have the satisfaction of successfully handling Hubbell (21-12), Schumacher (23-10), and Fitzsimmons (18-14).

Nineteen thirty-five turned out to be a repeat of the previous year. The Giants failed to win a pennant but not quite as painful. They finished third. Gus caught 128 games, and his hitting improved from .245 to .298. He also was selected for the All-Star Game. Hubbell, who always had high praise for

Mancuso, turned in his third straight 20-plus season, 23-12 on his way to the fabulous five.

In 1936 the Giants waited until August to put together a 15-game winning streak and pull ahead of the Cardinals to capture Terry's second National League pennant. Offensively, the team was led by Mel Ott, who had a monster season. The right fielder hit .328, drove in 135 runs, and had a .448 on-base percentage. He also led the league with 33 home runs, a .588 slugging average, and a 1.036 on-base plus slugging. Master Melvin was a one-man wrecking crew.

What Ott accomplished at the plate; Hubbell spun on the mound. King Carl led the league in victories 26-6, a winning percentage of .813, and a 2.31 earned run average. Of course, no team wins a pennant because of two players. It takes the efforts of a full roster. One of those was the tireless Mancuso, who caught 139 games and batted a cool .301 (only Ott and Moore were higher) and drove in 63 runs.

Gus had an explanation for his improved hitting, one that is still preached today. Use the whole field. " . . . I began to try hitting to right field, whereas previously, I had always been a dead left-field hitter. Not only did that get me a lot of valuable base hits that moved men from first to third, but it moved the outfielders over a bit so that I got more hits into left field too."[12]

But where Mancuso's efforts were most appreciated was behind the plate. In '36, Hubbell was almost the entire pitching staff, so much so that Edward T. Murphy of the *New York Sun* wrote, "Yet, with a so-called one-man staff, the team captured the league championship. Victories, and important ones, too, were registered in games in which less talented pitchers than Hubbell were in action. Mancuso's skill behind the plate did much toward carrying the team over the many rough spots which were encountered on days when King Carl was on the sidelines."[13]

Then in the 1936 World Series, the Giants met the mighty New York Yankees, led by Joe DiMaggio, Lou Gehrig, Bill Dickey, and a host of other superstars. The Bronx Bombers slugged their way to the World Championship four games to two. This Fall Classic victory would be the beginning of four straight championships for the Yankees. Gus caught all six games and apprised himself well. He batted .263, scored three runs, and drove in one.

The Giants won the pennant again in 1937 in a tight race with the Chicago Cubs. It was also the beginning of the end of Mancuso's stay with the Giants, despite Terry naming him the new team captain, replacing Travis Jackson, who would manage the Jersey City club in the International League. Also, Gus was selected to the All-Star Team for the second time in his career. The American League won 8-3. Gus went 0 for 1 as the backup to Gabby Hartnett. Less than a week later, Gus was injured and replaced by Harry Danning. Danning, who had been with the Giants since 1934 as Mancuso's backup, took over the full-time catching duties until Gus returned on September 3. The young backstop, however, took advantage of his playing time. In virtually the same number of at-bats as Gus, Danning had a higher batting average: .288 vs. .279, RBIs 51 to 39, and home runs 8 to 4. And then there was the age difference. Gus was 31 and Danning 25. But the final blow came in the World Series rematch between the Giants and the Yankees. The mighty Bombers won the Series four games to one. Mancuso started the first two games, went 0 for 7, and didn't return until game five as a pinch-hitter. It could have been a sign Gus was on his way out.

By February 1938, Gus Mancuso fell out of favor with Bill Terry, despite the praise he had heaped on him since 1933. Danning was now the number one catcher for the Giants and Gus the backup. Danning had a wonderful year. He caught 120 games, batted .306, and drove in 60 runs. In his new backup role, Gus hit .348 with an OBP of .411. The Giants finished third as the Cubs won the NL pennant.

The inevitable happened on December 6, 1938. Gus Mancuso, infielder Dick Bartell, and outfielder Hank Leiber were traded to the Chicago Cubs for outfielder Frank Demaree, infielder Billy Jurges, and catcher Ken O'Dea. Gus played one year with the Cubs as the backup to veteran catcher/manager Gabby Hartnett. Gus batted a weak .231 as Chicago finished fourth in 1939.

In almost a year to the day, Gus was on the move again. This time he and pitcher Newt Kimball were shipped to the Brooklyn Dodgers for catcher Al Todd. Chief Operating Officer Larry McPhail made the deal with the idea of using Gus in a dual role, primarily as a catcher but also helping the younger pitchers. McPhail was one of the all-time great innovators in baseball in the 1930s and 1940s. He also was against integration, a heavy drinker with a hot temper, a combination that gardened him many enemies. The good outweighed the bad. He was elected to the Hall of Fame in 1978.

During the 1940 season, Mancuso and Herman Franks were backups to Babe Phelps, as the Dodgers led by player/manager Leo Durocher finished second, 12 behind the pennant-winning Cincinnati Reds. The month of December was turning out to be a jinx for Mancuso. For the third December in a row, he was traded. This time he was sent to the St. Louis Cardinals, along with John Pinter, a minor league pitcher for the Dallas Rebels in the Texas League, and $65,000. In return, the Dodgers received catcher Mickey Owen. Ironically, the Cardinals were the club with which Mancuso began his major league career back in 1928, at age 22. Now at age 35, Mancuso was the starting catcher once again, albeit a little older. Gus caught 106 games and batted a weak .229, as the Cards finished second, 2½ games back of the Brooklyn Dodgers, led by Durocher.

After the 1941 season and December rolled around, Gus was shocked, but not because he wasn't traded. Like millions of other Americans, his emotional reaction, of total incredulity, was about the news of December 7. Japan had attacked Pearl Harbor, and as President Franklin Delano Roosevelt said it was, "a date which will live in infamy." It was the beginning of World War II for the United States and the total disruption of the country, and the loss of over 400,000 lives. It devastated major league baseball as many of the players joined up or were called to serve.

In the meantime, the 1942 season began, and Gus found himself sitting on the bench behind 27-year-old Walker Cooper, with little chance of seeing any playing time. He was correct; by May 23, Gus had played in a total of five games when the Giants purchased his contract. Back for the second time, the Giants' personnel had changed significantly. Most importantly, Gus would have a new manager. Terry was gone, and Mel Ott was at the helm. But the veteran catcher found himself in the same predicament before he was traded to Chicago as Danning's backup. In 39 games, Gus batted a feeble .193.

The following year Mancuso's performance at the plate was still woefully wanting as he batted .198, the second consecutive year he was below the Mendoza line. To his credit, the aging veteran caught 94 games. He was also classified 4-F because of the damaged first two fingers of his right hand, the result of all the years catching in both the minor and major leagues. But Ott had his problems too. He was in his second year managing and finished dead last with an embarrassing 55-98 record.

In 1944, the New York Giants improved but still finished a weak fifth with a 67-87 record, not much of a consolation, however, to the loyal fans. As he had been for the last several years, Gus was now the backup to Ernie Lombardi. "Schnozz," as he was affectionately called (because of his large nose), was picked up in a trade with the Boston Braves in April of '43. In 78 games, Gus improved his batting average to .251. Actually, during 19 days in May and June, he batted a cool .333. What was his secret? A lighter bat, different stance? Nope, none of that. It was Ott's B-1 vitamin tablets. "Yes, I've been taking the same pills Ottie has, and they're wonderful. I take a shot every night before I go to bed. Not only do I sleep well, but I get up fully refreshed," confirmed Gus.[14]

The B-1 vitamins weren't enough, as the Giants released Mancuso early in November of '44. The Phillies, managed by Mancuso's former battery mate Freddie Fitzsimmons, persuaded Gus to join the club as a part-time catcher sharing the duties with 24-year-old Andy Seminick. He also did double duty as their pitching coach. In 70 games, Gus batted a pathetic .199; so much for the B-1 vitamins. After the season, when Fitz was no longer the manager and Gus was pushing 40, he asked for his release. Gus Mancuso's major league playing career came to an end.

But the love of the game was still prevalent. As the saying goes, "it was in his blood." Over the next 15 years, Gus was involved in numerous baseball activities. He managed several minor league clubs in the late '40s and as a pitching coach for the Cincinnati Reds. He also ventured into the broadcasting business, the highlight of joining Harry Caray doing play-by-play for the St. Louis Cardinals.

Gus Mancuso, however, was best known for his six years with the New York Giants (1933-1938) as a vital member of the club. During this time frame, the Giants won three pennants and one World Series. His reputation was built on his defense, although in 1935 and 1936, he batted .298 and .301, respectively. Let's not forget, he hit .348 in 1938 even though it was in only 52 games. "Mancuso became captain of the Giants [1937] and the favorite for Carl Hubbell, whom the catcher called the greatest pitcher he ever worked with."[15] Gus Mancuso died October 26, 1984.

Back at the Polo Grounds, Hubbell missed pitching in the three-game series with Cincinnati but started the first game against St. Louis and Dizzy Dean. The outspoken Diz outpitched Hub, whipping the Giants 9-5 before 40,000 disappointed fans. Hubbell lasted only five innings, giving up six hits and seven runs. It was one of his poorest games of the season. Five of the runs came on homers as *Times* sportswriter Drebinger held back no punches when he wrote, "Hubbell was hammered unceremoniously." His record was now 5-3. Perhaps it was a wake-up call for the Meal Ticket. It would be a month before he lost another game.

On May 24, Hubbell bounced back quickly when he next faced the Cubs at the Polo Grounds. He allowed four singles in a 7-1 victory and inspired Drebinger to comment, "As for Hubbell's work on the mound, it was as fine a piece of pitching as could be desired, meriting a shutout, which would have been achieved but for a lone Giant error."[16] Hubbell's record was now 6-3.

The league-leading Pittsburgh Pirates were next on the Giants' schedule, winning the first game of the three at the Polo Grounds. However, they dropped the next two in a twin-bill sweep, starring Travis Jackson. In the first game, with the score tied 2-2, in the bottom of the 11th, the shortstop launched his fourth homer into the upper right-field stands for the victory. In the nightcap, Jackson homered in the second inning for a 1-0 lead, but that's all Hubbell needed. King Carl blanked the Pirates on five singles and zero walks. The victory dropped Pittsburgh out of first place as the Cardinals took over and the Giants moved up to third. It was Hubbell's second shutout of the season as his record went to 7-3.

During the Giants' first visit to Ebbets Field to meet the Brooklyn Dodgers, Terry chose not to start Hubbell, his ace, during the four-game series. His decision was by design. Strange as it may seem, Hub's track record against Brooklyn was not good. Up to this season, it was a miserable 9-20. But King Carl's absence didn't stop the Brooklyn fanatics from verbal abuse, remembering Terry's earlier quip about their existence in the league. According to author Noel Hynd, ". . . Terry had to have an inkling of what he was in for. The fans hurled verbal abuse at him that was rough even by Flatbush standards. When Casey Stengel tried to pose with Terry for some photographs, fans chucked firecrackers at both of them. Eventually, Stengel retreated to a safer spot, which was anywhere Terry wasn't."[17]

Hubbell opened the month of June facing the Philadelphia Phillies at the Polo Grounds. Behind the fine pitching of George Darrow, an unknown left-hander, who would last one season in the major leagues, the game would go into the seventh inning tied at 2-2. But Hubbell made a bad pitch to Irv Jeffries, who parked the ball into the upper left-field stands. In the bottom of the seventh, Hub was pinch-hit for as the Giants tied the game. Luque blanked the Phillies for the next two innings, setting up Memphis Bill's single with the bases loaded to win the game 4-3. Luque was credited with the win, and Hub came away with a no-decision for his afternoon's work—eight hits, three runs, no walks, and four Ks.

Hubbell bounced back in his next start at home against the Boston Braves. In reality, the game was over after the Giants scored five runs in the first inning, led by their manager, who drove in two of their five. Hubbell coasted along, tossing shutout ball through seven, but ran into trouble in the eighth with two out. A single, triple, single, and the Braves plated two runs, but it was not near enough, as King Carl won 6-2. His record was now 8-3. The victory was important because it moved the Giants into first place, one full game ahead of St. Louis.

In the final tune-up, before New York went on their second western swing, they routed the pathetic Phillies 18-7 at Baker Bowl during a rain-drenched game. New York scored four runs in the first, and it looked like, bad weather or not, Hub was in for an easy day. However, the master of the screwball gave three runs back after two outs. As the rain continued, Hub settled down until the fifth inning with two out and Johnny Moore on first. Al Todd hit back to the box, Hub deflected the ball and, when he spun around, slipped on the wet turf, landing on his left hand. Hubbell was removed from the game and replaced by Luque, who secured the final out after allowing a run. Hi Bell finished the game earning a save while Hubbell picked up his ninth win against three losses.

Beginning their second western swing, the Giants swept the three-game series with the Reds. Hub pitched in game two and picked up his third save. He entered the game in the seventh inning, with the Giants leading 6-4. He replaced Slick Castleman, who had replaced Joe Bowman. Hubbell pitched three scoreless innings, allowing three hits. The slight mishap Hub encountered when he slipped on the wet field in Philadelphia was not serious. Castleman earned the win. It would be the rookie's only victory of the season.

The next afternoon after the Giants had swept the Reds and were preparing to travel to Pittsburgh, New York fans were fixated on Madison Square Garden Bowl at Long Island. Primo Carnera, the 6 ft. 6 in. giant was about to defend his heavyweight title against Max Baer. Carnera, born in Italy, won his heavyweight title by defeating Jack Sharkey on June 29, 1933. Now he was facing Baer, born in Omaha, Nebraska, and responsible for Frankie Campbell's death in the 1930 fight. Baer was charged with manslaughter but eventually acquitted of all charges. Baer was also linked to the death of Ernie Schaaf after the severe beating he gave him in their 1932 match. Schaaf complained of headaches after the Baer pummeling but went on to fight Carnera five months later. He died in the ring after a left jab from the Italian. However, an autopsy revealed Schaaf had meningitis and was also suffering from a case of influenza.

It's clear why interest was so high for this world championship fight. Sadly, the hype and anticipation did not meet the results or even come close. It turned out to be a one-sided fight as Baer won the title by beating up on Carnera unmercifully. As the *Times* reported, "The Italian took every blow until he could take no more. Going down twelve times, he also fell once while delivering a punch. And twice in the first round, he stumbled against and almost through the ropes, helpless and almost on the brink of defeat."[18]

Carnera's next significant fight, after Baer, was against Joe Louis, "The Brown Bomber," who KO'd Carnera in the sixth round at Yankee Stadium in 1935. That ended any hope of Carnera recapturing the heavyweight title. Baer went on to defend his title against James J. Braddock, nicknamed "Cinderella Man," in 1935. Baer was a heavy favorite and failed to take the match seriously. Shockingly, he lost to Braddock in a 15-round unanimous decision. It was one of the biggest upsets in boxing history. It took until 2005 for Hollywood to finally make a movie of Braddock's life. It was titled, not surprisingly, *Cinderella Man* and starred Russell Crowe and Renee Zellweger. The director was Ron Howard, who, as a child actor played, Opie Taylor, the son of Sheriff Andy Taylor in the *Andy Griffith Show*, a big hit in the 1960s. After the humiliating defeat at Braddock's hands, a humbled Max Baer went on to fight the up-and-coming heavyweight Joe Louis. On September 24, 1935, Joe Louis knocked out Baer in round four. The quick and decisive defeat all but ended Max Baer's boxing career.

After the Cincinnati series, the Giants moved on to Pittsburgh to greet Pie Traynor, the newly appointed manager, and popular veteran third baseman. It turned out to be a harsh welcome for the new skipper. The Giants swept the three-game series, with the Meal Ticket winning the first game 5-2. It wasn't his finest hour, giving up 10 hits but only two runs. His pinpoint control (one walk) served him well and is often overlooked as an important element of his success. Hubbell's record now climbed to 10-3. Terry batting .360 and Ott .333 with 15 homers continued to lead the offense along with Moore and O'Doul at .352 each.

Schumacher (9-4) won the final game of the series 5-3 but needed help from Hubbell in the bottom of the eighth to get the last out. It was Hub's fourth save of the season. Moreover, the Giants have won eight of ten games on this current road trip and have increased their first-place lead over St. Louis to four games.

The next stop was Chicago. The Windy City was not kind to the Terry-men. After winning the first game 12-7 behind Fitzsimmons (7-5), the Giants lost the next three! Hubbell followed Fitz but lost the game in the second inning when he gave up a home run to shortstop Billy Jurges with two runners on. That's all Lon Warneke, the Arkansas Hummingbird, needed as he blanked

New York on four hits. The defeat snapped Hubbell's winning streak at five as his record went to 10-4.

After the Giants had their comeuppance in Chicago, the club moved to St. Louis with the Dean brothers anxiously waiting. New York won the first two games and Paul and Dizzy the last two. Hubbell pitched game two of the series, and his teammates gifted their ace with a seven-run outburst in the second inning. Oddly, a home run was not hit in the inning, but singles and doubles were aplenty, capped by Jackson's triple. The final score was 10-7, as Hubbell's record was now 11-4. By the time the series ended, St. Louis had dropped to third place as Chicago took over second, 1½ games back of New York.

Meanwhile, it was announced the All-Star Game was to be played on July 10 at the Polo Grounds. Bill Terry would manage the National League while the American League would be led by Joe Cronin. John A. Heydler, president of the National League, pointed out his counterpart, Will Harridge of the American League, had agreed a precedent had been established, the naming of the managers of the previous World Series. He further suggested it could be carried out in the future. Little did Heydler know Hubbell would make history during the '34 All-Star Game.

Back home from their successful western trip, the Giants won two of three from their bitter rivals, the Brooklyn Dodgers. The loss came at the hands of Hubbell. It was the first time Terry chose Hub to pitch against Brooklyn, knowing full well the difficulty his ace had with them. It was no different this time as the Dodgers pounded out 12 hits and six runs in 6 1/3 innings off the best left-hander in the league. Adding to the Giant's embarrassment, the Flatbush victory broke their eight-game losing streak. Brooklyn won 8-4 as Hubbell's record was now 11-5. Despite the loss, there was some good news for Giant fans. Terry was leading the league with a .369 batting average.

Four days later, in the second game of a July 4th twin-bill with the Boston Braves . . . and free from whatever psychological hold Brooklyn had on Hubbell, the master of the screwball threw his third shutout of the season. It was the King Carl, who Giant fans (and there were many among the 42,000) were accustomed to seeing. He allowed five hits, walked one, and struck out five as the Giants romped to a 15-0 victory. Ott had a monster day. The right fielder drove in five runs, going 3 for 4, including home runs number 20 and 21. Hubbell's record was now 12-5.

A week later, the Giants were facing those pesky Dodgers again, this time at Ebbets Field. The two clubs split the four games. Parmelee started game three and left in the fifth inning with a 5-1 lead, the bases loaded and one out. Terry, gambling against the jinx or whatever it was called, sent for Hub. Stengel countered by sending up Danny Taylor, a right-handed batter for Buzz Boyle, who batted from the left side. Taylor promptly tripled in three runs cutting the Giants' lead to 5-4. Hubbell gave up another run in the seventh, which tied the game. Brooklyn eventually won 7-5 with Luque, the losing pitcher. And Hubbell was still haunted and perplexed by his failure to beat the Dodgers.

In its second year of existence, the much-anticipated All-Star Game attracted a capacity crowd of 50,000 fans to the Polo Grounds on July 10. Another 15,000 fans were turned away when the gates were locked fifteen minutes before game time. As they did the previous year, the American League was victorious 9-7. The game was won in the fifth inning when the AL scored six runs beating up on Van Lingo Mungo. But the game would be forever remembered, not by the final score or which league won. It would be remembered for what happened in the first and second innings by the Meal Ticket. It would become forever a legendary part of baseball history. Top of the first, Carl Hubbell, the "invincible" left-hander, began inauspiciously "when Charlie Gehringer singled and went to second on Wally Berger's error in right. Then Heinie Manush walked. There were no outs, and coming up was the man who had won the first All-Star Game with a two-run homer, a fellow named Ruth.

"Hubbell threw four pitches to Ruth. One was a ball. The Babe swung at the second one and missed it. The next two were called strikes.

"Hubbell had, as they say, settled down. Gehrig, the next batter, swung and missed with the count 3-and-2; since the hit-and-run play was on, Manush and Gehringer advanced to second and third. Nevertheless, there were two outs now. Next on the menu was Foxx, whom Hubbell struck out on five pitches to end the inning."[19]

But that was only the beginning of Hubbell's unforgettable performance. Hubbell struck out Al Simmons with a 1-0 count on three straight pitches in the top of the second inning. Up next, manager/shortstop Joe Cronin with a 1-2 count, went down swinging. Carl Hubbell had fanned five of the greatest hitters in the history of the game. Years later, Hubbell commented on his magnificent performance. When the first two batters, Gehringer and Manush, got on base, Hubbell recalled, "Some fans were booing, yelling I should be taken out. Bill Terry, the manager, came out. Some players—Pie Traynor, Frankie Frisch, Gabby Hartnett—joined him. Terry didn't say anything. He just looked at me as if to say. 'Hey, you'd better get tough, or you'll have a short stay out here!' It was a breather—it relaxed me."[20] In all, Hubbell pitched three innings of shutout baseball. He allowed two hits, walked one, and struck out six.

The following day with the All-Star Game still being discussed, the Giants began a four-game series with the Pittsburgh Pirates at the Polo Grounds. New York won three of four, with Hub winning game three, 11-1. With an early six-run lead, the Meal Ticket dominated the Pirates on six hits, no walks while striking out eight. His record was now 13-5, and the Giants maintained their slim one-game lead.

When the Pirates left town, the second-place Chicago Cubs, only a slim two games back of the Terrymen, arrived. Although there was plenty of baseball remaining, it was an important series (five games) nonetheless. The Giants won the series three games to two. Hubbell was called upon in two of the games. He relieved Schumacher in the second game of the series, with the Giants leading 5-3. But Prince Hal got in trouble in the seventh, leaving two runners on, one out and a run in as Hubbell got the call from Terry. Hub promptly shut the door, pitching 2 2/3 scoreless innings, to register his fifth save of the season. Schumacher was credited with the victory, his eighth straight.

Two days later, Hubbell began a three-game losing streak. It started when, in the second game of a doubleheader, he was outpitched by Chicago's Bill Lee before 44,000, the largest crowd at the Polo Grounds this season. Although Hubbell lost 2-1, the tireless ace pitched extremely well. In seven innings, he allowed five hits, all singles. His record was now 13-6.

Hubbell was next matched up (July 21) against Cincinnati's Allyn Stout with a 1-5 record. The right-hander pitched an outstanding game, allowing six hits and two runs in a 3-2 victory, while the Giants' defense fell apart. Three errors in the first two innings contributed "directly or indirectly" to the Reds scoring. It was a frustrating loss for Hubbell as his record was now 13-7.

Unlike the game with the Reds, Hubbell's third consecutive loss was well deserved. Hub's demise occurred in the first game of a twin-bill when the Dean brothers ganged up on the Giants. Paul threw seven innings and gave up six hits and two runs for the 7-2 victory. His record was 11-4. Big brother Dizzy pitched the last two innings and blew the Giants away with nothing but goose eggs for his fourth save.

Conversely, Hubbell's screwball wasn't fooling many on this day. Hub's poor pitching and the Giants' sloppy defense resulted in King Carl leaving after four terrible innings. His final pitching line was seven hits, seven runs (three earned), leaving him with a 13-8 record. But there was a bright side. Schumacher had recently put together a nine-game winning streak, and Fitz had an eight-game streak going. Terry, with a .359 batting average, and Ott, with .345, were in the top six in the National League. These were just two of the positives to keep Terry smiling.

Before moving on, a quick word about the fabulous Dean brothers. For two years, 1934 and 1935, Dizzy and Paul were the best brother act in baseball. For those two years, the Dean boys won a combined 96 games and lost 42 for an outstanding .696 winning percentage. One can only speculate what the brothers could have accomplished if arm trouble hadn't shortened both their careers.

If many New York Giant fans worried about their ace left-hander suddenly losing his effectiveness, their concern was misguided. King Carl bounced back and won his next four starts, including save number six. His first victory of the four came on July 29 against Philadelphia. It was a brilliant four-hitter, blanking the Phillies 2-0 for his 14th victory against eight losses. The top of the order gave Hub all the runs he needed in the first inning. Critz singled, Terry tripled, and Ott singled for a quick two runs. The *Times* reported, "However, Carl never looked better than he did in this particular nightcap. It was not until the sixth that the Phils caught up with their first hit, and even that was an infield affair of a somewhat questionable sort. Three men got as far as second; only one reached third."[21] This was the Hubbell Giant fans knew and loved.

As the calendar turned over to August, Hubbell recorded his sixth save in an 11-2 victory over Boston at Braves Field. Second-year Giant Jack Salveson started the game and was handed a 6-1 lead after only two innings. But Salveson tired after five, and Terry immediately called for Hubbell, who pitched four scoreless innings, as the Giants tacked on more runs. Yes, it was Terry and Ott again going a combined 6 for 10 and five ribbies. Equally important, the Giants won the second game 10-3 behind Schumacher (16-5). Ott helped the cause by hitting home runs number 25 and 26 as the Giants increased their lead over Chicago by four games, the widest margin since their last western trip.

On August 3, Hubbell continued his mini winning streak with a 2-0 shutout of the Phillies at Baker Bowl. He allowed six hits, no free passes, and fanned five. His record was now 15-8. It was his fifth and last shutout of the season. All the scoring took place in the top of the fourth when Jackson singled, and Vergez launched a Euel Moore pitch into the left-field bleachers.

Victory number 16 for Hubbell came in a relief role and one that would elicit no more than a yawn against most teams, especially if you were a casual Giant fan. This victory was different. It was against the despised Brooklyn

Dodgers, a club that gave Hub fits. The last time Hubbell started against Brooklyn, he was pounded and left the game after giving up 12 hits and six runs in 6 1/3 innings. Once again, Terry defied history, defied the jinx theory, and called for his ace in the sixth when Salveson got in trouble. The inning ended in a 3-3 tie. But the Giants, led by Jackson, scored three in the bottom of the seventh to win the game 6-4. Hubbell picked up the victory (16-8), but his pitching line of five hits, one run in 3 2/3 innings, wasn't dominating. Did the Brooklyn jinx still linger?

The day Hubbell was to pitch against the Boston Braves, Wilbert Robinson's Mass was held at the Sacred Heart Cathedral in Atlanta. He had suddenly died the day before of a cerebral hemorrhage. As Jack Kavanagh and Norman Macht describe in their book *Uncle Robbie*, "Robinson was a major baseball figure for forty years. As a key member of the Baltimore Orioles of the 1890's he was a cheerful but tough-as-nails ballplayer in what was probably the roughest era the game has ever known."[22]

Robinson also worked for McGraw as a pitching coach and was instrumental in helping the New York Giants win pennants in 1911, 1912, and 1913. In 1914 "Uncle Robbie," as he was affectionately called, took over as the Brooklyn Dodgers manager. The name was changed to Robins in his honor and remained that way for 18 years. He won pennants in 1916 and 1920 but lost the World Series to the Boston Red Sox and Cleveland Indians, respectively. But after the 1931 season and almost 50 years in baseball, Robinson finally called it quits. Not for long. He was coaxed out of retirement to become president of the Atlantic Crackers of the Southern Association. When the club began to fail in August of '33, he took over as manager. A year later, Wilbert Robinson died of a brain hemorrhage. He was 70.

President John A. Heydler of the National League paid a marvelous tribute to Uncle Robbie. "All baseball will sorrow over the death of Wilbert Robinson. Aside from his achievements as a player and manager, he was beloved as a genuine character of the game. His fair fighting, his support of the umpires, his philosophy and good humor relieved the grind and stress of many a championship campaign."[23] In 1945, Wilbert Robinson was elected to the National Baseball Hall of Fame.

With saddened hearts, the Giants went on to beat Boston 6-3 at the Polo Grounds. It was Hubbell's 17th victory of the season, supported by three home runs. Critz, Vergez, and Ott all homered. It was Master Melvin's 30th and brought his RBI total to 120. Except for the second and seventh innings, Hub had smooth sailing all afternoon. Only one Boston player did all the damage, none other than Hubbell's former catcher Shanty Hogan. The big man drove in all three runs. Of Hub's 17 victories, five were at the expense of the Braves.

As important as the Giant's pennant race was, the big news of the day was Babe Ruth's announcement that 1934 was his last season as an active player. He also mentioned to the press that he would like to manage and singled out Boston, where his unprecedented career began. Perhaps he already had discussions with Braves owner Judge Emil Fuchs, knowing full well Yankees owner Jacob Ruppert wouldn't hire him. Who could ever forget Ruppert's hurtful but true words, "You can't manage yourself, Ruth. How do you expect to manage others?" Some say Ruppert never said those words or a variation, but the press has widely reported them and in numerous books for years.

It took 41-year-old Burleigh Grimes, the aging Pirates right-hander, to stop Hubbell and the Giants in the opening of a five-game series. The ageless one gave up six hits and two runs in eight innings and left with the score 2-2. It appeared Hubbell was on his way to his 18th victory by blanking the Pirates for seven innings. In the eighth, Hub ran into trouble. Arky Vaughn singled, Gus Suhr tripled for one run, and Critz booted a grounder for the second run. Waite Hoyt relieved Grimes and shut down the Giants in the ninth. In the bottom of the ninth, that man Suhr drove in the winning run, accounting for all the Pirates scoring in the 3-2 victory. Hubbell's record now stood at 17-9. It was a tough loss to swallow, and equaling frustrating, Hoyt was given the win and not Grimes.

While Terry had the Giants playing sound baseball and maintaining a respectable lead over the Cubs, the St. Louis Cardinals were causing all kinds of havoc. Frankie Frisch boldly fined Dizzy Dean $100 and brother Paul $50 for not accompanying the team to Detroit for an exhibition game. Dizzy went berserk and tore up his uniform . . . and another, then claimed he and Paul would go fishing. Not accepting fines gracefully, Frisch had enough of the brothers and suspended them both indefinitely. Two days later, Dizzy moved for a peace settlement, but Paul did not. Frisch refused and snapped, "Ten more days off the payroll."

A week later, the baseball czar, commissioner Kenesaw Mountain Landis, met with Frisch, the Dean brothers, and other principles in a boisterous meeting to finally settle the suspension. Frisch agreed to reduce the penalty from 10 days to seven, which meant Dizzy was immediately available to pitch. It cost Dizzy a total of $486, which included pay for seven days ($350), two destroyed uniforms ($36), and the initial fine of $100. Paul was reinstated earlier when he paid his fine plus the loss of two days' pay. The incident was about Dizzy's enormous ego.

King Carl got his revenge before the Giants left Pittsburgh. It was in the fifth and final game of the series. In his masterful style, he scattered 10 hits, allowed three runs, and didn't walk a Pirate. The final score was 8-3 as the Giants pounded out 18 hits, with Ott leading the way. The right fielder went 4 for 5 with three ribbies, including his 32nd home run. Hubbell's record was now 18-9.

With Hubbell's 18th victory, the Giants now led Chicago by 5½ games and St. Louis by 6, which meant it was going to be a three-team race to the finish line. Little did Giant fans know the Cards would finish strong with a bunch called the Gashouse Gang for their shabby look and rough and tumble play. They were led by a wild group, including player/manager Frankie Frisch, outspoken and feisty shortstop Leo Durocher, the "Wild Horse of the Osage," Pepper Martin, a daring and gutsy baserunner, outfielder Joe Medwick, another aggressive type, "Ripper" Collins, a switch-hitting power hitter, and catcher Bill DeLancey.

On the mound were the incomparable Dizzy and Paul Dean plus Tex Carlton and Bill Walker. The pitching alone was challenging for the opposition to handle, without dealing with the Cards' tenacious and gritty everyday players. Dizzy, at the time the Giants had a 6-game lead, had already racked up 21 victories! Paul had 13, and the two didn't stop winning with a month and a half remaining.

Dizzy ended the season, leading both leagues with 30 victories and only seven losses. The accomplishment of 30 wins in a season would not occur again, in either league, until 1968 when the infamous Denny McLain won 31 games. Not to take anything away from McLain, 1968 was later labeled the "Year of the Pitcher." The reason? The major leagues decided to increase the size of the strike zone from the top of the batter's shoulders to the bottom of the knees. Commissioner Ford Frick and the owners led the change because Roger Maris and others were hitting too many home runs. It finally took its toll in 1968. Both leagues suffered as batting averages dropped precipitously. It was so bad in '68 that Hall of Famer Carl Yastrzemski won the American League's batting title with a .301 average! The situation called for drastic action, so the mound's height was lowered from 15 to 10 inches. Also, the strike zone was shrunken to the area from the armpits to the top of the batter's knees.

During the next five games, Hubbell would save two, have a no-decision in two, and lose one to finish his work in August. In the second game of the Cincinnati series, the Giants used four pitchers, including Hubbell, in an 11 inning 6-4 victory. The game was tied at 4-4 after nine. In the 11th, Ott, who was having a marvelous year, singled with the bases loaded to put New York ahead 6-4. Terry immediately called for his ace. The Meal Ticket didn't disappoint. It was his seventh save of the season. Ironically, in his one inning of pitching, the man noted for his pinpoint control walked a batter. The other three Giant hurlers, Schumacher, Smith, and Salveson, walked NONE. Go figure.

The following day the Giants beat the Reds for the third straight game, 7-4. Again, Terry called on his part-time relief specialist to save the game. Parmelee started and was wild, in and out of trouble, all day. He allowed 10 hits and walked seven. Hubbell pitched 1 2/3 innings, allowing one hit. As he did the previous day, Hub was credited with the save, his eighth and last of the season.

New York moved into St. Louis for an important three-game series. The Cards were still mired in third place, six games back of the Giants, so a sweep by St. Louis would put them much too close with more than a month of baseball remaining. With the Giant fans breathing a sigh of relief, the Terrymen took two of three and left a frustrated Gashouse Gang seven back. Hubbell versus Paul Dean was the match-up in the first game. It was a rare day; King Carl's screwball wasn't very effective, as St. Louis chased him after giving up eight hits and three runs in five innings. Terry then opened the bullpen, as a parade of Giants pitchers—Smith, Luque, Bell, and Fitzsimmons—all took their turn holding the score to a close 3-2. Jo-Jo Moore, the slim Texan, took control in the top of the ninth. The Giants' left fielder walloped a home run into the screen atop the right-field bleachers with runners on first and third and two out. Bell allowed a double to the first batter he faced in the bottom of the ninth, which prompted Terry to call for Fitz, who shut down the attempted rally, clinching the 5-3 victory. Luque picked up the win, Fitz the save, and Hubbell a no-decision.

In the final game of the series, Hub was called on again in relief, a strategy that requires further comment. This practice, using a starting pitcher in relief, has not been part of a manager's playbook for decades. Moreover, the way a pitching staff is used has been completely revamped. Today, no manager would use a starting pitcher in a relief role, particularly his ace, during the regular season. When it comes to the playoffs, however, it is an entirely different story. Even more drastic is the revolutionary changes in the bullpen. In this author's opinion, the pendulum has swung way too far where you almost have a special-ist for each inning (a slight exaggeration). You have righty, lefty specialists, setup men, closers, and two-inning starters. Games today are four hours long. What next? It is all driven by that most annoying and overused word, analytics. But let's leave that discussion for another day.

Hubbell pitched two innings in relief of Parmelee and earned a no-decision. Schumacher picked up his 19th win in relief against only five losses as the Gi-ants came from behind to beat Dizzy Dean 7-6. The afternoon's hero was Travis Jackson, who drove in three runs, two of which came in the eighth, giving the Giants a 7-6 lead and eventually the game. It also was Dean's first loss to the Giants in six games.

The Meal Ticket finished August on a sad note. It was the final game of the Cub series, with Hub facing Lon Warneke in a classic pitcher's duel. Warneke (18-9) shut out the Giants on three hits. Hubbell had trouble with one batter all afternoon, Kiki Cuyler, a lifetime .321 hitter and future Hall of Famer. The speedy, line-drive hitter went 3 for 4 and drove in the winning and only run in the bottom of the ninth. Adding insult to injury, the run was unearned. It was the result of an error by Critz on Stan Hack's grounder. Hack was forced at second by Augie Galan. Cuyler then doubled (number 36), scoring Galan and winning the game 1-0. Hubbell's record was now 18-10. Six of his 10 losses were by one run!

The New York Giants entered September with a 5½ game lead over both Chicago and St. Louis. Baseball fans of the National League were now poised for a 3-way battle for the coveted pennant. The teams would not disappoint.

After the Giants took two of three from the Brooklyn Dodgers at Ebbets Field, the Terrymen traveled a short distance south to play the Phillies. Hubbell pitched the first game of a doubleheader and won 3-2 in typical fashion. He scattered nine hits and walked one batter. It was his fifth straight victory over the Phillies, as his record climbed to 19-10.

The Chicago Cubs arrived at the Polo Grounds tied with the Cardinals for second, both seven games back of the Giants and a comfortable lead. The Giants won the first two games from the Cubs, knocking them out of second place as the Cardinals were hot and continued to win. Hubbell pitched the final game of the series, disappointing the Ladies Day crowd of 10,000. He was matched against Warneke, the ace of the Cubs staff. They both had shutouts going until the fifth inning when Harnett homered with one on off Hub. In the bottom of the fifth, Terry sent in a pinch-hitter for Hubbell. Terry probably suspected Hubbell was getting arm weary from overuse. Who better to make this judgment than the manager, who overused his star pitcher. By season's end, Hubbell had pitched 313 innings, the most in his entire career. Salveson came on in relief and gave up two runs as the Cubs won 4-2. King Carl's record was now 19-11. It was Warneke's 20th win of the season.

New York split the next four games with the Pirates at the Polo Grounds. It was a tune-up for the big series with the Cardinals. Hubbell was tapped by Terry in game two, in relief of Schumacher, who, with 21 victories, was having a sensational season. Despite the Giants leading 7-4, thanks to home runs by Critz, Mancuso, and Ott (number 33), Prince Hal ran into trouble in the top of the ninth. He allowed four runs before a desperate Terry called on his ace (what a surprise) to only discover it wasn't Hub's day. He allowed one hit and a run aided by Mancuso's error, the fifth tally of the inning. The Pirates won 9-7. It was a no-decision for Hubbell but the loss, coupled with a Cardinal victory, put the Cards only four games back of the Giants.

Two days later, in the final game of the Pittsburgh series, the Meal Ticket redeemed himself with a classic Hubbell game. He allowed six hits, two runs, and one walk for a 3-2 win, his 20th of the season against 11 losses. More importantly, Philadelphia beat St. Louis 3-1 increasing the Giants' lead once again to 5½ games. Drebinger, writing for the *Times,* was a tad premature in his analysis of the National League pennant race, calling the Cardinal's chance as a "little more than a forlorn hope." He added, "The world's champions put on the finishing touches [beating Pittsburgh 3-2] to reinforcing their position until it was generally accepted as being practically impregnable."[24]

A day after Hubbell's 20th victory, Commissioner Landis made a startling announcement; he had sold the rights to broadcast the World Series games. The Ford Motor Company purchased the rights for a whopping $100,000, distributed to players participating in the upcoming Fall Classic. The length of the broadcasting rights was not mentioned in the announcement.

The Cardinals followed the Pirates into the Polo Grounds for four games, proving Drebinger might have been a bit premature in writing the Cardinals out of the pennant race. St Louis took three of four from the Giants, with the Dean brothers winning all three—two by Paul and one by Dizzy. Paul's second win was against Hubbell, with both hurlers going 11 innings during the second game of a doubleheader, which attracted an all-time record high attendance of 62,573. In the top of the 11th, with the score tied 1-1, Pepper Martin homered off Hub, and then the Cards added another run for good measure. It was not needed, as the Giants failed to score in their half, losing 3-1. The Giants' lead was quickly evaporating and was now 3½ games. Hubbell's record was 20-12.

The 1934 season was drawing to a close as Cincinnati arrived for a four-game series in which the Giants won three, with Hubbell winning the final game 4-3. Hub did it all against the Reds, on the mound, and at the plate. After escaping a bases-loaded no-out jam in the top of the ninth, the Giants ace batted in the winning run, in the bottom half, to win the game. It left the Giants still 3½ games in front. Hubbell's record was now 21-12.

The Giants traveled north to Boston, where they split a four-game series. New York won the first game 8-1 behind the outstanding pitching of the veteran Freddie Fitzsimmons. It was his 18th victory. That was wonderful news for Giant fans until they discovered the Dean boys had just won a doubleheader, in spectacular fashion, from Brooklyn at Ebbets Field. Dizzy (27-7) shut out the Dodgers 13-0 on a brilliant three-hitter. Believe it or not, that effort paled compared to what Paul did in the nightcap. The younger Dean pitched the first no-hitter in the National League since, of all people, Carl Hubbell in 1929. If it weren't for a walk in the first inning, Paul (18-9) would have pitched a perfect game. The Dean brothers were a force unto themselves, and it could not have been timelier. The Cardinals were now only 3 games back of New York.

The Giants lost the second game of the Boston series 3-2 and then had to play a doubleheader, which they split, winning the first game 8-0. It so happened, St. Louis was playing a twin-bill in Cincinnati, and they too won their first game 9-7. At this point, the Giants were 93-55 and the Cardinals 89-56, still trailing New York by an uncomfortable 2½ games. Before the second game of each doubleheader began, the Giants had five games remaining and St. Louis eight. Both lost their respective nightcaps, so the Giants maintained their 2½ game lead. It also was Hubbell's last start of the season. He left after eight innings when the Braves touched him for three runs on three hits and an error, which tied the game at 3-3. Bowman relieved Hub as the game went into extra innings. But he gave up the winning run in the 11th as the Braves won 4-3. It was a no-decision for a tired King Carl.

Hubbell would pitch again on September 26 in a 5-4 losing cause. He relieved Schumacher in the sixth and pitched two innings, giving up five hits and two runs, an uncharacteristic performance for the usual stingy left-hander. Luque, in relief, took the loss and Hubbell a no-decision. At this point, the Giants' lead was now only one game, but they were idle on September 27 and

28 while St. Louis continued to beat up on the Reds, resulting in a deadlock, both teams with identical 93-58 records.

Now the plot thickens. St. Louis had two more games with Cincinnati on September 29 and 30 at Sportsman's Park. The Giants had two more games at the Polo Grounds, same dates as St. Louis. Guess who the Giants were playing? The Brooklyn Dodgers, the club earlier in the year, Bill Terry asked, "Brooklyn, I haven't heard anything from them. Are they still in the league?" Hollywood couldn't write it any better.

So, one can only imagine how eager and anxious the Dodger fans were to get revenge on Terry. Author Noel Hynd described the fans' reaction. "They clanked cowbells, blew whistles, and howled at Bill Terry every time he poked his head out of the dugout or took his position on the field. They carried signs. BILL WHO? And YES, WE'RE STILL IN THE LEAGUE. Meanwhile, the Dodgers battered Tarzan Parmelee for five runs while Van Lingle Mungo held the Giants to one. Out in the Rhineland, Paul Dean [19-11] handled the Reds easily, winning 6-1. The Giants went home that day a game behind, after leading the league most of the season."[25]

The NL pennant race came down to the final day, September 30. A victory by the Giants and a loss by the Cardinals would result in a tie and a playoff. In New York, there was still hope, although fading, among Giant fans as Terry chose a well-rested Fitzsimmons to start the crucial final game of the season. In St. Louis, manager Frankie Frisch took no chances when he selected Dizzy Dean, after shutting out the Reds 4-0, *on one day's rest.*

Before 45,000 screaming fans, the New York Giants jumped out to a 4-0 lead in the first inning off Brooklyn right-hander Ray Benge. What looked like a hopeful afternoon for the Terrymen slowly and painfully developed into a 5-5 game and finally an extra-inning 8-5 loss. In relief of Fitz, Schumacher gave up two runs and eventually gave way to Hubbell, who allowed another run. Realistically, all hope for a Giant pennant disappeared early when the scoreboard posted a crooked number "3" for St. Louis in the fourth inning, giving the Cardinals a 5-0 lead. Dean made sure that was all the runs he needed. He went on to blank Cincinnati 9-0. It was his second consecutive shutout of the Reds in three days. It topped off one of the greatest pitching performances in major league baseball, as Dean won his 30th game of the season, a phenomenal accomplishment that wouldn't happen again until 1968.

With the 1934 season officially over for the New York Giants, the *Times* pulled no punches describing the team's failure. "As for the Giants, nothing now remains for them but the bitter reflection of having been made the victims of one of the most astonishing break-downs in major league baseball."[26]

Looking on the brighter side, there were some outstanding individual performances by the New York Giant players. Terry, in addition to managing at age 35, played in 153 games and batted .354. Moore batted .331 with 15 home runs, both career highs. Ott, still only 25-years-old turned in a slash line: .326/.415/.591 with 35 home runs and 135 RBIs, the latter two stats led the National League.

In the pitching department, Schumacher became a 20-game winner (23-10) for the first and only time in his career with a fine 3.18 ERA. Fitzsimmons went 18-14 with a 3.04 earned run average. Hubbell had a remarkable season, especially when you consider he was over-worked almost from the beginning of April. By season's end, Carl was arm weary. As one reporter said, in an obvious exaggeration to make his point, Hubbell "could not have baffled a boy scout." He threw 313 innings, the most in his career, which was after over 308 the previous season. Despite Terry over-using Hubbell, the lefty still managed to finish with a 21-12 record. He also led the National League in three categories: earned run average of 2.30, 25 complete games, and eight saves.

Although the 1934 season for the New York Giants players, front office, and fans was a huge disappointment, there was a bright side. The turnstiles were constantly clicking. For the second year in a row, attendance increased significantly. This time from 604,471 to 730,851, a 20% increase. The Giants' popularity and Hubbell's continued success would remain for the next several years.

Carl Hubbell is considered one of the greatest left-handers of all time. He pitched his entire career with the New York Giants winning 253 games and losing 154. He led the Giants to three National League pennants (1933, 1936, and 1937) and one World Championship in 1933. From 1933 to 1937 Carl Hubbell turned in five seasons of masterful baseball. He won 115 and lost 50 for an outstanding .697 winning percentage

CARL HUBBELL OF THE GIANTS, STILL THE ACE SOUTHPAW OF THE NATIONAL LEAGUE

Carl Hubbell pitched for the New York Giants for 16 years. He was a two-time MVP winner and a nine-time All-Star. One of his nicknames was the "Meal Ticket" for obvious reasons. What made Hubbell one of the great left-handers of all time was his phenomenal screwball and remarkable control. Pitching in almost 3,600 innings, he allowed only a mere 1.8 walks per nine innings. He was elected to the Hall of Fame in 1947.

William "Bill" Terry

Bill Terry played 14 years at first base for the New York Giants. The slick fielding left-hander finished his career as an active player in 1936 with an excellent lifetime average of .341. He won the batting title in 1930 with a phenomenal .401 average. On June 3, 1932, manager John McGraw suddenly resigned due to ill health. Terry was immediately named manager and remained through 1941. During his 10 year managerial rein the Giants won three National League pennants and one World Championship in 1933, led by Carl Hubbell.

Mel Ott, at age 16 was given a contract to play for the New York Giants and legendary manager John McGraw. McGraw made one of the great position switches in MLB. He converted Ott from catcher to the outfield. Young Ott played rightfield for the Giants for 22 years, from 1926 to 1947. He owns a lifetime batting average of .304, and was the first player in the National League to hit over 500 home runs (511). Labeled "Master Melvin" he had a highly unorthodox stance. As a left-handed batter, he would lift his right leg in the air and drop his bat low while the pitch was delivered. It helped generate power. In 1942 Ott succeeded Terry as the Giants' manager. His first season at the helm turned out to be the best of seven. He was elected to the Hall of Fame in 1951.

Mel Ott and Freddie Lindstrom are two scary Giant
hitters posing for the camera. Lindstrom took over
third base for the New York Giants in 1924 after an
injury to Heinie Groh. He played nine years with New
York, most at third. He batted a respectable .318 during this period before he was traded to the Pittsburgh
Pirates. During two of those years, 1928 and 1930,
Lindstrom batted .358 and .379 respectively. He was
inducted into the Hall of Fame in 1976 by the Veterans
Committee.

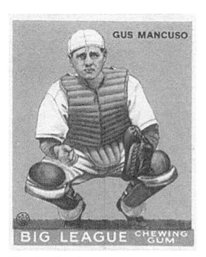

Shortly after the 1932 season was over manager Bill Terry acquired catcher Gus Mancuso. Terry wanted a young, durable, and talented backstop to handle his elite pitching rotation, led by Carl Hubbell. Mancuso would remain with the Giants for six seasons, before he was traded, and was a key factor in Hubbell's success. He was a workhorse behind the plate averaging 133 games for the first four seasons with the Giants. Mancuso was a major factor in Hubbell winning 20-plus games during his fabulous five seasons, 1933-1937. Gus returned to the Giants in 1942 and remained with them through the 1944 season

After McGraw resigned in 1932, new manager Bill Terry brought up Jo-Jo Moore from the minor leagues to play left field and lead-off. Beginning in 1933, and for the next nine years, Moore would play in 121 games or more each season, despite injuries. Moore, a consistent hitter finished his 12-years with the Giants batting .298. The man from Gause, Texas, played in three World Series for the Giants, winning in 1933 and losing in 1936 and 1937. He batted .274 in 16 games.

In 1924 Travis Jackson was the everyday shortstop for the New York Giants at age 20 as McGraw's men won their fourth consecutive National League pennant, a first in major league baseball. From 1925 until his retirement as an active player in 1936, Jackson batted over .300 five times. His lifetime batting average was a respectable .291. But defense was his strength. The 5' 10" 160-pound Jackson had a strong arm and could range far and wide. In 1927, 1928, and 1929 The Sporting News voted him the most outstanding shortstop.

Frank Hogan, nicknamed "Shanty" because, so it was said, he resembled a small hut. In other words, he was heavy. However, he was a fine defensive catcher with a strong arm. From 1928 to 1932, he caught most of the Giant games. Hogan surprised many, including McGraw, with his hitting. In his first four seasons, Hogan batted .333, .300, .339, and .301. But in 1932 weight became a serious problem for Hogan and new manager Bill Terry sold him to the Boston Braves. That move paved the way for the acquisition of Gus Mancuso. From Boston where weight continued to be an issue, Shanty went to the Washington Senators for a total of 40 games and was finally released, and out of baseball by 1937.

Carl Hubbell and Red Ruffing shaking hands before the first game of the 1936
World Series between the New York Giants and New York Yankees. The Meal
Ticket lived up to his well-deserved nickname and reputation. He handcuffed
the mighty Yankee hitters, beating them, 6-1. The Yankees were helpless against
Hubbell's screwball and pinpoint control. Not one Giant outfielder made a putout,
that's how dominating Hubbell was. Yankee's ace, Ruffing took the loss, giving up
nine hits. The Yankees went on to win the Series, 4 games to 2. It was their fifth
World Championship.

Carl Hubbell depicted on an early Play Ball baseball card with his signature follow-through.

9

Third Consecutive 20-Plus Season

"WHEN A PITCHER IS GOING GOOD, HE MUST GUARD
AGAINST COMPLACENCY. IT CAN SET IN UNCONSCIOUSLY.
I KNOW THAT I HAD TO LOOK OUT FOR IT."

As the Giant players quietly slipped away after the end of the '34 season debacle, manager Bill Terry was left to face the press. He made no excuses. He had no alibies, and he couldn't or didn't want to explain the tail end slump. It was time to forget and look to the new season. Terry was entering his third full season after taking over the managerial reins of the New York Giants. In 1932, Terry and the Giants finished sixth after replacing John McGraw, who suddenly quit on June 3. In 1933 Terry led the Giants, as player/manager, to the pennant and World Series. The following year ('34) turned out to be a disaster as the Giants inexplicably blew the pennant in the dwindling days of the season.

Not long after the season was over, Terry announced to the press, October 29, 1934, to be specific, he would "shake-up" the club. He was forthright and specific. He concentrated on the infield and ignored the pitching staff and outfield. "Almost anything anybody wants is for sale or trade. Not Ott or Hubbell, of course. I wouldn't think of selling either of them," he said.[1]

He also commented, laughingly, on a story he heard the Giants were going to trade Hubbell and $50,000 for Dizzy Dean. In fact, he said, "I wouldn't trade them even." The most significant point coming out of the interview was that Terry was looking for a shortstop . . . and he had the money to afford one, which meant Travis Jackson would move to third. After a "wonderful year," Critz would remain at second. Terry also included himself in the shake-up as he was looking for a first baseman to replace him. Terry batted .354 with a .414

OBP and an OPS of .878 at age 35. Those numbers would be difficult, if not impossible, to replace.

Terry was true to his word. Two days later, in a blockbuster trade, he obtained the shortstop he coveted. He sent third baseman Johnny Vergez, infielder Blondy Ryan, outfielder George Watkins, rookie pitcher John Puzzello and a reported $75,000 to the Philadelphia Phillies for the incredibly talented 27-year-old shortstop Dick Bartell.

Author Hynd described Bartell's reputation at the time of the trade. "Bartell was better known around the league as 'Rowdy Richard.' He was an infielder in the old John McGraw mold, meaning he approached baseball the way a modern hockey player might. He was well known for two spiking incidents, both involving the Dodgers. Nowhere in baseball was he more hated than at Ebbets Field. He was, then, a natural for stardom at the Polo Grounds.[2]

As author Williams points out, Terry met with strong resistance from the Giants' owner regarding the amount of money involved. "Charles Stoneham had resisted at first, reminding Terry about the Depression and saying the price was way too high, but Terry had insisted. He told Stoneham the trade would bring the Giants a pennant in two years, and the owner gave in."[3]

Terry's prediction of a pennant in two years was wrong. It only took the Giants one year. A few days later, New York Giants fans, in particular, and baseball fans around the country forgot about Terry's trade.

John A. Heydler suddenly announced his retirement. At age 65, citing poor health as the reason, Heydler would continue to serve until December 11. Heydler had a long and varied 40-year career in baseball, the last 16 as president of the National League. He began his career as a printer when he met Nick Young, then president of the National League. His friendship with Young was the inspiration that sparked his interest in baseball. Although he had played the game and even umpired, it was not until he became a sportswriter and then editor for *The Washington Post* that he developed his love for the game. Eventually, Heydler became the private secretary to Harry Pulliam, then president of the National League. He continued to move up the ladder of success when, in 1907, he was elected secretary and treasurer of the league.

In 1909, Pulliam died, and Heydler was named acting president to complete the term, which he did. Thomas Lynch was elected the new president and was eventually succeeded by John K. Tener, former Governor of Pennsylvania. Heydler served both presidents as secretary-treasurer. Tener served as National League president from 1913 until 1918, when he resigned after the league owners refused to support his decision in the Scott Perry case. With Tener gone, Heydler completed the term as acting president once again. In 1919, the magnates unanimously elected him as president as well as secretary and treasurer. During his 16 years as president of the National League, ". . . Heydler had revealed himself an able baseball executive, a kindly disposed and even-tempered man with an uncanny faculty for healing breaks between turbulent factions . . ."[4]

Terry wasn't nearly finished shaking up his club with the acquisition of Bartell. Although Hank Leiber only batted .241 in 1934, Terry must have seen something in the 24-year-old. He moved him to center field between Ott and Moore. The youngster responded with a career season, batting .331 with 22 homers and 107 RBIs.

The other important move was using newly acquired (December 14, 1934) infielder Mark Koenig, a veteran who made his reputation with the New York Yankees as their shortstop for five years. Eventually, Koenig would replace a slumping Critz at second, despite Terry's earlier comments.

As they did in 1934, the Giants trained in Florida, but in the exhibition games, the club got off to a poor start with Hubbell losing to Connie Mack's A's. They also lost to the St. Louis Browns, Boston Red Sox, and the Cardinals. As the Giants headed north along with the Cleveland Indians to play their exhibition schedule in southern towns, devoid of major league baseball, Terry's patience with the club was quickly running out. It snapped in New Orleans when the Giants took a drubbing from the Indians, 14-2. What angered Terry was he had his regulars in the lineup, unlike some of the earlier defeats. In those losses, he was trying out players he wanted to evaluate and get to know their abilities. But his regulars losing games; that was too much. The result was he sent two rookies, outfielder Jim Asbell and pitcher John Leonardo to the minors. More importantly, he warned the rest of the club it could happen to anyone, and he meant it. Ironically, the following day, 77 sports editors and writers, participating in the ninth annual Associated Press pennant poll, picked the Cardinals to win and the Giants second.

The Giants, after a grinding four weeks on the road, including 12 games with the Cleveland Indians, finally were ready for opening day. The 12-game series with the Indians, which began in Tallahassee through eight states, ended with each team winning five and tying two.

Regardless of what the sports writers and editors predicted, three National League managers selected the Giants to win: Stengel of Brooklyn, Charlie

Dressen of the Reds, and Frankie Frisch of the Cardinals. Whether they were sincere or simply pandering to the Giants, hoping they would be overconfident, who knows? But Terry's club did have the best four-man pitching staff in the National League, at least on paper. Terry believed it himself. "This is the best team I have ever managed, and I like its chances for the pennant. The Cardinals will give us plenty of opposition, but I do not expect the Dean brothers to have the success against us they did last year."[5]

The 25,000 fans that attended opening day at Braves Field will never forget the game. In hindsight, it should have been named Babe Ruth Day. The Bambino, at age 40 and now a Boston Brave, single handily beat the Giants and Carl Hubbell, 4-2. The Babe drove in three of the four runs with a single and a 430-foot home run . . . all off the left-handed screwballer. Perhaps Ruth remembered the 1934 All-Star Game and was looking for sweet revenge. Hubbell lasted only six innings, giving up nine hits, four runs but didn't walk a batter.

After the game, sitting in the locker room, Ruth commented on his opening day performance. "I didn't even dream that I'd get off to such a start," he said while accepting congratulations from his new teammates. Never lost for words, he continued. "The start sure overshadows my first game as an American Leaguer, when I pitched the Red Sox to a 3-2 victory over the Cleveland Indians."[6]

Four days later, the Giants won their first game, after two losses, of the new season, beating the Phillies 6-4, but it wasn't easy. It took 11 innings and a key single by Terry, with Bartell and Hubbell on second and third respectively, to drive in both and break the 4-4 tie. Hub picked up his first victory of the year in relief. Schumacher allowed 11 hits and six walks in 7 2/3 innings but only three runs. Hubbell relieved in the seventh but in the tenth allowed the Phillies to tie the game. The following inning, Terry provided the key hit, and Hub blanked the Phillies to even his record at 1-1.

Two days after his relief appearance, Hubbell started the last game of the Philadelphia series and pitched a masterful four-hitter. The 8-1 victory began a four-game winning streak for the Giants. Hub allowed one run on Dolph Camilli's home run in the fourth inning; otherwise, his screwball was unhittable. The Giants' new acquisition, Dick Bartell, finally broke out of his early slump (5 for 19), going 4 for 5 to give new life to the expensive trade. Hubbell's record was now 2-1.

After Philadelphia, the Giants swept the Boston Braves at the Polo Grounds, improving their record to 5-2. Next, the Giants met the Phillies again, this time at the Polo Grounds, for three games. The first game of the series went 13 innings and, to everyone's frustration, ended in darkness, 3½ hours later (a typical nine-inning game today) a 5-5 tie. Moreover, it was ladies' day, and the women were treated to a rare triple play pulled off by the Phillies. Eight hurlers were used during the marathon game; three for Philadelphia and five for New York. Hubbell started and was gone after five and a third innings, allowing four runs and six hits. His record remained at 2-1.

Human nature as it is, one wonders if the salary dispute Hubbell encountered before the season opener was on the left-hander's mind. Despite Hubbell's remarkable season, the Giants offered him the same $17,500 he received in 1934. Hub was upset, claiming, "I'd done everything they asked, started and relieved."

May 3 began the first invasion of the Western clubs to the Polo Grounds with the appearance of the Cincinnati Reds in a three-game series. The Reds were met with two unbeatable forces in the opening game, the Giants' relentless hitting and Hubbell's screwball. The Giants pounded out 16 hits, including home runs by Moore and Ott, while King Carl sailed along, giving up six hits and two runs. The final score was 9-2. His record was now 3-1.

The second game of the Cincinnati series was rained out, while the final game ended in a 2-2 tie. The Chicago Cubs next visited the Polo Grounds, only to lose a doubleheader 3-1 and 6-2, extending the Giants' modest winning streak to four games.

As the weather cleared, the Pirates arrived for four games, and the Giants continued their winning ways, taking three of four, with the opening contest another gem by the Meal Ticket. Hub scattered eight hits in typical fashion, pitching his way out of tight spots and allowing one run. If not for Arky Vaughan's homer in the eighth, Hubbell would have had his first shutout of the season. The final score was 3-1. Hubbell's record was now 4-1.

The Giants won the next two of three from the Pirates, giving them a record of 14-4 and a slim 1½ game lead over the surprising Brooklyn Dodgers. Although one would not characterize the Giants as high flying this early in the season, Terry had his club looking like they were determined to win another National League pennant. But there was someone who was flying higher, and that was Amelia Earhart. Actually, the day before Hubbell beat the Pirates 3-1, the young lady from Atchison, Kansas, set another record by being the first person to fly solo from Mexico City to Newark, New Jersey. It was one of many firsts for this incredible woman, who began her flying career in 1921. By 1928 she became the first woman to fly across the Atlantic (20 hours and 40 minutes). Four years later (1932), she became the first woman to fly solo across the Atlantic (14 hours and 56 minutes). The list of firsts goes on and on. Then in 1937, Amelia Earhart, along with her navigator, Fred Noonan, made a valiant attempt to be the first woman to fly around the world. The two left on June 1. They landed in Lae, New Guinea, on June 29 and had completed all but 7,000 miles. Their next stop was Howland Island, a small dot in the Pacific Ocean. Sadly, on July 2, the pair took off, never to be heard from again.

"On July 19th, after spending $4 million and scouring 250,000 square miles of ocean, the United States government reluctantly called off the operation. In 1938, a lighthouse was constructed on Howland Island in her memory, and across the United States, streets, schools, and airports are named after Earhart. Her birthplace, Atchison, Kansas, became a virtual shrine to her memory. Amelia Earhart awards and scholarships are given out every year."[7]

The world champion St. Louis Cardinals was the last Western club to complete their arrival at the Polo Grounds. Proving they were the world champs, the Cards took two of three from the Giants, including the series opener 3-2. Hubbell and Bill Walker, two left-handers, battled each other for nine innings until the fatal tenth. With the game tied 2-2, in the top of the tenth inning, light-hitting Leo Durocher stepped to the plate with two out. Durocher took the first pitch for a ball. On Hub's next delivery, Leo drove the ball into the upper left field deck to win the game, as the Giants failed to score in their half of the inning. During his 17-year playing career, Durocher hit a grand total of 24 home runs. No doubt, both he and Hubbell remembered this one for years to come.

It was now the Giants' turn to invade the Western clubs, beginning with a three-game series in Cincinnati. Although the Giants won two of three from the Reds, the first game, a 6-2 loss, was a near disaster. Jo-Jo Moore was hit on the wrist by a foul ball off the bat of Roy Parmelee. Moore was rushed to the local hospital. Later, Bartell was injured in a collision with Red's huge catcher Ernie Lombardi. In addition, Terry, still believing the Giants had a chance to win with the score 4-2, brought in Hub with the bases loaded. King Carl didn't have it this afternoon, as he allowed a single to score two runs and seal the victory for the Reds.

In the opening game of the Pittsburgh series, Hubbell continued his poor pitching as he was hammered for five runs on six hits after only four innings. In relief of Hub, Allyn Stout and Frank Gabler didn't help as the Pirates had their hitting shoes on this day. The final score was Pittsburgh 11 New York 4. Of the 14 hits for Pittsburgh, there were five triples, two doubles, and one home run. To ease the pain, the Giants won the next two games to take the series. Hubbell's record was now 4-3.

The next stop for the Terrymen was Wrigley Field in Chicago. Hubbell started the last game of the series and finally shook off whatever hindered his dominant pitching style. His screwball was working to perfection, as he limited the Cubs to two runs on four hits. The 3-2 victory brought Hubbell's record to 5-3. There was no mistake; King Carl had to be on the top of his game for several reasons: he was facing Chicago's ace right-hander Lon Warneke; and behind him was a makeshift infield (due to injuries) with Mark Koenig at short, Al Cuccinello at second and Ott at third. The victory was also important because it continued, what turned out to be, a seven-game winning streak for New York.

On the same day Hubbell pitched brilliantly against Chicago, the immortal Babe Ruth overshadowed his accomplishment. Now playing for the Boston Braves, the Sultan of Swat blasted three home runs against the Pittsburgh Pirates at Forbes Field. Turning back the clock to his younger years, Ruth hit home runs in the first, third, and seventh innings. He went 4 for 4 and drove in six runs for the afternoon. The Bambino left the game in the seventh inning, after his last prodigious blast, to a standing ovation from the partisan Pittsburgh crowd. Despite the herculean efforts by the 40-year-old, the Braves lost the game 11-7.

The next game Hub pitched was on May 31 against the hapless Boston Braves. It was the second game (Schumacher won the first) of a doubleheader. The Meal Ticket delivered again, spreading 12 hits and narrowly missing a shutout as the Braves pushed across two runs in the ninth but came up short, 4-2. The ninth inning was also marred by a downpour of rain, which some felt might have affected Hubbell's screwball. Ruth didn't play in either game, disappointing many fans due to "water on the knee." Hubbell's record was now 6-3. The Giants were now leading the National League and second place St. Louis by 5½ games.

Hubbell won his third straight game, this time against the Philadelphia Phillies 7-4. He pitched the second game of a twin-bill. Once again, Hub gave up plenty of hits (10) but only four runs (two earned). As is almost always the case, Hubbell's control was near perfect. He allowed one walk but struck out seven. His record was now 7-3.

But in Pittsburgh, all hell was breaking loose. St. Louis Cardinals manager Frankie Frisch and his irascible star pitcher, Dizzy Dean, were at it again. The brouhaha began the previous day when Dean was pummeled for eight hits and nine runs in six innings. Rather than accepting he had an off day, Dean blamed his teammates for lack of support and claimed they were "jealous" of him. The emotional and cantankerous Dean even went as far as to request he be traded.

The no-nonsense Frisch made it quite clear he was in charge when he told the press, "Dean is lucky he didn't get a stiff fine and suspension, a result of the way he acted. Yesterday was the climax. He wasn't doing his best out there in the box, and he knows it. He has twice in previous games with the Pirates disobeyed my instructions and pitched wrong to Arky Vaughan, with the result that we lost both games. He seems to think he can throw the ball past the good hitters just because he's Dizzy Dean. That's not baseball, and he can't play that way for me."[8]

No disciplinary action was taken at the time, but Frisch had the support of Branch Rickey, vice president and business manager of the world champions. "Whatever Frisch does, I'll back him up. If he sees fit to impose a fine, I'll see that it is paid, and maybe the figures in the fine will be hiked a bit."[9]

Hubbell's next victory was the Cincinnati Reds, a club mired in sixth place, 12½ games back of the first-place Giants. Hub pitched a superb game, winning his fourth straight. Throughout the afternoon, King Carl was in total command, giving up four harmless runs late in the game, with a 10-0 lead. He allowed eight hits, walked none, and fanned six. Hub set the pace early by retiring the first 14 hitters he faced. Ott and Terry did most of the damage, accounting for six of the ten runs. Ott hit his 11th homer and now led the league. Hubbell's record improved to 8-3.

It is interesting to note Hubbell's approach to a game when he has a big lead. The Cincinnati game is a good example. When Hub has a big lead in a game, he purposely eases up and coasts to the game's victorious end. In so doing, he would often give up meaningless hits and runs late in a game. On the contrary, give King Carl a one-run lead, and, more often than not, that's as close as the opposition would come in defeat. Some of his teammates were aware of this approach.

Four days later, the Meal Ticket faced the tough St. Louis Cardinals, winning his fifth game in a row with the help of a first-inning five-run barrage by his teammates. The red-hot Ott led the assault with a three-run homer. The final score was 7-3. Hub's record was now 9-3, and the Giants lead was 5½ over Pittsburgh and six over St. Louis.

The next two outings for Hubbell came against Pittsburgh and Chicago, both at the Polo Grounds. The Giants lost both games as Hubbell came away with two no-decisions. In the game against the Pirates, in which the Giants lost 5-4, Hub left after seven innings, trailing 3-1 (only two of the runs were earned) on seven hits. Once again, his control was impeccable, as he didn't walk a batter. Smith relieved Hub and gave up a run in the eighth, but the Giants scored three in the bottom of the inning to tie the game. Smith gave up a run in the 11th and took the loss 5-4.

On the same day, an interesting situation occurred in Bradenton, Florida. Apparently, the Bradenton baseball fans took the game very seriously and the Dean brothers as well. Dizzy and Daffy both live in Bradenton during the winter months. The Bradenton fans were quite upset over the fact that both Deans were not pitching as well as the previous year when they helped lead the Cardinals to a World Championship. There was no mention of Dizzy's childish antics.

However, their performances to date were enough to prompt the Mayor of Bradenton, A.M. Sparks, to issue a city proclamation calling upon the brothers to "get down to business and bring home the bacon." No mention was made whether the brothers voiced any comments.

The next no-decision Hubbell recorded was against Chicago, a game the Giants lost 10-5. Hub started and left after seven innings when he gave up a hit in the top of the eighth. He was leading at the time 5-4, then the onslaught. Four Giant pitchers followed: Stout, Smith, Gabler, and Fitzsimmons. When the tsunami ended, the Cubs had scored four runs and led 8-5, wiping out Hubbell's potential 10th win. Adding fuel to the fire, Chicago scored two more in the ninth, making the final score 10-5.

After Chicago left to go back to the Windy City, the Giants traveled a short distance to the Flatbush section of Brooklyn to play a four-game series with the Dodgers. New York won three of the four games, the lone loss coming in game two when Hubbell, in relief, gave up a run to give Stengel's Dodgers a 3-2 victory. Fitz started and left after five, with the game tied 2-2. In the sixth, Hub walked Tony Cuccinello, who went to third on a single by pitcher Mungo. With the infield drawn in, Buzz Boyle singled up the middle for the lead and eventual winning run. The loss for Hubbell (9-4) is rich with irony. The left-hander, who arguably has the most perfect control, lost the game by walking the first batter he faced.

However, the next day, all was forgotten when the Giants won both ends of the Brooklyn doubleheader, 7-4 and 5-4. There were many stars during the long afternoon, but Master Melvin shined the brightest. Ott hit home runs number 15 and 16 and made a spectacular one-handed catch in the nightcap. Prince Hal notched victory number 11 in the second game, quietly making it nine in a row. Schumacher, at age 24, appeared ready to replace Hubbell as the ace of the staff. Time will tell, and Terry wouldn't have long to wait. The double victories increased the Giants' lead to 8½ games over second-place Pittsburgh. Although still early in the season, at this point, it appeared the Giants were headed for another National League pennant. But that refrain had been heard before.

Hubbell continued his mediocre pitching against the Philadelphia Phillies, losing a ten-inning game 4-3. He and Phillies right-hander, Curt Davis, were locked in a 3-3 tie when his adversary took control of the game. In the top of the 10th, Davis selected one of Hub's mistakes and shockingly parked the ball into the upper left field stands for the eventual victory. It was the only home run Davis hit all season! Hubbell's record was now 9-5.

The 1935 All-Star Game was soon approaching, and unlike the two previous years, the fans would not select the starting lineups. Instead, they would be picked by the managers of the 1934 World Series teams—Frankie Frisch of the St. Louis Cardinals and Mickey Cochrane from the Detroit Tigers.

In the meantime, Bill Terry, along with other managers, were submitting their worthy choices to participate in the All-Star Game on July 8. Their selections went to Frisch to make the final decision. The players on the '35 All-Star Game roster from the Giants were: Bill Terry, Carl Hubbell, Gus Mancuso, Jo-Jo Moore, Mel Ott, and Hal Schumacher.

The American League won 4-1, led by Jimmy Foxx (A's), who drove in three of the four runs and the pitching of the Yankees, Lefty Gomez, who went six innings, giving up three hits and one run. Almost 70,000 fans turned out at Municipal Stadium in Cleveland to witness the game. It was the National League's third loss in a row and resulted in a change of rules, a limit on innings pitched. Beginning in 1936, no pitcher was allowed to go more than three innings unless the game went into extra innings.

All the Giants on the National League roster played in the game to a greater or lesser degree. There was one exception, Carl Hubbell. Hub had pitched the day before and beat Brooklyn 9-2. King Carl allowed 12 hits but was stingy in the clutch, whiffing seven and allowing only two runs. The big blow of the game came early, in the third inning, when Ott teed off on a Ray Benge delivery and parked the ball in the upper right-field stands for a grand slam homer. It was his 18th of the season. It must have been a gratifying victory for Hubbell since he had trouble beating Brooklyn in the past. His record improved to 10-5. Over the years, the Dodgers had handled Hub pretty well with a stunning record of 24-11.

With a little more than half the season remaining, the Giants have a comfortable lead over both St. Louis (7 back) and Chicago (8½ back), but the race to the flag would be a bumpy one for all three clubs.

On July 13, a well-rested Hubbell faced the Pirates at Forbes Field and notched his 11th win against five losses. The final score was 7-6. Perhaps, Hub had too much rest. He allowed 13 hits and blew a four-run lead in the fourth inning, giving up five runs. But the Giants fought back, handing Hub the gift victory. Clearly, Hubbell is in a slump but still manages to wiggle his way out of jams. Right now, King Carl's crown is slightly tarnished. In the last three games, he allowed 12 hits once and 13 hits twice but still won two games. The Giants now lead St. Louis by 7½ and Chicago by 9.

In Cincinnati, the Giants split the four-game series. Hubbell pitched twice, the first time in a 13-6 loss in relief of Schumacher (13-3), who was hammered for the first time this season. Hubbell, in relief, and newcomer Leon Chagnon, were also hit hard. Hub gave up two hits and two runs in two-thirds of an inning as the slump continued. Schumacher took the loss. Ott hit his 20th home run and continued to lead the league, while Terry (.350) and Hank Leiber (.330) were in the top five in batting average.

At this point in the season, author Peter Williams in his book, *When the Giants were Giants*, claimed the Giants luck began to run out. "Freddie Fitzsimmons chipped a bone in his elbow. Terry broke Clydell 'Slick' Castleman's finger with a line drive in practice, and both pitchers were lost to the starting rotation. There were nearly three months left in the season, but Schumacher would win only six more games. In an ominous echo of 1934, it became apparent that the Giants pitchers, the ones who weren't injured, were wearing down while the Cardinal staff was still strong. Not only were Hubbell, Parmelee, and Schumacher pitching too often for the good of their arms, but the Giants also had the misfortune of playing many extra-inning games in 1935."[10]

The other game Hubbell pitched at Crosley Field more closely resembled the man who earned the sobriquet, the Meal Ticket. Hub started and won 6-3, giving up three runs on nine hits and issuing zero free passes. It was his 12th win against five losses.

In St. Louis, the Cardinals won their 13th consecutive game, beating the Boston Braves 2-1 and now trailed New York by four, shades of 1934. The Gas House Gang won the following day making it 14 in a row, but it ended on July 19, when Brooklyn's Johnny Babich threw a five-hit shutout while striking out eight.

After Cincinnati, the Terrymen ran into an ill-timed funk as the Chicago Cubs won all four games at Wrigley Field. Hub pitched game three and lost 5-4. It was the first game of a doubleheader and went 11 innings before the "biggest crowd in ten years at Wrigley Field." *Times* sportswriter James P. Dawson further commented, "Every inch of space was utilized in the huge park as interest went to fever heat in this critical series. Those unable to gain admission watched from rooftops, porches, fire escapes, and telegraph poles. So great was the crowd that it overflowed on the field, dictating ground rules that made a two-bagger of any blow into the overflow."[11]

Hub pitched the entire game, allowing ten hits, five runs, and an unbelievable, for him, six walks. His record was now 12-6. The Cubs won the nightcap 11-5 while the Cardinals were winning a doubleheader from Brooklyn, putting St. Louis only 1½ games back of the Giants. And now New York had to move to St. Louis for a wild, wild six-game series. Yes, you read correctly, six games.

Not surprisingly, the Giant meltdown continued in St. Louis. New York lost the first game, 8-5, and the opener of a twin-bill, 6-1. Schumacher and Parmelee took the losses as the Giants dropped out of first place by a half-game but only for a short time. In the second game of the doubleheader, behind Al Smith, the Giants won 8-2 as the Cards had to use four pitchers.

The next day Hubbell outpitched Dizzy Dean 4-2, giving the Giants a little more breathing room, albeit a 1½ game lead. It was a skillful pitching performance by the Hubbell of old. He allowed only two runs on six hits. He was aided by a four-run seventh before a crowd of 29,000, of which 17,000 were of the opposite sex, enjoying Ladies Day. Although two of the four runs resulted from a throwing error by Pepper Martin, Hub helped his cause by driving in run number three. His record now stood at 13-6.

The Giants made it four in a row the following day, winning both ends of a doubleheader. Schumacher (14-5) pitched brilliantly in the opener, beating

Paul Dean 3-1. In the second game, the Giants mauled St. Louis 13-2. That defeat, coupled with a Chicago Cub victory, dropped St. Louis down to third place. Here are the standings as of July 25:

TEAM	W	L	GB
New York	57	30	–
Chicago	56	35	3
St. Louis	54	34	3½

As the National League became an unpredictable and exciting race among three teams, the Giants headed back home for a three-game series with Brooklyn. After the Giants lost the first game, 6-4, at Ebbets Field, the next day, the Terrymen got their revenge by winning the doubleheader, 6-0 and 1-0. It was vintage Hubbell in the first game. He pitched a marvelous five-hit, 6-0 shutout, his first and only of the season. His pinpoint control was perfect, and his record was now 14-6. If Dodger fans were unhappy with the results of the first game, it must have been frustrating to see Dutch Leonard pitch an inspiring game, only to be topped by another shutout, 1-0, a four-hit outing by 22-year-old New York Giant Slick Castleman (9-2).

Then the surprising Phillies took two of three from the Giants. The last game was a 5-3 win over a tired Hubbell, who gave up 11 hits and four of the five runs. What a difference from the previous game, the 6-0 shutout, when he walked none. In this game, he gave up five, a clear sign of fatigue. Moreover, Hub was on his way to pitching over 300 innings for the third straight season. His record was now 14-7.

The same day Hubbell lost to the Phillies, Emil Fuchs, president of the Boston Braves, forfeited his majority of stock holdings to Charles F. Adams. The move was not a surprise. The Braves had been bleeding money for years; so much so, Fuchs made one last valiant effort to save the club by hiring Babe Ruth for the '35 season. Ruth was offered a contract that included the titles of assistant manager and vice president. Neither of which he was. Ruth played in only 28 games, batted .181 with six home runs. As previously mentioned, on May 25, he did hit three homers, including number 714. It was his last hurrah. He played his last game on May 30. Fuchs' ill-conceived effort had failed. It was now Adams's job to run the club until National League president, Ford Frick, could find someone with deep pockets to buy the franchise.

The Giants began August by sweeping the trouble-riddled Braves four games. Hub pitched the last game of the series and won 3-1. The Braves jumped to a 1-0 lead in the third, but the Giants came back in the bottom of the fifth to score three, led by Terry's two-run single. Hub coasted the rest of the way, scattering eight hits and walking none. His record was now 15-7.

Hubbell didn't pitch again until the Phillies series, six games at Baker Bowl. The Giants lost four of six with Hub pitching twice. He started the second game of a doubleheader and lost 6-3. His downfall came in the fourth inning. The Braves scored four, capped by catcher Al Todd's three-run homer. The Terrymen weren't hitting until the ninth when they scored three, but it was too little, too late. Hubbell's record was now 15-8.

Hub made his second appearance in relief of Schumacher (16-7). Prince Hal was the victim of the Giants hitting slump. Bucky Walters, in a masterful pitching job, blanked New York 2-0. Hub pitched only one inning, allowing one hit. However, the Giants continued to lead Chicago by 2½ games, a flimsy lead at best.

In the American League, the New York Yankees appeared to be running out of time. They were six games back of the Detroit Tigers. That was bad enough, but now the Yankees, led by Joe McCarthy, were headed west to play 21 games on foreign soil. When they returned in late August, the Bombers had won 11, lost ten, and were nine games back.

By September 18, the Yankees were still floundering and only had cut the Tiger lead by a measly ½ game. Then the Yankees went on a tear, winning eight of their nine games but finished three off the pace as the Tigers won their second consecutive American League flag, and deservedly so.

The difference between the two clubs was overwhelmingly pitching. The Tigers had four outstanding starters: Tommy Bridges (21-10, ERA 3.51), Schoolboy Rowe (19-13, ERA 3.69), Elden Auker (18-7, ERA 3.83), and General Crowder (16-10, ERA 4.26). If that wasn't enough, the Tigers offense featured 24-year-old MVP Hank Greenberg who hit .328 with 36 home runs and 168 RBIs; Charlie Gehringer, who hit .330 while smashing 19 home runs and driving in 108; and Goose Goslin, who batted .292 with 111 ribbies.

Although the Yankees had a powerful club, they paled in comparison to the Tigers. The ace of the pitching staff, Lefty Gomez, had an off-year with a poor 12-15 record while Red Ruffing was 16-11. No other Yankee had more victories than Ruffing. Lou Gehrig was the Yankees' lone threat with Ruth gone, the only player to drive in more than 100 runs.

Leonard Koppett, in his book, *Koppett's Concise History of Major League Baseball,* points out the Yankees had five un-played games due to rainouts and the Tigers three. He elaborated further, "In 1935, nobody said a word. It was the Depression. Trying to play them would mean extra travel, and eight games is a lot. The World Series was to start in two days, and radio was paying good money for that. Besides, the Yankees would have to win four, and the Tigers lose two to create a tie, which would then mean a playoff."[12] So it appears everyone looked the other way since nothing was done. Times, indeed, have changed.

Back in the National League, the third-place Cardinals were at the Polo Grounds for five games. Hub pitched the first game of a twin-bill before 52,000 against Paul Dean (13-10), who was having trouble this season. It was reported to be "the largest mid-week gathering in the history of the National League."

Dean was gone after only two innings, heading for the showers, behind 5-1. Given an early lead, Hub pitched a solid game. He did, however, give up three home runs, luckily with no runners on base. The Giants won 6-4. It was Hubbell's 16th victory against eight losses. The hero of the game was left fielder Jo-Jo Moore who ignited the Giants to a fast start by tripling in the first inning and homering, with two on, in the second. It was Moore's 15th round-tripper of the season.

Joseph Gregg Moore was born to Charlie and Rowena (nee Gregg) on Christmas Day, 1908, in the farming town of Gause, Texas. The population of Gause in 1915 was about 1,000. After that, it declined slowly, and by the 1960s, Gause had less than 300 people. Like so many other youngsters of his day, the school was not interesting or more likely not available to them. Joe did attend grammar school and graduated from Crystal City High School in 1927. He also attended Texas A&M. After one semester, he left the Aggies to pursue a career in the game he loved; baseball. It was part of his DNA.

Years later, he gave credit to a man named Joe Scheffield who "was running a semi-pro team at Crystal Springs, Texas, and he gave me a job as a shortstop. I was about 16 and had played some baseball, but never under a competent manager. Scheffield, although he'd never played in organized ball, was a smart baseball man. He coached me in my batting and gave me my first real instructions along those lines."[13]

In 1928 Moore signed with the Coleman Bobcats in the West Texas League (Class D). He played two years with the Bobcats. He batted a creditable .293 his first year. "But in 1929, he enjoyed an outstanding season: in 103 games, he batted .352, with 21 doubles, 12 triples, and 15 homers. These figures won him a one-game trial with Waco of the Texas League."[14]

Not surprisingly, the following year, 1930, Moore found himself with the San Antonio Indians of the Texas League (Class A). In 124 games, Moore batted .329 and was exceptional in the outfield, recording 26 assists. The manager at the time was George Burns, who had played left field for the New York Giants under John McGraw. Burns had a distinguished 15-year career with the Giants as a lead-off man. In 1,853 games, he batted .287, with 1,188 runs scored, 2,077 hits and a .366 OBP. So, Burns was no slouch. More importantly for Moore, after Christy Mathewson, McGraw believed Burns "was the best player he ever managed."

After an outstanding season with the Indians, *The Sporting News* ran an article about the greatness of Jo-Jo Moore. The paper claimed outright, "Joe is going to the majors; there is no question about it anymore. The boy . . . has proved the sensation of the Texas loop. President J. Alvin Gardner of the league has done something unprecedented by coming out with an enthusiastic statement that Moore looks like "the best outfield prospect in the Texas League since Tris Speaker went up." *The Sporting News* went on to say, "Every manager, every league official, every sportswriter, has had something to say about the sparkling, all-around brilliance of young Moore."[15]

With all the compliments and hype surrounding Moore's play with the Indians, plus the Burns-McGraw connection, it was inevitable when the Giants purchased the contract of the 21-year-old left fielder. *The Brooklyn Daily Eagle* claimed, "The sale has created a record price for the Texas League." There was no mention of the price.

With that introduction, Moore was ready for the New York Giants and major league baseball. Not so fast. At 5'11" and 150 pounds, give or take a few, McGraw considered him too small to succeed. He was skinny, looked undernourished, and bore little resemblance to a professional baseball player who might not be able to handle the wear and tear of a full season. Oh, how that assessment was off the mark.

So, Moore was shipped back to the minor leagues. In 1931, playing for the Newark Bears of the International League (AA), he batted .347 in 79 games. During the same season, Moore also played for the Bridgeport Bears of the Eastern League (A). He batted .359 in 30 games. The Giants were still not impressed. The following year, back in the International League, this time with the Jersey City Skeeters, he hit .312.

As fate would have it, McGraw's health was failing, and after 40 games, he resigned as the New York Giants manager. Bill Terry replaced him. Terry's first move was to bring up Moore, who became his lead-off man and left fielder. Moore finished the season playing in 86 games and batting .305. That contribution reaffirmed Terry's confidence in the young rookie. The Giants finished sixth. For the next nine years, Moore would play in 121 games or more each season, despite the many injuries he would sustain.

In 1933, Terry brought the Giants from sixth place to win his first pennant as a manager. Moore, among others, made a major contribution to the victory. He batted a .292 and was a steady performer in left field, "often with spectacular fielding plays, accurate throws, and timely hits." A perfect example came on July 21 against the Pittsburgh Pirates. Hobbled with a "truss strapped around his middle," he went 5 for 5, driving in two runs and scoring the same to help beat the Pirates, 6-5.

Moore was keenly aware of the contrast between the managerial style of McGraw and Terry. McGraw was autocratic and rarely consulted with his players. Terry, in contrast, was open to all players' suggestions and sometimes implemented some. Author Peter Williams, discussing the managerial change with Moore, said, "Joe Moore put the difference between the two more succinctly, telling me simply that "McGraw was a driver; Terry was a leader."[16]

Moore also confided in Williams about the unity the 1933 team possessed. "Joe Moore told me that 'back in our day we were called the family team—we were very close. All of us lived in the same neighborhood in New York, up in Washington Heights. And . . . our families were very close; we visited, we sat in the park together and whatnot. But we were a pretty close ballclub."[17]

Terry's bold leadership, the dominating pitching led by Hubbell, team unity, along with a solid offense earned the Giants the National League pennant. Their opposition in the World Series would be the Washington Senators, a club that led the majors in hitting. But the Giants won four games to one, behind the brilliant pitching of Hubbell and Schumacher and hitting of Ott. Moore, who was now being called any one of three names, Jo-Jo, "The Thin Man," and "The Gause Ghost," batted a puny .227, with one RBI and one run scored but contributed with his excellent defense.

If nothing else, Jo-Jo did tie a World Series record with two hits in one inning. It came in game two when the Giants scored six runs in the sixth inning. Moore led off with a single and his second at-bat singled again, driving in the sixth and final run of the game.

After the World Series, Jo-Jo gathered up his winning share and headed back to Gause, Texas, where he built a six-room house for his wife with all the modern conveniences and prepared for the 1934 season. But first, Jo-Jo underwent surgery to repair stomach muscles. The surgery was a success, and the future All-Star felt much better heading into the new season.

As a team player, Jo-Jo Moore had to have had mixed feelings after completing the 1934 season. The Giants blew the pennant in the final days, while Jo-Jo was having one of his best seasons of his 12-year career. He batted .331, a career-high, scored 106 runs, collected 192 hits while driving in 61 runs, a substantial amount for a lead-off hitter. He also hit 15 home runs, the result of a new batting stance. Moore was voted on to the All-Star team along with Terry, Jackson, Hubbell, and Ott. He also came in third in the Most Valuable Player award voting, behind the winner, Dizzy Dean, and second-place finisher Paul Waner.

In 1935, the Giants finished third with a respectable 91-62 record. Terry had the Giants leading the league into late August, but then the club fell apart, as the Cardinals and Cubs were streaking. Despite the Giants' third-place finish, Jo-Jo turned in another remarkable season. He played in 155 games and led the league with 681 at-bats. For a lead-off man, he was noted to be very impatient at the plate. In *The Ballplayers*, editor Mike Shatzkin points out, "Because Moore was a notorious first-ball hitter, some managers insisted their pitchers start him off with a ball outside the strike zone, fining those who allowed Moore a first-pitch to hit. Often Moore had to duck an opening delivery. When Hank Leiber was Moore's roommate, he told Dizzy Dean to quit throwing at Joe, or he'd break every bone in Dean's body."[18]

Jo-Jo continued his steady play in 1936, both at-bat and in the field. He hit .316 with career highs in both runs scored (110) and hits (205), 160 of which were league-leading singles, helping the Giants win their second National League pennant under Terry. For the second straight year, Moore made the All-Star team, which the National League finally won 4-3, after three consecutive losses.

The Giants lost the World Series to the New York Yankees in six games. Moore batted a meager .214 but did excel in game five to help extend the series. After nine, the game was tied at 4-4. The Gauze Ghost led off the top of the 10th with a double down the left field line. Bartell sacrificed him to third, and Terry, who hadn't hit a ball out of the infield all day, drove a long fly to Joe DiMaggio in center as Jo-Jo raced home with the eventual winning run, as 50,000 fans were on their feet screaming. Sadly, for Giants fans, that moment was their last opportunity to cheer. The next day the Yankees crushed the Giants 13-5.

Unknown to Giant fans, 1937 would be the team's last hurrah. They wouldn't win another pennant until 1951 when Bobby Thompson hit the "shot heard round the world" to win the final game of the three-game playoff against their rival, the Brooklyn Dodgers. But 1937 turned out to be a two-team race with the Chicago Cubs. The Giants won out in the end, rewarding Terry with his third National League pennant. The Thin Man, the epitome of consistency, was chosen for the All-Star Game for the third consecutive year. Moore made a brief appearance late in the game, pinch-hitting and grounding out. The American League won 8-3.

Jo-Jo turned in another laudable season in '37. The man from Gauze, Texas, batted .310 with an OPS of .810. He set a new personal record of 10 triples and tied his '34 mark with 37 doubles. Once again, Jo-Jo led the league with 11 assists, despite a head injury in June. But his major contribution to the pennant came in September when the race had tightened up. From September 8 to September 27, Jo-Jo unleashed a timely 20-game hitting streak, going 34 for 91 (.374), including 10 RBIs and 18 runs scored. No wonder Brooklyn manager Casey Stengel had high praise for Jo-Jo. "Every time we play the Giants, Moore is robbing one of our hitters of an extra base with a great catch. Every time I look up from the bench, Moore is rounding second base or throwing out a runner at third or home. He's a REAL Giant."[19]

Although Moore's contribution helped win the pennant, the Giants, once again, had to face the unstoppable New York Yankees in the World Series. Again, the Yankees won, this time in five. Jo-Jo hit a blustery .391 in the losing cause.

During the next four years, 1938-1941, the Giants would finish no higher than third place. Jo-Jo would continue to hold down the left-field position with the same poise and deftness as in the past. In addition, the Gause Ghost was a member of two more All-Star teams in 1938 and 1940. In 1938 he batted .302, the last time he hit over three hundred during his career.

Moore's remarkable 12-year career with the New York Giants ended abruptly after the 1941 season. Years later, in an interview with Brent Kelley for *Sports Collectors Digest*, Jo-Jo explained what happened. "I would have still been with the Giants the next year [1942]. I was gonna have to take a little cut, and the Indianapolis (American Association) ball club wanted me. Gabby Hartnett was the manager there, and Gabby and I were good friends, so I went there and was actually making more money."[20]

Then in September 1943, Philadelphia A's manager, Connie Mack, traded Roberto Estalella and cash for Moore. Jo-Jo never reported to the A's because, in February of '44, he was drafted into military service but was reclassified. He never wore an "Athletic or Uncle Sam uniform." Eventually, Mack canceled the deal and recalled the Cuban-born Estalella.

Moore managed and played in the minor leagues for a while and then finally retired to Gause, Texas, to work his ranch. Moore's final 12-year major league stats are quite impressive: .298 hitter, helped Giants win three National League pennants, one World Series, six-time All-Star, and a defensive whiz in left field with a strong and accurate arm.

As the pages turned on the calendar and the years flew by, Moore moved to the Grand Court retirement home in Bryan, Texas. It was in 1995, four years after his wife, Jewell, died. Jo-Jo celebrated his 90th birthday party at his son's house. Now gray-haired, with two hearing aids and minor health issues, he told a delightful story to his grandchildren and great-grandchildren. It went like this; there was a rhubarb in the infield, at the Polo Grounds, between the Giants and St. Louis Cardinals players. Moore sat down in left field, waiting for it to end. "Suddenly, he saw Pepper Martin, the Cardinals third baseman, coming out there. 'I thought, 'oh, oh, this doesn't look so good. I said, 'What are you doing out here?' And he said, 'I'm gonna sit with you. The last time I got into one of those scraps, I got hit in the mouth and never saw it comin', turned me upside down.'"[21] Jo-Jo Moore died April 1, 2001, at age 92.

After Hubbell beat Dean, the Giants lost the series to St. Louis as Cincinnati arrived at the Polo Grounds. The Giants regrouped and won all four games, with the Meal Ticket winning the opener, 8-4. The Giants staked Hub to a 7-0 lead. He sailed along, maintaining the shutout, until the eighth when he faltered. The Reds plated four, the big blow a three-run homer by Billy Sullivan, not known as a power hitter. Hub weathered the ninth for the 8-4 victory. Hub's record was now 17-8. Of late, Hubbell has had difficulty keeping the ball in the park, a dangerous habit, especially with runners on. By season's end, King Carl's crown was showing signs of wear. He would lead the National League, giving up 27 homers.

As the saying goes, there was no rest for the weary. Terry would see to that, at least for Hubbell. After eight innings of game three with the Reds, the score was knotted at 4-4. In the top of the ninth, Euel Moore pitching for the Giants found himself in trouble with runners on first and second with two outs. At that point, Terry was taking no chances and called on his Meal Ticket, with one day's rest! Hubbell promptly fanned left-handed swinger Ival Goodman for the final out. The Giants failed to score in their half of the ninth as the game went into extra innings. After getting two out in the 10th, it looked like an easy inning for Hub. Not so. Lew Riggs singled for the Reds, and Ernie Lombardi doubled, and just like that, Cincinnati took the lead 5-4. Hub retired Gordon Slade to end the inning.

If there were any gloomy faces in the stands or dugout, they brightened in a hurry. Hank Leiber homered off Benny Frey in the 10th, tying the game. It was the center fielder's 18th of the season. The 24-year-old, in his third season with New York, was having a career year. He would finish with a .331 average, 22 homers, and 107 RBIs.

Frey, a little shaky after Leiber's homer, gave up a single to Mancuso (Critz ran for him), and Bartell sacrificed Critz to second. Emmet Nelson replaced Frey. Hubbell flied out. Cincinnati manager Chuck Dressen brought in Don Brennan. Moore was intentionally walked, whereupon Jackson singled to end the game. Final score Giants 6 Reds 5. Hubbell was credited with the win, his 18th against eight losses.

After the sweep of the Reds, the tight National League race looked like this:

TEAM	W	L	GB
New York	73	41	–
St. Louis	69	43	3
Chicago	72	48	4

Fresh from sweeping Cincinnati, the Giants took on the pesky Cubs, who quickly whisked away New York's broom, winning three of the four games. While the Giants and Cubs were battling each other, the St. Louis Cardinals put together an eight-game winning streak knocking New York out of first place.

Hubbell pitched two of the four games. He started the opener against the Cubs fireballer, Lon Warneke, and left after eight innings, behind 3-2. Hub allowed eight hits but didn't walk a batter. Ott, who was having a fabulous season, hit his second homer (number 27) of the day in the bottom of the ninth to tie the game and avoid a loss for Hub. But the Giants lost the game in the 11th when second reliever, Al Smith, with runners on first and second, and two out, failed to retire pinch hitter Woody English, as he singled to left.

Game three, the only contest the Giants won, was a wild game when the Giants exploded for eight runs in the second inning, handing starter Parmelee an easy victory, or so it seemed. Ott and Leiber accounted for six of the eight runs. Master Melvin hit his 28th with two runners on base, and Leiber hit two. The first was with the bases empty, the second with a man on. With an 8-0 lead Terry could sit back, relax and enjoy watching Parmelee coast the rest of the game. It was not to be. Parmelee, nicknamed "Tarzan" by *New York Daily News* writer Jimmy Powers, not because of his muscular build but rather his tendency towards episodes of wildness. In the third inning, Tarzan went wild! He managed to get one out but hit a batter, walked three (which brought his total to five), and allowed two runs. There went Terry's relaxed day. He immediately called on Hubbell to halt the craziness, even though Hub had pitched eight innings two days prior. King Carl pitched almost seven innings, allowing five hits, two runs, and, of course, did not walk a batter. The final score was New York 9 Chicago 4. His record was now 19-8.

If Terry and the Giants thought their ouster from first place was temporary, Pittsburgh made it permanent. The Pirates swept the three-game series at the Polo Grounds, putting the Giants 2½ back of St. Louis and Chicago 3 behind. Hubbell started the first game of the doubleheader and was in a pitching duel with Cy Blanton (16-9), that is, until the eighth inning. Hub and the Giants were trailing 3-1 when Pittsburgh scored three, which might have been prevented. Hubbell loaded the bases with one out when Pie Traynor "pushed a grounder to the right of second," which could have resulted in a double play by a more agile second baseman. Mark Koenig, at the end of his career and a self-proclaimed "lousy infielder," couldn't get to the ball, which scored two runs. A sacrifice fly brought in run number three. The game ended 6-1 as Hub gave up nine hits and a rare four walks. His record was now 19-9.

September 4, 1935, was a date for Giant fans that will live in infamy. Pardon the partial literary theft of President Franklin D. Roosevelt's immortal words, but it is appropriate. This was the day the Chicago Cubs began their 21 consecutive game winning streak and the march to the National League pennant. As the Cubs beat the Phillies 8-2, New York, behind Hubbell, trounced Cincinnati 6-4.

Hub spotted the Reds two runs in the first inning but then held them in check for the next six until his teammates gave him the lead. The over-worked left-hander gave up single runs in both the eighth and ninth innings but still managed to win 6-4. It was his 20th win as his record now stood at 20-9. It's too bad pitch counts weren't in vogue during Hubbell's career. It would be very interesting to see the number of pitches thrown in a game and not just for Hubbell.

It was reported in *The New York Times* Babe Ruth was given a lifetime pass to all National League games. As most baseball fans know, Ruth spent 21 of his 22-year major league career in the American League. However, National League president Ford Frick saw fit to honor the Babe with this gift. Speculation as to Frick's motive is open to discussion. The Babe was gracious in his acceptance of the pass, which contained the number 500, a tribute to the first major league player to hit 500 home runs.

In a thank you letter to Frick, Ruth wrote, in part, ". . . I want you to know that this touch of sentiment and appreciation will never be forgotten. It is nice to know that the National League has a heart."[22] The Babe was not one to mince words. His last sentence could easily be meant for the American League and the New York Yankees.

Four days later, Hubbell pitched his second road game in September as the Terrymen traveled to Forbes Field in Pittsburgh. Hub pitched a marvelous game, allowing only six hits and one run for a 3-1 Giant win. Terry, who has been on a tear since leaving the Polo Grounds, had another perfect day going 4 for 4. Counting this game, the player/manager has been hitting at a torrid .636 clip. Hubbell's record was now 21-9.

While the Cubs were routing the Dodgers 13-3, New York was losing to the St. Louis Cardinals 5-2. It was the Cubs' ninth straight win and put them only two games back of the league-leading Cards. The Giants were in third place, now 4½ back. The 5-2 loss was the opening game of the series and poor timing for the Giants ace to have an off game, especially against Dizzy Dean. Hub gave up four runs on seven hits and was gone after five innings. Dean, on the other hand, was at the top of his game. The boisterous one limited the Giants to seven hits and two runs while striking out eight. It was his 26th victory of the season against eight losses. Hub's record was now 21-10, and the future for the Giants was bleak as the season was quickly coming to an end.

Then, when all looked lost, the Giants came to life and won the next three games of the series, 13-10, 5-4, and 7-3. Even though Hubbell lost the first game of the series, Terry felt confident calling on his Meal Ticket to pitch on two days' rest. His mound opponent was the one and only Dizzy. But this time, the outcome was reversed. Dean was gone after five innings, trailing 5-0. Hub kept the Cards at bay, giving up nine hits but only three runs even though he walked four Cardinals. He weakened in the eighth under the oppressive St. Louis heat but managed to call upon that little bit extra all the great pitchers possess. Hubbell's record was now 22-10.

The Giants were now headed for Chicago to play the sizzling hot Cubs, winners of their last 12 games. Here is what the standings looked like as the Terrymen contemplated the next four games:

TEAM	W	L	GB
Chicago	91	52	–
St. Louis	87	52	2
New York	84	52	3½

Bill Terry and his New York Giants were now facing the most crucial four-game series of the 1935 season. A sweep could put the Giants back in first, depending on how St. Louis played. Regardless, the Giants had to win at least three of four from the Cubs to keep their hopes alive, and back in the pennant race, they squandered in August. And a sweep there was, only not by the Giants. Hub lost the final game of the humiliating four games, 6-1. Bill Lee, nicknamed "Big Bill," living up to his sobriquet, pitched a masterful game. He allowed a mere six hits and only gave up one run, late in the game when the outcome was certain. Hubbell pitched only seven innings and gave up five runs and 10 of the 13 hits. His record was now 22-11.

Author Williams summed up the Cubs' season after they swept the Giants. "The Cubs proved to be the story of 1935. They had great defense—three regulars led the league in fielding average—and two of these, catcher Gabby Hartnett and second baseman Billy Herman, also batted .344 and .341, respectively. It was Herman's best season as a hitter, Hartnett's second best, and both men are now in the Hall of Fame. Add to this a pitching staff with two twenty-game winners and four more in double figures, and the result is a formidable outfit."[23]

There is one more individual to single out, the manager Charlie Grimm. He was affectionately called "Jolly Cholly, "and for good reason. He was always in good cheer and rarely in a bad mood. Grimm was a solid first baseman, a good hitter, and popular with Cub fans and players. He took over the managerial job on August 3, 1932 (five games behind league-leading Pittsburgh), when then-manager Rogers Hornsby, one of the greatest right-handed hitters in baseball, was fired. Hornsby's managerial style, outspoken and demanding, was off-putting even though his players respected his on-field play. Conversely, the Cub players and fans loved Grimm, and it showed on the field as Charlie led the '32 Cubs to the National League pennant but lost the World Series to the powerful Yankees. In 1933 and 1934, the Cubs finished third each year, but this season Jolly Cholly's leadership and personality, had his club playing timely and magical baseball, and he deserves credit.

After leaving Chicago, the Giants with their heads hung low, and Terry offering no excuses or alibis, the future looked impossible, at best. Adding insult to injury, the Terrymen now faced six doubleheaders out of 13 games remaining! Clearly, it was an insurmountable task.

The Giants won 7, lost 6, and finished the season in third place, 8½ games back. Now back at the Polo Grounds, Hubbell pitched and won the first game of the Braves doubleheader. New York scored three runs in the first inning and then went to sleep as the game tightened up when Hub gave up single runs in the fifth and sixth. The final score was 3-2, and in the end, Hubbell had pitched his typical game—six hits, two runs, and no walks. His record was now 23-11.

Most baseball fans were now focused on the crucial and all-determining five-game series between the Cubs and Cardinals. The Cards were three games back of Chicago. Paul Dean (19-12) lost the opening game, a heartbreaker, to 20-game winner Lon Warneke (20-13) by a score of 1-0. Nineteen-year-old Phil Cavaretta accounted for the lone score, hitting a home run in the second inning, and that's all the Arkansas Hummingbird needed as the Cardinals fell four games back and were faced with winning the rest of the series. Brother Dizzy was handed the ball to put a stop to the Chicago juggernaut but was not up to the task as Bill Lee (20-6), pitching a superb game, held the Cards to six hits and two runs in the 6-2 victory. Dizzy (28-12) was smacked around for 15 hits. The victory clinched the National League pennant for the Cubs. They also won the second game of the twin-bill, ending their marvelous and timely 21-game winning streak.

On the same day, Chicago clinched the pennant, Hubbell pitched his last game of the season, no doubt, an exhausted and tired competitor. He lost to the lowly Boston Braves in ugly fashion. After only two innings, the pathetic Braves clobbered Hub for eight hits and six runs. The final score was Boston 6, New York 4. Hub finished the season 23-12.

With the Giants eliminated from the pennant race weeks before the season ended, it raises serious questions as to why manager Bill Terry would choose to pitch Hubbell or any other of his starting pitchers in meaningless games. Why not give a younger, unproven kid the opportunity? These many years later, it boggles the mind.

The Giants, for the second consecutive year, squandered golden opportunities to win back-to-back pennants. Once again, tight races and not the outcome accounted for the Giants increasing their attendance during the Depression to a league-leading 748,748. Now, talk began to circulate the Giants were a club that choked in the clutch. If the Giants had a clear identifiable weakness, it was not easy to find. Terry, Ott, Moore, and Leiber all had exceptional years. The rest of the offense and defense were competitive. However, Schumacher, with a 2.88 ERA, was the only starting pitcher under 3.00. Castleman, Parmelee, Fitzsimmons, and Stout were above 4.00. It came as no surprise when the Giants were ranked fourth in the National League with a team ERA of 3.78. They were also ranked number one in innings pitched. Could there be a correlation?

Hubbell's 1935 season was the only one of the fabulous five when he didn't lead the National League in some important and positive pitching category. However, Hub did lead in one unwanted category, home runs, giving up 27. It would be the highest total of his 16-year career and impossible to explain, with any certainty, after all these many years. One possibility could be a fatigued arm. It was Hubbell's third consecutive year logging over 300 innings on the mound, 302.2 to be exact. Many of the innings pitched were with little rest. Then again, it could be Hub had an off year in the sense he didn't dominate as in 1933 and 1934.

But a look at where Hubbell finished in important pitching stats reveals he had a season most pitchers would eagerly accept. He was second to the leader, Dean, in three categories: complete games 29 to 24, strikeouts 195 to 190, and wins 28 to 23. In the other categories, he ranked fifth in winning percentage and eighth in earned run average.

The next two years would find the New York Giants and Carl Hubbell back in the middle of the National League pennant race but with an entirely different outcome. Hubbell would put together a dream season, living up to both his nicknames, King Carl and the Meal Ticket. He would lead the National League in wins, highest winning percentage, lowest ERA, and named the MVP. Oh yes, he would set a record that still stands today, winning 24 consecutive games over two seasons.

10

Most Wins. Highest WP. Lowest ERA. MVP

"WHAT MADE IT [SCREWBALL] WORK FOR ME WAS I THREW IT WITH THE SAME OVERHAND MOTION AS MY FASTBALL AND CURVEBALL. IT SERVED AS MY CHANGE OF PACE TOO."

Bill Terry, once again, did not stand pat with his infield. He made two important changes, one of which was himself. It began with the retirement of second baseman Hughie Critz who went home after the '35 season. The player chose to replace Critz was St. Louis Cardinals' second baseman, Burgess Whitehead, who graduated Phi Beta Kappa from the University of North Carolina. To obtain the services of Whitehead, the Giants gave up starter Roy Parmelee (14-10, ERA 4.22), relief pitcher Allyn Stout (1-4, ERA 4.91), along with 20-year-old second baseman Al Cuccinello and utility player Phil Weintraub. "Critics of the deal conceded that Whitehead was fast, an agile second baseman who could make the double play, an occasional hitter, and a good-hit-and-run man, all of which they needed."[1]

But some skeptics were unsure of the trade. They believed Whitehead could not play an entire season because he was a slim, frail-looking guy. He was listed at 5'10" and 160 pounds. Well, the critics were wrong, as often they are. The 26-year-old would play in all 154 games and bat a decent .278. For the next two seasons, Whitehead would team up with Dick Bartell to form one of the tightest infields in the league. That defense would go a long way in helping the Giants to succeed in 1936-1937.

Terry, who had been sending signals recently he was looking for a replacement, finally made the move. At age 37, with a damaged knee and other aches and pains, it was time to take a permanent seat on the bench. Replacing Terry was an impossible task. Where could you find a future Hall of Famer with a lifetime batting average of .341? Not an easy job. The best Terry could do was acquire Sam Leslie from Brooklyn, who had a solid season with the Dodgers in '35, playing in 142 games, batting .308, and driving in 93 runs. The Giants picked up two other experienced players, both relievers, Dick Coffman from the St. Louis Browns and Firpo Marberry, age 37, who had pitched for the Senators (11 years) and Tigers (3 years). Rounding out the everyday players, Gus Mancuso was back catching, Travis Jackson at third, along with Jo-Jo Moore in left, Hank Leiber in center, and Mel Ott in right.

The pitching staff added up to one man, Carl Hubbell, with surprising help from the inexperienced Harry Gumbert. Although Hubbell was the ace of the Giants' staff, his performance in '35 was not as dazzling as '33 and '34. In early January of '36, it was believed Hub signed for $18,500, the same amount as the previous year. That figure made him one of the highest-paid pitchers in the National League. To be sure, Hubbell was satisfied, especially during the Depression when millions of people couldn't find work, let alone at the salary the left-hander signed for.

Before the Giants headed for Pensacola, Florida, for spring training, president Charles Stoneham died at a hotel in Hot Springs, Arkansas. He was 59 years old and suffered from nephritis. The life of Stoneham is a classic rag to riches story. He was a complex man, to say the least. He began his career as a "board boy" in a brokerage house and rose to senior partner in a Manhattan firm. Eventually, his success led to his firm, Charles A. Stoneham & Co. He was also known as a gambler and was attracted to the nightlife.

Stoneham's success led to a syndicate, headed by him, that purchased the New York Giants. The syndicate included two partners: at the time, Giants' manager John McGraw and Manhattan magistrate Frank McQuade. Stoneham held the overwhelming number of shares in the syndicate and, was what you would call, an absentee manager. He left all the baseball decisions to McGraw. It was a successful arrangement as the Giants won four consecutive National League pennants and two World Series between 1921 and 1924.

But his financial success was not without serious and major problems from his brokerage days, which resulted in lawsuits and counter lawsuits. It turned out to be a huge legal mess. The most sensational case was with E. M. Fuller & Co. It resulted in Stoneham being charged with fraud, theft, and related criminal wrongdoing. However, after a long trial, Stoneham was acquitted. This left the Giants' owner with a renewed interest in his club's financial position.

Stoneham's troubles, however, were far from over. In May 1928, after ousting his junior partner, Giant treasurer McQuade, lawsuits began flying between the two. The battle ". . . dragged until 1934, when the Court of Appeals denied that Mr. McQuade was entitled to a judgment of $42,827 from Mr. Stoneman and Mr. McGraw."[2]

In 1933 Stoneham did live to enjoy another World Championship with his new manager, Bill Terry. But as his health continued to limit his activities, Stoneham's son, Horace, took over more of the responsibility of the front office. The end for the controversial and complex man came much too early to see the Giants win two more National League pennants. Shortly after Charles died, his son replaced him.

By early March 1936, the entire Giants squad had arrived at Pensacola to begin spring training. Even at this early stage and with the weather hot but ideal for baseball, Terry was not in a good mood. The reason was Hank Leiber, his star center fielder, was now a major holdout.

Despite Leiber's absence, the Giants opened their 17-game exhibition schedule against the Cleveland Indians with three contests. It would not resume for another two weeks. Well, if Terry was upset over Leiber, losing all three to the Indians, 4-2, 5-3, and 6-0 wasn't a mood lifter.

Before the Giants met with Cleveland again, they had played 12 games against the likes of the Pensacola Naval Air Station, Atlanta Crackers, Kansas City Blues, Nashville Volunteers, and the Chicago Cubs. Their record was 9-3, but the good news was the signing of Leiber. The center fielder, who had a wonderful season, playing in 154 games, batting .331 with 22 home runs and 107 RBIs, was asking for $12,500. Terry, however, did not want to exceed $10,000. No figures were revealed, but the speculation was the two compromised at $11,000.

With the Leiber signing, the Giants were at full strength and began their trek home playing the Indians as both teams headed for opening day. As the exhibition schedule was drawing to a close, Carl Hubbell was fine-tuning his repertoire of pitches, especially the screwball. In one of his last exhibition games, he whipped the Indians 10-2. Hubbell went the full nine innings. After Cleveland scored two runs in the first (one earned), the gifted southpaw slammed the door shut. He blanked the Indians the rest of the way with three measly hits.

The final game of the Giants' spring series came to an end in Cleveland in a dramatic fashion. The barnstorming series, which began in Florida and moved westward to Arkansas, finally ended with the Giants trouncing the Indians 7-0. Jo-Jo Moore was the hero of the game, walloping two homers, one a grand slam. He drove in five of the seven runs. The victory tied the series at seven each. The barnstorming back north was an annual tradition between the two clubs that began in 1934 and continued for more than 20 years.

The Giant victory was a positive ending to a long and tiresome journey beginning in Pensacola, especially the trip north battling Cleveland. The fans in the communities along the way were hungry for baseball. Remember, this was before television. The ball games became major events with local bands and politicians. As author Williams claimed, "There were usually dogs on the field, sometimes even sheep."

Opening day was just around the corner. Of the eight managers in the National League, Charlie Grimm was the most positive. He stated emphatically the Cubs would win the pennant. Frisch and Terry hedged slightly. Terry said, "It's a one-two-three proposition for us. I think this is the best team I ever had. I like our chances."[3] In the American League, the Detroit Tigers were picked to repeat.

The New York Giants opened the season with a three-game series against, of all teams, the despised Brooklyn Dodgers. Terry held back Hubbell for the entire series, perhaps due to Hubbell's poor showing against Brooklyn in the past. Terry chose Schumacher, Gumbert, and Fitzsimmons as the Giants swept the Dodgers. It was a wonderful start for the Giants, but not without incident. The altercation came in game two, "Bartell grounded to first baseman Buddy Hassett for what appeared to be a routine, unassisted putout by Hassett. Mungo, coming over to cover the bag, appeared to give Dick a hard jolt with his hip. From a bleacher vantage point, Bartell seemed to fly through the air as though shot out of a cannon. He turned a couple of somersaults and landed flat on his back."[4]

Without hesitation, Bartell jumped to his feet and yelled at Mungo, claiming he did it on purpose. Words were exchanged as the two men began throwing punches. Both dugouts emptied. Umpire Beans Reardon finally separated the two combatants and restored order. Then Reardon kicked out both men. Welcome to a New York Giant, Brooklyn Dodger match. And it was only the second game of the season!

The following day, National League president Ford Frick fined both Bartell and Mungo $25 each. Frick admitted the fine was the "smallest for a fistfight." He also discussed his new non-fraternization rule he had announced before the opening of the season. The new edict stated that if players on opposing teams were caught talking to each other, they would be fined. The rule became even more ridiculous when he added managers would also be fined.

Terry finally unleashed his staff ace, Hubbell, in Boston, against the team with a new owner and name (Bees). However, the results were the same. The Giants and Hubbell won 6-4, but it wasn't a typically commanding performance by the ace. In five innings, he gave up seven hits and three runs. Fitz relieved and picked up the save.

After four days of rest, Hubbell returned to the mound to face the Philadelphia Phillies and pitched more like King Carl. He beat the Phillies 7-2 and had only one bad inning, the seventh when he allowed two runs. His pitching line read: nine innings, eight hits, two runs, two walks, and five strikeouts. His record was now 2-0 and the Giants 7-1, both off to a fast start with the team in first place.

The Giants next visited Ebbets Field. But before their two-game series, Terry wisely asked for increased police protection even though Bartell was ill and didn't play in either game. One might conclude Terry had an ulterior motive . . . let's say hyping the rivalry. Whatever, the request was granted. The games were played with no altercations as Brooklyn won both, 4-3 and 8-2. Although it was only two losses, it stopped the Giants' fast get-away and set them on a course of playing mediocre baseball until early May.

In an ironic twist of events, Hubbell lost his first game of the season 2-1 to the St. Louis Cardinals. It was the initial game of the Giants' first western trip. His opponent was Roy Parmelee, former teammate, who was part of the trade to get Whitehead. Both hurlers went the distance until the bottom of the 17th when with one out, two misplays by the Giants' infield cost Hubbell the game. The irony is that Parmelee outpitched Hub while showing superb control. He walked four batters, this from a pitcher noted for wildness, so much so, he was tagged with the nickname Tarzan. Hubbell gave up 11 hits (Parmelee, six), one earned run, and walked four batters. His record was now 2-1.

After the marathon 17 inning loss to the Redbirds, Hubbell still carried the jinx into Cincinnati. Right-hander Lee Stine, not quite a household name throughout baseball circles, probably pitched the game of his short four-year career. Young Stine (23) blanked the Giants on eight hits while not walking a batter. Hub, as described in *The New York Times,* turned in "another commendable performance." He had one bad inning, which came at the bottom of the ninth when Kiki Cuyler led off with a triple. One out later, Hub intentionally walked Babe Herman and Ernie Lombardi, setting up a possible double play. That strategy ended when former Yankee Sammy Byrd flied out to short right, scoring Cuyler for the 1-0 victory. It was the second tough loss for Hub as his record evened at 2-2.

Four days later, Hubbell took his regular turn facing the Phillies. The hard-luck hurler was sailing along in a 1-1 tie until the fourth inning when the Phillies erupted for three runs, chasing the left-hander in favor of Harry Gumbert, who put out the fire a bit too late. The final score was Philadelphia 5 New York 3. Hubbell's record was now 2-3. For the last ten games, the Giants' record was an embarrassing 3-7, dropping them to fourth place with an overall record of 10-10. The good news was the Giants won the next nine in a row!

During the streak, King Carl won two games and saved one as the Giants were back in first place. Hubbell also pitched an inning in a wild 13-12 win over the Phillies with three runs in the ninth, compliments of Master Melvin. With two runners on, Ott smacked a long home run into the right-field stands. It was his fifth of the season. Gumbert (3-0) won the game, Gabler earned a save, and Hub a no-decision.

Two days later, Hubbell was back in form, tossing a five-hit shutout over the Chicago Cubs. He allowed one walk and fanned five. Hub finally received support from his teammates, which he hadn't during his last four starts. The 5-0 victory evened Hubbell's record at 3-3. It was his first shutout of the early season.

Next, the Giants won a short two-game series from the Cincinnati Reds at the Polo Grounds. In the first game, Prince Hal blanked the Reds 2-0 with help from Al Smith in relief. The next day the Giants beat the Reds 4-3, but not before some serious nail-biting by the local fans. Gumbert had pitched a commendable game, holding a slim one-run lead when he began to weaken in the top of the ninth. Gumbert began by walking pinch-hitter Gilly Campell and fell behind 2-0 to another pinch-hitter, Ival Goodman. Terry quickly called on the Meal Ticket, despite having only one day's rest, after blanking the Cubs 5-0. Hub induced Goodman to hit into a force at second. Then he struck out Kiki Cuyler, a career.321 hitter. Lee Handley, a 23-year-old rookie, was up next. After one swing, he looked so helpless, the third pinch-hitter of the inning was sent up in the person of Sammy Byrd, who popped up to Bartell, ending the game. It was Hubbell's first save of the season. His won/lost record remained at 3-3.

Coming off his clutch relief performance, Hubbell faced the visiting Pittsburgh Pirates and won 4-2 for the Giants' eighth straight victory. Hubbell's guile and fortitude got him through a complete game, despite giving up 12 hits. Two crucial factors earned him his fourth victory against three losses. He didn't walk a batter and was unhittable with men on base.

After the Giants split a two-game series with the St. Louis Cardinals, Philadelphia was next at the Polo Grounds. In the opening game of the series, the last-place Phillies demolished the Giants 15-0. The following day, however, the Giants returned the favor, pummeling the Phillies 9-0; eight of the runs crossed the plate in the bottom of the fifth. It was another masterpiece by King Carl and his second shutout in the last three games. Hub's record was now 5-3. Newcomer, second baseman Burgess Whitehead had a huge day going 4 for 5 along with three RBIs. Although early, it appears Whitehead is fulfilling all of Terry's expectations.

Burgess Whitehead was born June 29, 1910, in Tarboro, North Carolina. Little is known about his parents except for his father, Clifford, who was a dentist and all his uncles were peanut farmers. The family moved from Tarboro to Lewiston, approximately 35 miles northeast, where he attended Lewiston High School. After graduating, the young man attended Augusta Military Academy in Virginia. During his two years at the Academy, Whitey, as he was called, impressed the coaches to the point, they predicted a bright future for him in the game. From the Academy, he went on to the University of North Carolina. He spent three years as a Tar Heel, where he earned the distinction of being a member of the most prestigious honor society, Phi Beta Kappa.

His college attendance was during the Depression, and money was tight. Whitehead, in his spare time from studying, worked various jobs to help with the finances. During the school week, he "sold football tickets and worked in a dormitory laundry." No doubt, the most joyful job was during the summer when he played semi-pro ball for $35 a week.

Whitehead played shortstop all three years at UNC with rave reviews. "By that time, major league scouts had heard of him and were offering him contracts to play professional ball." One of the scouts was Art Devlin of the Giants, who sent Whitehead to the Polo Grounds for a tryout. McGraw was impressed, but apparently not enough. He advised the youngster to finish his schooling. Branch Rickey's brother, Frank, scouting for the St. Louis Cardinals, made him an offer he couldn't refuse (long before the phrase became popular). "Just as the 1931 college campaign was about to start, it was disclosed Whitehead, along with two players from Wake Forest and one from North Carolina State, had signed contracts to play in Organized Baseball."[5]

With a signed contract, Whitehead joined the Columbus Red Birds, a minor league club of the parent St. Louis Cardinals. The year was 1931, and 21-year-old Whitehead played in 135 games, batting an impressive .328 to compliment his fine fielding. Ironically, one of his teammates was a pitcher by the name of Roy Parmelee.

Back for another season with Columbus, Whitehead played in 162 games, hitting .313 with 211 hits, a team high. He also showed off his speed with 36 doubles, placing him third on the team. During these two years, Whitehead was shifted from short to second, where his play was equally brilliant.

In 1933, a disappointed Whitehead was back with Columbus for the third time. Again, Whitehead had another outstanding season. He batted a stellar .346 with 20 doubles in 89 games. The Cardinals finally called him up late in the season, where he batted .286 in 12 games.

For the next two seasons, Whitehead backed up Frisch and Durocher at second and short, respectively. He even filled in for Pepper Martin at third. In 1934, the utility infielder batted .277 in 100 games. But the following year, playing in 107, mostly as a replacement for the aging Frisch, he hit .263. His playing was good enough to be selected to the 1935 All-Star team, in which the American League won 4-1. Whitehead's playing time was limited to running for Jimmie Wilson in the seventh inning.

During Whitey's three seasons at Columbus, it was freely discussed that the young second baseman would eventually replace Frisch. It was reported that when Frisch was ready to step down, it would be a smooth transition. Cardinal scout Charley Barrett and vice-president Branch Rickey both believed Whitehead could do the job at second. He was the logical successor.

On December 9, 1935, when Whitehead was traded to the New York Giants, it came as a shocker to St. Louis and North Carolina fans, not to mention Whitey. Asked if he was upset over the trade, Whitey offered this candid reply. "I had been led to believe that I was being groomed as Frankie Frisch's successor with St. Louis, of course, the disillusionment upset me momentarily. But I'm happier than ever now that I'm a Giant—and a regular at that."[6]

In hindsight, it was a fortuitous trade for Whitehead. The next two seasons (1936-1937) with the Giants, he was the regular second baseman. Critz,

Cuccinello, and Koenig shared second in '35, making the position a weak link in the already patchwork infield. Whitehead's arrival solidified the position along with shortstop Bartell to help bring two National League pennants to the Polo Grounds. Terry had high regard for his new second sacker, and the feeling was mutual. Terry paid little attention to the St. Louis critics. The critical question was, could the 5'10", 160-pound frame of Whitehead standup during a long, competitive season? Whitey gave the critics their answer, making them eat their words. He played in all 154 games, batted a steady .278, and stole a team-leading 14 bases. He also scored 99 runs and, along with Bartell, formed an excellent double-play combination. It silenced the naysayers, at least for a while.

The Giants won the pennant with a 92-62 record, five games ahead of Chicago and St. Louis. Terry and the Giants, after a three-year hiatus, were back in the World Series. Unfortunately, their opponents, the Yankees, were as strong as ever, even without the services of Babe Ruth. His "replacement" was rookie Joe DiMaggio, who turned in a fabulous season: 29 home runs, 129 RBIs, and a batting average of .323. In all aspects of the game, the Yankees had a distinct advantage and won the Series in six games. Whitehead played in all six, but at the plate was a disappointment. He went 1 for 21 (.048) with two RBIs.

In 1937 the Giants improved on their record (95-57) and won another National League pennant by three games over the Chicago Cubs. It would be understandable if Whitehead was gloating since his former team, the Cardinals, finished fourth, a distant 15 games back. Once again, Whitey fooled his critics and played in 152 games with a .286 batting average. He also had the distinction of collecting 164 hits, second to Jo-Jo Moore, the team leader with 180. By the end of August, he had played in 270 consecutive games, far from the "Iron Man" tag given by the press, but more than enough to stifle his critics. Whitehead made the All-Star team for the second time in his short career. The American League won 8-3. Once again, Whitey was used as a pinch-runner for Gabby Hartnett in the sixth inning.

Regrettably, the Giants' opponent in the World Series was the New York Yankees, winning their pennant by 13 games over the Detroit Tigers. They were led by DiMaggio, Gehrig, and Dickey, plus the only American League twenty-game winners, Lefty Gomez (21-11) and Red Ruffing (20-7). It was a classic mismatch. The Giants couldn't compete with the Yankees offense but did boast of two twenty-game winners, Hubbell (22-8) and Cliff Melton (20-9).

The Yankees won in five games for their second consecutive World Series championship. Whitehead played in all five games, this time improving his performance going for 4 for 16 (.250) with two doubles. The Yankees would beat the Cubs in the '38 Series and the Reds in '39, making it four straight World titles for manager Joe McCarthy.

With two National League pennants and two World Series appearances, the future for Burgess Whitehead looked bright. Then on February 19, 1938, Whitehead was not feeling well and was taken to a doctor by his brother, Louis. "The doctor found appendicitis so acute that gangrene had already set in, and Whitehead was operated on immediately, barely surviving the illness. Worse, the experience scared the daylights out of him, putting him in very precarious emotional shape for most of the subsequent year."[7]

Whitehead missed the entire 1938 season, often described in the press as a "nervous breakdown." By November of '38, he was ready to rejoin the Giants and looked forward to a comeback. As predicted, Whitey returned in 1939 and played in 95 games, but the season was riddled with problems. He reported late to spring camp at Baton Rouge, which didn't sit well with Terry, although the manager did keep his cool, at least for a while. Terry's patience ran out after Whitehead complained about being tired, arriving late at the ballpark, and overall acting strangely. It finally came to a head in the middle of August when Terry suspended Whitehead for an "infraction of training rules." Speculation was rampant Whitehead would quit the game. But that blew over, and Whitehead was back playing on August 21. The inevitable happened in early September when Whitehead left the club and went home. Besides Whitehead, Terry had his hands full with a club that lacked consistency along with mediocre pitching and hitting. The Giants finished fifth (77-74), 18½ games back of the pennant-winning Cincinnati Reds.

Surprise, surprise, Whitehead returned to the Giants in 1940 with a vengeance. Installed at third base, the man from Tarboro played in 133 games, batted .282, and led the team with 162 hits. Towards the end of the season, sportswriter, Joe King, had high praise for Whitehead. "Whitey is one of the steadiest of the Giants this season and one of the most useful. He's played second and third bases, and his stickwork—not under .285 since June—has enabled Terry to switch him from the lower to the upper part of the batting order in shakeups. This is indeed a reconstructed Whitehead; there is no suggestion of the flighty, uncertain Whitey of 1939."[8]

Despite Whitehead's solid season, Terry simply didn't have the talent to compete. Ott continued to show signs of slowing down while first baseman Babe Young led the club with 101 RBIs. Hubbell (11-12) was no longer the

Meal Ticket as age, and a weak arm finally caught up with him. Schumacher led the pitching staff with a 13-13 record, which explains, in part, why the Giants finished sixth with a 72-80 record, a whopping 27½ games back of the league-leading Reds.

For Terry and the New York Giants, their 1941 performance was a repeat of the previous season. The club finished in fifth place (74-79), an embarrassing 25½ games back of the Brooklyn Dodgers. Whitehead returned and had a mediocre season, at best. He played in 116 games and batted a pathetic .228, the lowest of his eight-year career.

With the United States entry into World War II only months away, Burgess Whitehead's future in major league baseball was not looking good. By the middle of October, every American male between the ages of 21 and 36 was required to register for the Selective Service. Adding to Whitehead's demise, rumors began flying Terry would be replaced as manager by either Dick Bartell or Billy Jurges. Neither received the job. It went to Mel Ott. Then the Japanese bombed Pearl Harbor, and Whitehead's future, along with millions of other young men, would see their lives change drastically.

Among the many changes new manager Ott made was "selling Whitehead to the Toronto Maple Leafs of the International League on December 11. As a result, Burgess spent the 1942 season playing second base in Toronto, where he hit .259 and stole 26 bases in 148 games for the sixth-place Maple Leafs."[9]

After the season, the Pittsburgh Pirates purchased Whitehead's contract. Before Whitey had a chance to play for manager Frankie Frisch, his teammate from the Cardinal days, Uncle Sam came a calling. Whitehead was inducted into the Army at Fort Bragg, North Carolina. "Staff Sergeant Whitehead served as a physical instructor with the Army Air Force at Daniel Field, Georgia and Miami Beach, Florida. In 1945, he was player-coach for the Second Air Force at Buckley Field, Denver."[10] In 1946, after three years in the military, Burgess Whitehead returned to major league baseball, playing for the Pirates. Frisch was still the manager; the former Cardinal second baseman Whitehead was groomed to replace in the '30s. However, Whitey was up to his old tricks again for "breaking training rules." Frisch suspended and fined him $200. He was reinstated in April and played the remainder of the season sporadically, finishing with a .220 batting average in 55 games.

Not surprisingly, in January 1947, Whitehead was given his unconditional release ending his major league career with a lifetime batting average of .266. In a 1975 telephone interview with sports editor Bob Broeg, Whitehead said, "at

Carl Hubbell's request, I did go over to Jersey City in '47 to play second base next to a young shortstop the Giants were grooming."[11]

At Jersey City, Whitey played in 141 games and batted .257. He was third on the club with 26 doubles as Jersey City finished with an impressive 94-60 record. However, they were defeated by the Buffalo Bisons in the playoffs. Whitey returned to Jersey City the following season, but at age 38 plus injuries, he played in only 79 games but batted .284 with a poor club that finished with a 69-83 record and a seventh-place finish. That ended the baseball life of one of the most puzzling players of his era.

At the time of the interview with Broeg, Whitey and his two brothers had, ". . . a prosperous feed business and livestock auction in Windsor, N.C. Whitehead, married nearly 37 years to the former Ruth Lyon, has a son and daughter, but no grandchildren."[12]

In 1981 Whitehead was inducted into the North Carolina Sports Hall of Fame, joining such notables as Clyde King, Tony Cloninger, Roger Craig, Whitey Lockman, Jim "Catfish" Hunter, and brothers Gaylord and Jim Perry, to name a few. Then on Thanksgiving Day, November 25, 1993, Burgess Whitehead died at home of a heart attack at age 83. He was survived by his wife, Ruth, son Charles, daughter Susan, and four grandchildren.

After the Giants won three of four from the Phillies, Casey Stengel brought his Brooklyn club into the Polo Grounds for two games. It was Hubbell's first start of the season against the Dodgers at home. It was a dandy. Hub won in 12 innings, 5-4. The Giants scored the winning run on a bases-loaded walk to Kiddo Davis in the 12th. King Carl outlasted three Brooklyn hurlers, including starter Mungo. Hubbell's record was now 6-3 as the Giants clung to first place.

When the Giants moved to Ebbets Field four days later, Terry disregarded the so-called jinx and called on Hubbell to face Brooklyn and Mungo again. After seven innings, Hub was hanging on by his fingernails to a 1-0 lead but still in command, then the bottom of the eighth. Two doubles, two singles (one of which was a fluke) scored three runs and sent Hub to the showers. The Giants came right back and scored two runs to tie the game at three. That took Hub off the hook for the loss. The Dodgers scored in the bottom of the ninth for the 4-3 victory. Hubbell's record remained at 6-3. The Giants were now in second place, 2½ games in back of St. Louis, as the team hastened to catch the train for another western trip.

Hubbell relieved in the second game of the Chicago series. Castleman started and was roughed up for 11 hits and six runs in only four innings. Dick Coffman, who the Giants acquired from the Browns in November of '35, relieved Castleman and pitched a scoreless inning. When the Giants scored two in the top of the sixth, Chicago still led 6-4, but with three innings remaining, Terry, no doubt, believed his club could win the game. The logical choice was Hubbell to stop the Cubs from further scoring. Hubbell was horrible! There is no other way to explain his outing. In one-third of an inning, he allowed three hits, one walk, and two runs. Fitz relieved Hub and held Chicago in check, but it was too late as the Cubs won 8-5. Castleman (1-5) took the loss as Hub's record remained at 6-3.

The Giants moved on to St. Louis, where they split the four-game series. Hubbell won game two, 4-3. The Cardinals nicked Hub for single runs in the first three innings, tying the game at three all. From that point on, the ace left-hander didn't allow another run, as New York scored, what turned out to be, the winning run in the seventh on a ground ball that went through Durocher's legs. Hubbell's record was now 7-3.

After the St. Louis series, the Terrymen moved on to Cincinnati and lost both games, then moved into Forbes Field for a three-game series with the Pirates. Hubbell pitched the opening game and lost another squeaker, 3-2. How Hub lost was tragic. The Pirates Bill Swift and Hub were locked in a 2-2 duel until the bottom of the ninth with two out. The game looked like it was headed for extra innings until Hub's teammates failed him. Woody Jensen smacked a low liner to right field where Ott tried to make a shoestring catch to end the inning but when he realized he couldn't, pulled up. He was "handcuffed" as the ball skipped by him and Jensen pulled up at third. Fred Schulte was up next. He was already 3 for 4. He slapped a grounder towards right. Whitehead lunged for the ball, knocked it down but could not make a play at first as Jensen scored. It was the Giants' fourth consecutive loss on the road. Hubbell record was now 7-4

If that wasn't a heartbreaking moment, all Terry had to do was check the other scores around the league. The Cubs were beating up on the Boston Bees, 17-1 at Wrigley Field. But that's not even the good news for Cub fans. It was the ninth consecutive victory for the hard-charging Cubs, led by Charlie Grimm. His club wouldn't stop winning until they had run the streak to 15 (June 4-21). At the moment, Chicago was in second place as New York dropped to fourth.

It reminds one of the 1932 Cubs, led by newly appointed manager Grimm, who had zero experience leading a baseball team. When Grimm took over on August 3, the Cubs were five games back of the Pittsburgh Pirates. A little more than two weeks later, the Cubs, led by Grimm, put together a magical 14-game winning streak. It left the Cubs seven games in first place, not too shabby for a rookie manager. The Cubs went on to win the pennant, and it would be nice to say they went on to beat the Yankees in the World Series, but they didn't. The Yankees swept the Cubs in '32 when Ruth hit the controversial "called" home run off Charlie Root.

Back home at the Polo Grounds after their disastrous road trip, Terry was looking for his club to straighten out and play up to their abilities. Although the Giants beat Cincinnati 5-2 behind Hubbell's impeccable pitching, the club did not look sharp. As the *Times* reported, ". . . there was a woeful lack of finesse." Hubbell allowed seven hits and two runs (both unearned) as he walked only one batter and fanned five. His record was now 8-4.

If there was any joy in the Cincinnati clubhouse after the game, it probably was subdued, even though Kiki Cuyler collected his 2,000th hit off the great Carl Hubbell. The milestone came in the third when he doubled off the right-field wall driving in two runs. Cuyler would eventually finish his 18-year career with 2,299 hits, 1,305 runs, and an outstanding .321 batting average. He was elected to the Hall of Fame by the Veterans Committee in 1968.

After the two-game split with the Reds, the first-place Cardinals arrived at the Polo Grounds for three games, looking to increase their lead over the Giants. St. Louis won the opener 7-5 behind the pitching of Dizzy Dean (13-2). Schumacher started (7-4), lasted two innings, while Terry used four more pitchers only to lose eventually.

However, the next day Hubbell stopped the Cardinals for his ninth win of the season. King Carl needed help in the eighth inning from Coffman. With one out in the eighth, Hub gave up three singles (two of them scratch), a Bartell error, and then a clutch double plated three runs. Coffman stopped the rally but gave up two runs in the ninth. The final score was New York 7 St. Louis 6. Hubbell's record was now 9-4.

The offensive star of the game was manager Bill Terry who went 3 for 5, driving in two runs, one of which won the game. Since opening day, Terry had been alternating at first base with Sam Leslie due to his chronic knee problem, which flared up during spring camp. In fact, it was so bad Terry left camp to visit Dr. Spencer Speed in Memphis. He was the same physician who helped

Travis Jackson in 1933. "Happily, Dr. Speed said an operation wouldn't be necessary. He drained fluid from the knee, said that a couple of weeks of rest would suffice, and agreed to go back to the camp with Terry."[13] It would only be a matter of time before Terry would give into the knee and age.

Hubbell's ninth victory was the beginning of a New York Giant five-game winning streak. During this period, the Giants moved up to third place after a 4-3 win over Pittsburgh. In the first game of a doubleheader against the Pirates, Hub was buzzing along with a 3-1 lead thanks to Ott's 13th homer, a two-run blast in the first inning. However, Hub gave up a run in the eighth and a homer by Woody Jensen in the ninth to tie the game. But in the bottom of the ninth, Johnny Welch uncorked a wild pitch with the bases loaded with Giants to end the game. Hubbell went the distance giving up eight hits for the victory. His record was now 10-4.

During his next four starts, Hubbell and the Giants ran smack into some tough pitching. Hub would lose two and come away with a no-decision in the other two. During this period, the Giants would struggle to win consistently until the middle of July. During this span, they had losing streaks of 4, 6, and 3. It would put them under .500 at 40-41.

On June 28, the first game of a twin-bill, Chicago left-hander Larry French handcuffed the Giant hitters in a 3-0 shutout. He allowed seven hits, all singles except for Ott's double. As one writer said, "The Giants were helpless . . ." Hub pitched a decent game. In seven innings, he allowed five hits and two runs and surprisingly struck out seven. His record was now 10-5.

On July 2, the Giants defeated the Boston Bees at Braves Field 7-6 in a wild game they nearly blew. Hubbell started and was happily handed a six-run lead in the very first inning. With the Meal Ticket on the mound, one would think the game was all but over. Not so. Hub was hit hard in the second inning, giving up two runs. Then in the fifth, he beaned Billy Urbanski (who left the game), followed by a passed ball, a single, and a double for two runs. Terry quickly yanked Hub in favor of Gabler, who gave up a single for the third run of the inning. Boston scored again in the sixth, tying the game at 6-6. Once again, Master Melvin saved the day with a run-scoring double in the ninth. Gabler (2-2) was credited with the win, while Hub's record stayed at 10-5.

James P Dawson, writing for the *Times,* speculated that "Hubbell probably was unnerved by the toss which laid Urbanski low in the fifth. The ball landed on Bill's temple and dropped him. But he seemed all right after the game."[14]

Hubbell didn't pitch again until July 7 at the All-Star Game; this year played at Braves Field in Boston. Hub was selected for the fourth consecutive time and apprised himself well. The National League, after three straight losses, finally topped the American League. The final score was 4-3. Dean pitched the first three innings and didn't allow a hit or run. Hubbell worked the next three, giving up two hits and no runs. Both performances were not surprising, considering the two All-Stars combined for 50 victories during the season.

The National League scored two off Lefty Grove in the second inning and two more off Schoolboy Rowe in the fifth. The American League batted Curt Davis around for three runs in only two-thirds of an inning. Interestingly, rookie Joe DiMaggio started in right field, made two major errors, and took the collar, 0 for 5 at the plate. Nervous jitters? That's hard to believe when reflecting on his fabulous career.

Three days after the All-Star Game, Hubbell was back on the mound pitching against the St. Louis Cardinals. The redoubtable Hub, working in 102-degree heat, shut out the Cards for six innings and led 4-0. It looked like King Carl was headed for his third shutout of the season. It was not to be. The Cardinals scored a run in the seventh and three more in the eighth to tie the game. Gumbert replaced him and was yanked after allowing two hits in favor of Fitzsimmons, who was having a bad year. The game ended in the 13th on Frisch's double. Fitz took the 5-4 loss, and Hub received another no-decision.

It was the second loss at the hands of the Cardinals and was sinking the Giants further back of the league leaders. On top of the defeat, Giant fans received more bad news. Manager Bill Terry was back from another visit to Memphis for treatment of his left knee. Dr. Speed told Terry that an operation was necessary. The diagnosis was a "torn semi-lunar cartilage."

The *Times* reported, "Terry also has a broken bone in the little finger of his right, or glove hand. He wore a steel splint on the finger today but made light of this injury. 'A broken finger means nothing; the leg is what gets me down'"[15] Terry continued to play sporadically for the rest of the season, his last as a player.

The following day the Cardinals beat the Giants 9-3, making it a three-game sweep. It should have been a joyous day for St. Louis fans, but it was not. In the sixth inning, Whitehead came to bat with a runner on first and no out. According to author Robert Gregory in his biography of Dean, Whitehead ". . . smacked a line drive straight at ol' Diz's noggin. It struck him on the forehead, just above the right ear, caromed into left field, and as Dizzy slumped unconscious to the ground, the runner, Kiddo Davis, scored from first, and

Whitehead pulled into second with a double. The crowd of 10,000 was up and very still as players from each team ran to the mound to check on him. A few, detecting life, called for cold towels from the dugouts.

"I wanted base hits," said Whitehead, "but not that way. He was such a good friend and such a great player, and I feel just terrible."[16]

Whitehead, a former teammate of Dean and friend, was understandably upset. "A later medical bulletin would calculate that Diz was out for seven minutes, five on the field and two in the clubhouse before ice packs brought him around."[17] From the clubhouse, Frisch and the Cardinal players learned that Diz would be okay. Back on the field, they went in their half of the inning and promptly scored six runs to win the game and series.

In Chicago, the Giants continued their downward slide losing three of four. In the July 13 game, Hubbell lost 1-0 as the Giant bats went AWOL. Bill Lee, who blanked the Giants and Hub on June 28, was again almost unhittable as the Cubs moved into first place. Hub pitched a quality game. In six innings, he allowed two hits and one run, good enough to win most games, of course, assuming run support. His record was now 10-6.

The 1-0 loss at the hands of Chicago and Lee would be the last game Hubbell would lose for the rest of the season! Obviously, no one knew it at the time—Terry, Hubbell or his teammates, the opposition, Giant fans, no one. After one more relief appearance, the Meal Ticket would win 16 straight games without a loss. But let's not get ahead of this phenomenal story.

After Chicago, the floundering Giants moved to Pittsburgh for four games. The teams split the opening doubleheader. The Giants lost the first game in the bottom of the 10th inning. The game was tied 4-4. The bases were loaded, two out and a 2-0 count on Woody Jensen. Terry called on Hubbell, who relieved Fitz, who had relieved Castleman. Terry wanted his best control pitcher in this situation, for there was no place to put Jensen. Hubbell promptly walked Jensen! Go figure. The loss upset Terry to the point he dragged his painful and troubling knee, plus a broken finger on his glove hand, into the lineup in the nightcap. It was also an upsetting no-decision for Hub. His record remained at 10-6.

Terry inserting himself into the lineup unleashed the Giant bats. Terry led the assault, going 3 for 6 with three RBIs. In all, the Giants rapped out 16 hits, including Ott's 16th home run. The final score was 14-4. It also kicked off four consecutive victories, one of which Hubbell picked up.

It was the final game of the Pittsburgh series, and it looked like the Meal Ticket was back. Heck, it was more than that. He was close to perfection, blanking the Pirates on five hits and zero bases on balls for a 6-0 win. Only one runner reached second. It was the first of 16 straight and the third shutout of the season as the Giants wallowed in fifth place. Hub's record was now 11-6, and his consecutive win streak at one.

On one day's rest, Terry continued to call on his workhorse, Hubbell, to salvage the opening game of a doubleheader with Cincinnati. The Giants were leading 3-2, entering the bottom of the seventh. Fitzsimmons gave up a single, and Terry, lacking patience, gave Fitz the hook in favor of Coffman. The right-hander yielded a wild pitch and a double to tie the game. Two free passes later, Coffman was replaced by King Carl. Hub induced a double-play ball, and the Giants were out of the inning. The Giants scored in the top of the ninth for the 4-3 victory as Hub pitched 2 2/3 innings of hitless baseball. His record was now 12-6, and his consecutive win streak at two.

After a miserable 6-8 western road trip, back at the Polo Grounds, the Giants faced the Cardinals in a three-game series. The opener pitted Hubbell against Dizzy Dean. Surprisingly, it was their first meeting of the season, and it was a classic. The two best hurlers in the National League matched each other pitch for pitch. The Giants struck first in the bottom of the fifth when Mancuso homered to left. Not to be outdone, the next inning Pepper Martin homered. The game remained tied until the bottom of the 10th. What happened next sent the Giant fans home a happy bunch. With two out, Bartell homered to deep left to end the game and give the Giants a 2-1 victory. Hubbell's record was now 13-6, and his consecutive win streak at three. Moreover, the Giants were now closing in on Pittsburgh for third place.

The Giants moved into third place five days later when they split a double-header with Cincinnati while Brooklyn edged the Pirates in both games of their twin bill. Hubbell started the opener against the Reds and worked seven innings. He gave up ten hits and left the game trailing 4-2. Castleman relieved and did a marvelous job. He kept the Reds at bay with two scoreless and hitless innings. Then the bottom of the ninth and Hub's teammates scored three runs, capped by Leiber's game-winning RBI. If not for Castleman and the three-run outburst, Hubbell's streak would have ended at a puny three. The come-from-behind victory gave Hubbell's winning streak new life.

On July 30, King Carl tossed a magnificent game against the league-leading Chicago Cubs. Hub even spotted Jolly Cholly Grimm's club a run in the first inning, giving up a home run to lead-off batter Augie Galan. That's all the Cubs would get for the entire game. Patience was Hub's strong suit. It paid off in the sixth inning when the Giants scored three runs. The victory put the Giants back in third place, six games back of the Cubs. Hubbell's record was now 14-6, and his consecutive win streak at four.

On only two day's rest, Hubbell faced the tough Pirates and almost hurled another shutout. He allowed a hit in the first inning, a ball that bounced off Terry's glove. The Giants were leading 3-0. He didn't allow another hit until the ninth, when the Pirates scored two runs on three hits as Hub finished off the inning and the 3-2 victory. Considering Hubbell was pitching on two day's rest, he hurled one heck of a game. Hubbell's record was now 15-6 and his consecutive win streak at five. Also, the Giants were now 5½ games back of the Cubs.

Hubbell next pitched against the Phillies and had the last-place club fooled all afternoon. Hub, who has been pitching exceptionally well, even helped out with the bat. With the game tied at 2-2, Hub led off the top of the seventh with a line-drive single to right field and eventually scored when Whitehead singled to take the lead and game, 3-2. King Carl got the final six outs to record his 16th win against six losses. His consecutive win streak was at six. More importantly, the Giants were playing exceptional baseball. Since August 1, when they beat the Pirates 6-0, the Terrymen would win 21 of 22 games. Hubbell would play a major role in that streak.

But first, in St. Louis, the heat must have gotten to ol' Diz. Playing the Cubs in a crucial game for first place, a fight erupted between Dean and pitcher Tex Carleton. Here's the scene: Dean on the mound, two out, and Billy Herman at-bat. Dean suddenly left the mound and raced towards the Chicago dugout. Halfway there, he was greeted by Carlton (slated to pitch the next day). They met near the first baseline, and the fight began. They were separated by the umpires and players of both teams. Dean returned to the mound, astonishing the 30,000 plus fans. So, you ask, what's so unusual about that? Fights between players have been going on since the National League was formed in 1876.

Here's what was unique. Chicago manager Grimm, for whatever reason, pleaded with the umpires to keep Dean in the game! According to the umpires, upon Grimm's insistence, they acquiesced. Grimm's magnanimous gesture might have cost the Cubs the game as Dean went the distance in a 7-3 St. Louis victory.

According to author Gregory, Grimm called the umpires together and said, "Look, there's a big crowd here (31,040), and they came out to see Dizzy.

Don't disappoint them. Let him stay in the game. That fight didn't amount to anything." Several sportswriters disagreed. In particular, Dan Daniel, of the *World-Telegram,* among others, said, "Our boy Charlie was a sucker."[18]

The following day against Brooklyn, Terry sent Hubbell to the mound to rescue the 35-year-old Fitzsimmons. The Giants were leading 8-1 as Fitz entered the seventh inning, viewed by most as a comfortable lead. But when Fitz was tagged for a double and a run-scoring single, then walked a batter, Terry made his move. Hub stopped the Dodgers from scoring but gave up a run in the eighth for the save, his second, as the Giants won the game, 8-3. The fact that Terry brought in his Meal Ticket with an 8-2 lead clearly illustrates how tight the race is among the Cubs, Cardinals, and Giants. While the Giants were winning, the Cubs beat the Cards 6-4 and were back in first place. The Giants now trailed the Cubs by 3½ games. Unknown at the time, this victory kicked off a timely 15-game New York Giant winning streak.

Hubbell was called upon again the following day to pick up his third save of the season as he helped beat the Dodgers 2-1. Frank Gabler was brilliant, both on the mound and at the plate. The game was scoreless as the Giants entered the 12th inning at Ebbets Field. With two Giants on base, two out, Terry let Gabler hit. The young hurler whacked Mungo's first pitch for a bases-clearing triple to left-center.

In the bottom half of the inning, the leadoff hitter, Eddie Wilson, doubled. Immediately, that sent Terry out of the dugout, calling for the peerless one. Not at his best, Hub was touched for a run and saved by Ott's throw home, cutting off another run. Hubbell fanned the next batter to end the game. Here were the standings as of August 12.

TEAM	W	L	GB
St. Louis	66	43	–
Chicago	64	43	1
New York	62	46	3½

Before a crowd of 18,000 the following day, the Giants celebrated a victory over the Phillies, 6-4. Hubbell didn't pitch as Terry wisely rested his ace. With both the Cubs and Cards idle, the Terrymen picked up a half-game on both. In addition, the Giants also celebrated the National League's 60th anniversary at the Polo Grounds. It began with a "parade that started at 110th street and

Lenox Avenue, hard by the site of the first Polo Grounds and wound its way slowly through mechanized traffic over to Broadway, to 155th Street and the Polo Grounds."[19]

A second celebration was a little more elaborate, with another parade and the introduction of some old-timers, the oldest being 91-year-old Jim Mutrie. He was the first manager of the New York Giants. He and Terry shook hands at home plate as the crowd went wild. The game finally commenced as, "The New York Knickerbockers downed the Brooklyn Atlantics—revered club names carried by disguised youngsters of the present day—in a three-inning game by a score of 2 to 1, and laughs were enjoyed as today's fans saw a replica of a ball game of sixty years ago with all the attending 'atmosphere.'"[20]

With a whopping two day's rest, Hubbell started against the Phillies and won 4-1, his 17th victory against only six losses. The scoreboard was more interesting than the game, which Hub had under control. The board showed the Cardinals, and the Cubs lost their respective games, moving the Giants up a full game in the standings. This was a club, a month ago, that was in fifth place and now occupied third, one and a half games out of first. It was the Giants' fifth straight victory and King Carl's seventh consecutive win.

After the Giants swept the four games from the Phillies, the Brooklyn Dodgers arrived for three games. The Giants won the doubleheader 5-3 and 11-5, behind Fitz, and Smith in a dandy relief performance, which brought the Giants' winning streak to eight in a row. After losing both ends of the twin bill to their rivals, the Dodgers now had to face the red-hot Carl Hubbell. Surprisingly, there was a small crowd, but they were treated to plenty of excitement. The Dodgers Max Butcher was pitching a marvelous game, as was Hub. The score was 1-1 entering the bottom of the eighth when, in a matter of minutes, Ott hit his 27th homer and Ripple his sixth to give the Giants a 3-1 lead.

No doubt Stengel, on the verge of his club being swept, must have experienced some anxiety, for he questioned quite vigorously Ripple's homer. Apparently, Stengel complained that a fan had reached over the right-field wall and caught the ball before it would have hit the wall and should have been only a double, according to the ground rules. Umpire Lee Ballanfant disagreed, and when Casey continued to argue, Ballanfant gave him the old heave-ho to the delight of the Giant fans. It reminded one of the Yankees' Derek Jeter's home run in Game One of the 1996 ALCS against Baltimore when Jeffrey Maier deflected the ball.

Entering the top of the ninth with a 3-1 lead, it looked like a cinch win for Hubbell. But it was far from a cinch. Perhaps Hub tired or the delay caused by Ripple's controversial home run resulting in a loss of concentration. Whatever the reason, the lefty ace found himself with one out and the bases loaded. He got the ground ball he was looking for, but a hard slide by George Watkins at second resulted in a force out as a run scored. As the great ones usually do, Hubbell struck out the next hitter to end the game, 3-2. His record was now 18-6, and it was Hubbell's eighth consecutive victory as the Giants headed for a western swing sporting a nine-game winning streak of their own.

Jimmy Ripple, in his short seven-year major league career, as they say, was in the right place at the right time. After bouncing around in the minor leagues for seven years, the New York Giants bought the young outfielder from Montreal of the International League. As a rookie with the Giants in '36, Ripple finished the season batting .305 in 96 games and a trip to the World Series. In a losing cause, he played in five of the six games, batting .333 with an OBP of .467 as the Yankees won the Series. The following year he helped the Giants to another pennant, playing in 121 games and hitting .317. In the World Series, against the Yankees, in another losing cause, Ripple played in all five games. He batted .294 with a .400 on-base percentage.

Ripple played one more year with the Giants and then was traded to their rivals, the Dodgers, where he stayed until 1940 when Brooklyn placed him on waivers, and Cincinnati selected him. Ripple played in 35 games down the stretch for the Reds with a .307 batting average as the team won the National League pennant. Cincinnati beat the Detroit Tigers in seven games, with Ripple, a major contributor. In game two, Ripple's two-run homer helped pitcher Bucky Walters beat Detroit 5-3. After a see-saw battle, the Series rested on game seven. With the Tigers leading 1-0, entering the bottom of the seventh, Cincinnati's Frank McCormick doubled, followed by another two-bagger by Ripple to tie the game at 1-1. Then Jimmie Wilson bunted Ripple to third. Pinch-hitter Ernie Lombardi was given an intentional pass. Billy Myers, the next batter, drove Ripple home with the lead and eventual winning run. Playing in all seven games, Ripple batted .333 while driving in six runs, the most of any player on either team.

As mentioned earlier, Jimmy Ripple was one lucky ballplayer. Having zero control over his destiny, in seven major league seasons, the outfielder was an active and valuable player on three pennant-winning teams and one World Series club. Very few major league players can make that claim. Yes, Jimmy Ripple was in the right place at the right time.

After sweeping the Boston Bees three games, the first stop in the Giants' western trip was Cincinnati. However, before the raging Giants swept the Reds, the club moved into a first-place tie with the St. Louis Cardinals. While New York continued their outstanding play, the Cardinals began a poorly timed six-game losing streak.

In the second game of the Reds series, Hubbell won 6-5 with the help of a four-run Giant first inning. He pitched a masterful game, if not a courageous one. With a 6-3 lead in the bottom of the ninth, Cincinnati began hitting Hub, scoring two quick runs with only one out. The whiz from Meeker, Oklahoma, was not accustomed to a substantial lead. Most of the time, he pitched with a one-run advantage, at best. Then again, Hub could have tired. Whatever the cause, King Carl found his crown and retired the next two Reds for the victory. His record was 19-6, along with his ninth consecutive victory. More importantly, it was the Giants' 14th straight win, increasing their now first-place lead over the fading Cardinals to 2½ games . . . and 3½ over the Cubs.

The Giants' 15-game winning streak finally ended on August 29, losing to the Pittsburgh Pirates, 7-4. From that point on, the Terrymen would play slightly better than .500, while St. Louis and Chicago would play under .500. While the pennant race remained tight, there was little doubt manager Bill Terry was headed for his second National League title and his Meal Ticket headed for an exceptional year.

On August 30, before an overflow gathering of 45,000 boisterous fans at Wrigley Field, Hubbell beat the Cubs 6-1 in the first game of a doubleheader. Hubbell had reached the magic number, his 20th victory of the season and 10th consecutive win. He whipped Bill Lee, the right-hander, the last pitcher he lost to back on July 13, which must have made his 20th win extra rewarding. Hubbell allowed seven hits; four scattered over the first eight innings. He was still the master of pinpoint control, walking only one batter.

After winning three of four from the Cubs, the Giants moved to St. Louis for two crucial games. They lost the first 4-3 as their first-place lead narrowed to three games. But the next day, the margin was back to four as Hub beat Dizzy Dean, 2-1. As Dawson of the *Times* reported, "Hubbell, in as masterful an exhibition of pitching as he has provided this year, scored his eleventh straight, tying this season's major league record of [Bump] Hadley of the Yanks, and gained his twenty-first triumph [21-6] of the campaign, a four-hit effort."[21]

It was the most exciting game of the season. Entering the top of the ninth, with the score 1-1 and one out, Mancuso singled. Bartell doubled as Mancuso pulled up at third. Terry, in a strategic move, sent in the speedy Whitehead to run for Mancuso. In addition, Terry left Hubbell bat. As fate would have it, Hubbell hit a fly ball into short right-center that "fell only a scant few yards back of the clay infield." Whitehead gambled, took off from third as Martin fired the ball home. Catcher Virgil Davis put the tag on Whitehead but not before the speedster slid between his legs in a mighty crash.

The Giants surprisingly lost a three-game series to the lowly Boston Bees back home at the Polo Grounds. Hubbell quickly put a stop to the losing streak, beating Philadelphia 6-2. It was another superb effort by the redoubtable southpaw. He allowed seven hits and two runs as his record went to 22-6 and continued his now 12-game winning streak.

It appeared as the season was winding down and the race uncomfortably tight; Carl Hubbell kept pitching better and better. On September 11 against the Cubs, he tossed yet another masterpiece. With the game tied at 1-1 after 5 1/2 innings, the Giants scored three runs on a bases-clearing triple by Mancuso. That's all Hub needed as he tossed another four-hitter (all singles), winning 5-1. Adding to his dominance, King Carl faced the minimum of 21 batters over the last seven innings. Hub's record was now 23-6, along with a 13-game winning streak.

With the Giants now boasting a four-game lead over St. Louis and six over the Cubs, talk began to speculate about the number of victories New York needed to win the pennant. With 17 games remaining, the Giants would have to win 14 to clinch, coupled with St. Louis winning all 17 of their games. The immediate future was looking very bright for the New York Giants.

On September 14, the Giants beat St. Louis 7-5 before a crowd of 25,000. Gabler started for the Giants and gave up two runs in the first, but the Giants came roaring back with six in the third, led by Moore and Ripple. Both managers desperately wanted this game. Not to be outdone, the Cards scored two runs in the fourth, sending Gabler to the showers. Coffman replaced him to end the inning with the score of 6-4. Terry, taking no chances, called on Hubbell to begin the fifth. In the sixth, the partisan crowd was shocked when Hub allowed a home run by pitcher Ed Heusser to make the score 6-5. It was the only home run Heusser hit all season. The Giants got the run back in their half of the inning, making it 7-5, and that's where the game ended as Hubbell blanked the Cards in the last three innings. In all, Hub pitched five innings and allowed six hits, one run, and "received official credit for the victory." His record was now 24-6, and his consecutive win streak at 14.

So as not to go unnoticed, Dizzy Dean pitched the last 2 1/3 innings, retiring seven in a row. Some might question why Frisch didn't bring in Dean sooner. Perhaps they didn't realize it was Dean's fourth appearance in the last five games, covering three days. That alone tells how badly Frisch wanted to win this game and the series. The Cards now trailed the Giants by 4½ games with 13 to play, plus the two teams would not meet again this season.

Hubbell next pitched against Brooklyn at Ebbets Field and beat his archrival, Mungo, 9-1. It must have been quite boring and discouraging for anti-Giant fans as Hubbell spun another magical four-hitter. He walked one and fanned five as the Giants increased their first-place lead to five and a half games over the Cardinals and six ahead of the Cubs.

In the top of the fifth, the Giants erupted for five runs on Ott's 33rd homer with a runner on, breaking the 1-1 tie. That's all Hub needed, even though his teammates tacked on three more runs before the game was over. His record was now 25-6, and his consecutive winning streak reached 15. All the Giants had to do now was win four of their remaining nine games to capture the National League flag.

The Giant/Hubbell victory wasn't the only celebration that occupied New York baseball fans. In the Bronx, Mayor La Guardia presented an inscribed Morocco-leather scroll, marking the 1,800th straight game Lou Gehrig played. His unprecedented streak began June 1, 1925, when he pinch-hit for Pee Wee Wanniger. As most baseball fans know, the "Iron Man" played in 2,130 consecutive games. Cal Ripken Jr. broke it with an unbelievable number of 2,632.

Hubbell pitched his last game of the regular season on September 23 against the Phillies and won 5-4. He was staked to a five-run lead but was touched up for four runs, three in the eighth and one in the ninth, to hold on to the win. King Carl gave up eight hits and, as he often does, walked only one batter. He finished the season with an awesome record of 26-6. His consecutive winning streak reached 16.

The *Times* had high praise for the Giant's top pitcher, reporting, "Hubbell, in bagging his sixteenth straight today, established himself beyond question as one of the greatest hurlers of modern times. His is the longest winning streak to be hung up in the National League since Rube Marquard's memorable nineteen in a row in 1912, wiping out the hitherto second-best mark since then of fifteen by Dazzy Vance . . ."[22]

The following day, the Giants clinched the National League pennant behind the solid pitching of Schumacher (11-13), who was having an off-year. It was a thrilling game, won in the 10th inning when Schumacher singled home Jackson on a close play at the plate. The Giants had won the pennant in one of the most outstanding comebacks in baseball. They ended the season with a record of 92-62, five games ahead of the Cubs and Cardinals (tied for second).

Strangely, the expected celebration was not forthcoming. For whatever reason, the players were taking the victory in stride. Perhaps it was the concern of facing the Yankees, their World Series opponent, across the river. The Bronx Bombers had clinched the American League pennant on September 9 in dominant fashion, winning both ends of a doubleheader with the Cleveland Indians, 11-3 and 12-9. The overpowering Yanks finished the season with a 102-51 record, 19½ games ahead of second-place Detroit.

Now it was time for the much-anticipated World Series between two New York rival clubs; the Giants managed by Bill Terry and the Yankees by Joe McCarthy. The last time these two clubs met in the Fall Classic was in 1923 when the Yankees won their first-ever World Series, led by the immortal Babe Ruth. And the fare for the subway series still cost a nickel. Fan enthusiasm and interest could not be higher, so large crowds were anticipated at both the Polo Grounds and Yankee Stadium. Taking a close look at the matchups between the two clubs, it was no surprise the Yankees were heavily favored to win the Series. It simply boiled down to the Yankees crushing and devastating offensive attack versus the Giant's invincible and unassuming, Carl Hubbell.

Position by position comparisons revealed what Terry was up against.

CATHER	BA	HR	RBI
Dickey, Yankees	.362	22	107
Mancuso, Giants	.301	9	63

FIRST BASE	BA	HR	RBI
Gehrig, Yankees	.354	49	152
Terry, Giants	.310	2	39
Leslie, Giants	.295	6	54

SECOND BASE	BA	HR	RBI
Lazzeri, Yankees	.287	14	109
Whitehead, Giants	.278	4	47

THIRD BASE	BA	HR	RBI
Rolfe, Yankees	.319	10	70
Jackson, Giants	.230	7	53

SHORTSTOP	BA	HR	RBI
Crosetti, Yankees	.288	15	78
Bartell, Giants	.298	8	42

LEFT FIELD	BA	HR	RBI
Powell, Yankees	.302	7	48
Moore, Giants	.316	7	63

CENTER FIELD	BA	HR	RBI
DiMaggio, Yankees	.323	29	125
Leiber, Giants	.279	9	67
Ripple, Giants	.305	7	47

RIGHT FIELD	BA	HR	RBI
Selkirk, Yankees	.308	18	107
Ott, Giants	.329	33	135

It didn't take a genius or a bookie to figure out the Yankees had a huge advantage at the plate. At every position, the Yankees were superior except for Jo-Jo Moore in left field, who had the advantage over Jake Powell (not by much) and Ott over Selkirk. As a team, the Yankees hit .300. As author Hynd quipped, "Watching the Yankees in operation, one gained the impression that even the groundkeeper could come off the bench, take a couple of pitches, then line a double to right."[23] They also scored 1,065 runs, 323 more than the Giants.

There was also a confidence builder lurking in the background. The Yankees had won 12 straight World Series games, entering Game One of this Series.

The streak began with the 1927 Pirates and continued with the 1928 Cardinals and the Cubs in 1932.

Pitchers			
YANKEES	**W**	**L**	**ERA**
Ruffing	20	12	3.85
Pearson	19	7	3.71
Broaca	12	7	4.24
Gomez	13	7	4.39
Hadley	14	4	4.35
Malone	12	4	3.81
GIANTS	**W**	**L**	**ERA**
Hubbell	26	6	2.31
Schumacher	11	13	3.47
Smith	14	13	3.78
Fitzsimmons	10	7	3.32
Gumbert	11	3	3.90
Gabler	9	8	3.12

The Giants' pitching staff had a 3.46 earned run average compared to the Yankees elevated 4.17. Was this an advantage? It would be difficult to determine considering different leagues, teams, and players. Clearly, Hubbell was the best pitcher between the two teams. The pitching burden for the Giants was Hubbell's. Hub was arguably the best pitcher in baseball in 1936. However, there is just so much you can ask from one talented player. Remember, it's a team effort. Some followers were even strategizing that Hubbell could pitch three games. It would depend on how effective Schumacher, Fitz, or Gumbert (who had a worthy season) would be when facing the Yankees' dangerous lineup.

There was also another way of looking at the upcoming World Series that just might favor the Giants, as reported by Dan Daniel in *The Sporting News*. On July 15, the Giants were 11 games behind the first-place Cubs and came back to capture the pennant. It was no easy task, similar to the Boston Braves in 1914. The Braves were in last place on July 4, 15 games back, and won the pennant. The Giants had the momentum. Could lightning strike twice in the National League?

The other part of Daniel's theory was the Yankees won easily, coasting the latter part of the season. Perhaps, the edge and spark were gone. When Lou Gehrig heard about the theory, he laughed. He said, "In fact, I would rather go into a series from an easy race like ours than from a tough, nerve-racking affair such as the Giants have been going through."[24]

There is only one way to find out who is correct, as the umpire bellows, "play ball."

Game 1, September 30, 1936, at Polo Grounds

The Meal Ticket lived up to his well-deserved nickname and reputation. He handcuffed the mighty Yankee hitters, beating them, 6-1. The Yankees, except for Jake Powell (3 for 4), were helpless against Hubbell's screwball and pinpoint control. Hub allowed seven hits, walked one batter, and surprisingly struck out eight. A Giant outfielder made not a putout, that's how dominating Hubbell was. He allowed one bad pitch all afternoon, on a rain-soaked field, which was to George Selkirk who homered in the third. The Giants clinched the game before more than 39,000 in the eighth inning, scoring four runs. The victory broke the Yankees Series winning streak at 12. More importantly, it allowed Terry to pitch Hubbell two more times should the Series go seven.

Game 2, October 2, 1936, at Polo Grounds

Commissioner Landis postponed game two due to wet grounds, but it was played the next day. One would expect Terry to be pleased since it gave Hubbell another day of rest. With President Franklin Delano Roosevelt and his entourage of 48 looking on, the Yankees showed the 43,000 plus why they were favored to win the World Series. The Bronx Bombers unloaded on starter Schumacher for two runs in the first and two more in the second before Terry yanked him for Smith, and then the parade began. In all, the Giants used five pitchers during the game with a final score of 18-4. The Yankees scored seven runs in the third inning, led by Lazzeri's grand slam, which tied Elmer Smith's feat for Cleveland, when he hit a bases-loaded homer in Game Five of the 1920 World Series against Brooklyn. The Yankees set or tied a dozen records during this massacre. With all the runs, Lefty Gomez coasted to an easy victory.

Game 3, October 3, 1936, at Yankee Stadium

The following day the teams moved across the river to Yankee Stadium for game three. After mauling the Giants the previous day 18-4, the Yankees edged the

Giants 2-1 in a tight game. Veteran knuckleballer Fitzsimmons was the hard-luck loser, allowing only four hits while the Giants racked up 11 off of Hadley and Malone. The crowd of 64,842 was the largest ever to see a World Series game. They watched Gehrig homer in the second inning and Ripple in the fifth. That was all the scoring until the fateful bottom of the eighth. With runners on first and third, Crosetti won the game when he bounced a single off of Fitz's glove as Powell scored from third. Some speculated that if Fitz let the ball go by, Whitehead would have had an easy play for the third out, and Powell not score. Gloomy Giant fans cheered up as best they could when they discovered Hubbell was pitching game four.

Game 4, October 4, 1936, at Yankee Stadium
The record crowd of 64,842 the day before at Yankee Stadium lasted about 24 hours as 66,669 baseball fans poured into the Stadium to see Hubbell perform his magic. But it was not to be. The rabbit was out of the hat. The quiet left-hander from Meeker did not have enough in that wonderful left arm to stop the Yankees juggernaut as the Giants went down to defeat 5-2. Hub allowed a run in the second and three more in the third, led by Gehrig's second homer of the Series, a two-run blast.

The Yankees Monte Pearson pitched a remarkable game, especially considering the right-hander was a doubtful starter before the Series. He had injured his back during the last week of the season. His healing was speedy and thorough since he pitched the entire game. He allowed seven hits (all singles), two runs, and whiffed seven Giants. The victory capped a fine season by Pearson, who finished with a 19-7 record. Terry and the Giants were now on the brink of elimination.

Game 5, October 5, 1936, at Yankee Stadium
What a difference a day or two makes. Hal Schumacher, who was banged around in game two, pitched one of the greatest clutch games of his young career. With elimination staring the Giants in the face, the fastball hurler gave up ten hits, walked six, but still managed to limit the Yankees to four runs in 10 innings. He struck out an incredible ten batters, mainly using his curveball, he admitted to the press. And there was no bigger out for him than in the bottom of the ninth, with the game tied at 4-4. Pat Malone, who relieved Ruffing in the seventh inning, led off with a single. Malone was forced at second when Crosetti failed to advance him. Then Rolfe forced Crosetti at second on a

grounder to Whitehead. DiMaggio walked, putting runners on first and second as the mighty Gehrig came to the plate. Keep in mind, Gehrig finished the season with 49 home runs. He ran the count to three and two as the fans began buzzing. On the next pitch, Gehrig grounded to Whitehead to end the inning, as Giant fans gave a collective sigh of relief.

In the top of the 10th. Moore bounced the first pitch from Malone into the left field stands for a ground-rule double. Bartell sacrificed Moore to third. On a 3-2 count, Terry belted a long fly to DiMaggio in left-center as Moore tagged and scored the winning run. The Yankees were retired easily in the tenth. Final score: Giants 5 Yankees 4.

After the game, the Giants' clubhouse was a boisterous, congratulatory scene. The center of attention was Schumacher and Moore. Cameramen and sportswriters surrounded the two as flashbulbs were popping, and questions were fired at each. One of the questions directed at Schumacher was about the tense moment in the bottom of the ninth. Was he "worried" when the Yankees had the winning run in scoring position and Gehrig coming up? The star of the day replied, " I didn't have time to think about that. All I had to do was get him out. We had to get those fellows out a lot of times to stay in that game."[25] Now back to the Polo Grounds and a friendlier crowd.

Game 6, October 6, 1936, at Polo Grounds

Despite Schumacher's outstanding pitching the day before, all it did was delay the inevitable. The Yankees routed the Giants 13-5, although the final score is somewhat misleading. The game was much closer. In fact, the Yankees only had a slim 6-5 lead after eight innings. Gomez had started for the Yankees and was relieved in the seventh. The trio of Ott, Moore, and Terry drove in all five runs to keep the game close and the Series alive. The Yankees ninth was the killer. Dick Coffman began the fateful ninth for the Giants after relieving Castleman, who relieved starter Fitzsimmons. Coffman gave up three hits, a walk, and five runs and didn't get an out. Mercifully, Coffman was relieved by Gumbert, who was slightly better. He allowed two hits, three walks, and two more runs to complete the ninth inning fiasco. Johnny Murphy retired the Giants in order in their half of the ninth. It was the fifth Yankee title under Jacob Ruppert's ownership and second for manager McCarthy as a Yankee.

In his first interview after losing the World Series, Terry was quite blunt about the club's future needs. He was emphatically clear he needed a third baseman. Travis Jackson was finished, and he knew it too, claimed Terry. He also said Johnny McCarthy, a recent purchase from Newark, would be given a chance to be the starting first baseman in 1937. Terry was also looking for a left-handed batting catcher to help rest Mancuso.

Players from both the Giants and Yankees headed home for relaxation. Specifically, Moore was traveling south to Gause, Texas. He had a farm that needed serious repair. Ott was headed to New Orleans, his current residence, while Carl Hubbell was on his way to the Oklahoma City Golf and Country Club as the guest of honor. Athletes from all sports were to attend to pay homage to Hub and the extraordinary season he had. In the afternoon, Hub visited his hometown of Meeker for another homecoming party. It was reported 3,000 fans jammed into Meeker, a town of under 600, to see their hero. The Meeker town team, in which Hubbell pitched four innings, defeated a club of semi-pro stars, 2 to 1. Cy Blanton of the Pittsburgh Pirates pitched for the semi-pro club. He is a native of Shawnee, Oklahoma.

Several days later, the Baseball Writers Association of America chose Hubbell as the National League Most Valuable Player. It was his second MVP award. He was chosen in 1933. The 1936 MVP award was unanimous and deservedly so. To summarize, here's what Hubbell and his nasty screwball accomplished as he led the Giants' pitching staff and team into the World Series:

Led the league with 26 victories and only six losses.
Led the league with a .813 winning percentage.
Led the league with a 2.31 ERA.
Pitched in 304 innings.
Concluded the 1936 season winning 16 straight.
Threw three shutouts.
Saved three games.
The six losses were by scores of 2-1 (lost in the 17th on two misplays) 1-0,
    5-3, 3-2, 3-0, 1-0.

Now the question before Bill Terry and the New York Giants was: could they repeat in 1937? Equally important, could Carl Hubbell duplicate the phenomenal season of '36?

II

Most Wins, Highest WP, Most Strikeouts

"I KNEW I COULDN'T HAVE WON THOSE GAMES [24 CONSECUTIVE] WITHOUT THE HELP OF THOSE OTHER SEVEN MEMBERS BEHIND ME AND THE MAN BEHIND THE PLATE. THEY DESERVE THE CREDIT."

As he did in past years, Terry set out early to improve his club for the 1937 season. He was set with Whitehead at second, Bartell at short, and an outfield, from left to right of Moore, Ripple, and Ott. Terry's hope for a left-handed hitting catcher never materialized, so Mancuso and Danning split the catching duties throughout the season.

The pitching staff would remain intact. Hubbell, Schumacher, Gumbert, Castleman, and Coffman all returned for another pennant-winning season. There was one important addition, a 6'5" skinny southpaw named Cliff Melton. The Giants purchased Melton from Baltimore of the International League on July 27 of the previous season. He would team up with Hub to make a dynamic duo.

Tom Meany, writing for *The Sporting News* in their April 8, 1937, issue, had high praise for the rookie. "With the rough spots ironed out of his control, Melton has everything to make the grade. There's a real buzz to his fast one, and his curve is good enough to get him by, too. Everything depends upon his control, and that has been letter-perfect . . ."[1] Terry liked what he witnessed at spring camp and was planning on using Melton as his second left-hander in the starting rotation.

Filling the third and first base positions would pose a difficult hurdle. True to his word, Terry filled the hot corner on December 8, 1936. The Phillies sent

Lou Chiozza to New York for shortstop George Scharein and $25,000 in cash. For the Phillies in 1936, Chiozza hit .297 in 144 games. He played second, third and was even used in center field but lacked power at the plate.

Chiozza would turn out to be a mediocre player for the Giants. In 117 games, the man from Tallulah, Louisiana, would bat a paltry .232. He played two more years for Terry as a utility man and then was out of major league baseball for good. But he did leave one mark of distinction. According to Mike Shatzkin, editor of *The Ballplayers*, "Chiozza became the first man to bat in a major league night game when he led off for the Phillies in Cincinnati on May 24, 1935."[2]

Other than cash, Terry didn't give up much for Chiozza. Scharein would play for the Phillies the next three years, mostly at short. Then in 1940, after seven games, he was sent to the Yankees to complete an earlier deal. He never played for the Yankees but was relegated to the minor leagues until 1950. His lifetime batting average, as a major leaguer, was a weak .240.

Terry's promise to give minor leaguer Johnny Murphy more playing time met with contrary rumors that the Chiozza trade was only a partial deal. There was more to come between the two clubs. Supposedly, Hank Leiber and a rookie first baseman (although not named, it could have been Murphy) to the Phillies for Dolf Camilli. It would have solved Terry's first base problem, but it never happened. The following year Camilli was traded to the Brooklyn Dodgers, where the slugger starred for the next six seasons.

The first base problem continued to linger before spring training. Terry wanted to "conditionally retire." In other words, return to playing when he desired. Legally, that didn't fly. "As a result, Stoneham drew up a new contract that somehow got around the legal technicalities; Terry would officially quit for good, but Horace Stoneham would maintain the freedom to hire him again as a player if necessary. Terry signed the new paper and went home, where he made adjustments to the spring training schedule."[3]

In 1937, the spring training location became a new experience for the New York Giants. They were to begin workouts and games in Havana, Cuba. The plan was to stay in Havana for 3½ weeks, then play a few games in Florida and finally hook up with the Cleveland Indians in Gulfport for their annual fine-tuning, on the way north for opening day.

It sounded wonderful until Terry took ill and was fighting a heavy cold in Memphis. He wouldn't be there when the team arrived. That responsibility was left to secretary Eddie Brannick until Terry arrived. The next problem that arose was the holdout of Hank Leiber because he didn't want to travel by train and boat to Havana. He preferred the more modern convenience of flying. The answer from Stoneham was an emphatic no. Also holding out were Bartell, Moore, and Danning but not for the reason of travel inconvenience. Eventually, all three signed when Terry arrived and added some clout to the negotiations.

After numerous workouts in beautiful Havana weather, the time came for the Giants to face the local competition and play baseball. It so happened, the first game fell on Independence Day, a Cuban National Holiday. A crowd of 7,000 watched the festivities, including a military band and a 7-4 victory over a sloppy Giant club that committed four errors.

In the next game, the Havana club clobbered New York, 9-1. When the Giants lost their third consecutive game, this time by a score of 6-1, instead of being upset, Terry was quite calm. He even took time to praise the Havana pitcher, Ramon Bragana, who allowed only six hits in the victory.

The Giants finally got around to winning a game, beating a group of Cuban amateurs, 7-2. Officially, they were called the Fortuna Sporting Club. Pitching for the Giants was a right-hander by the name of Hubbell. No, it's not a typo. He was the brother of the Meal Ticket. John pitched three innings, did well until the ninth, when he gave up two runs. The genes in the Hubbell family stopped at Carl, for John never played in a major league game.

Two days later, the Almendares professionals shut out the Giants, 4-0. The following day, Hub made his first appearance and performed credibly, as did his successors, Fitzsimmons and Gumbert. The final score was 7-3, led by Danning's home run in the fifth when the Giants scored all three runs for the easy win. The final game of the Havana series was against the All-Star team, made of Cuban professionals. It ended in a 1-1 tie. In all, the Cuban players won the series, four games to two and one tie.

In a lengthy interview, at least for Hubbell, a man of few words, with Drebinger of the *Times*, the ace left-hander discussed the time in Havana, his curveball, and pitching changes. When asked about the weather and training in Havana, Hub was forthright. " Yes, it has been hard work out there under that sun, but I'm certain it has put all of us in wonderful shape. I think, though, that two weeks of this would have been enough. You know, we still have five more weeks of training after we leave here."[4]

When the subject switched to possibly developing a new pitch to fool batters, the unobtrusive and modest Hubbell replied candidly. "No, I'm not tinkering with anything new this year. Not that I may not need something new before the season is over. But I'd rather wait to see what the batters will do to me before I start working on something else. You know, it takes a lot out of a fellow my age to start working on a new delivery, and I want to be sure of what I want to try before making any attempt.

"I put in a lot of work perfecting my curveball the last two years. I had to. In 1934 the batters convinced me the screwball no longer was enough to get by on alone. It was getting to be old stuff. So, I worked on the curve, and last year I think I threw more curves than screwballs."[5]

The Giants returned to Gulfport, Mississippi, to begin their traditional 18-game barnstorming series with the Cleveland Indians. They headed north via New Orleans, playing Cleveland in Mississippi, Georgia, Alabama, Arkansas, Texas, and Oklahoma until they arrived in their respective cities for opening day.

The big attraction in 1937, during the barnstorming trip, was an 18-year-old fireballing right-hander by the name of Bob Feller. The young phenom made his first appearance against the Giants in Vicksburg, Mississippi. A local crowd of 4,000 packed the ballpark in biting cold weather to see this young farm boy from Van Meter, Iowa, face the pennant-winning New York Giants. Rapid Robert, as he later would be called, didn't disappoint. He pitched three innings, baffling the Giants with his blinding speed. He allowed no hits and struck out six, including all three Giants in the third inning. Feller hit a batter and walked one. Hubbell also made his debut against the Indians, giving up a run in his three innings of work. The fans were there, however, to see Feller as Cleveland won 4-2.

As expected, the newest pitching sensation created a great deal of talk among the Giant players. Surprisingly, the reactions were mixed. Bartell and Leslie thought Brooklyn's Mungo was faster; Whitehead and Schumacher praised the youngster. Hubbell, always straightforward in his remarks concerning his peers, thought Feller was "mighty good." He should become "a very great pitcher." Indeed, he would. He became one of the greats.

Bob Feller pitched for the Cleveland Indians for 18 years, winning 266 and losing 162 games. He lost three years to military service and, when he returned, pitched in only 72 innings in 1945. If not for this interruption, he would have easily had more than 300 victories. Feller led the league six times in wins and seven times in strikeouts. He claims his strikeout records were due to his curve and slider. Early in his career, he struggled with his control, leading the league in walks four times. Throughout his career, the hard-throwing right-hander was the ace and mainstay of the Cleveland pitching rotation. It came as no surprise he was elected to the Hall of Fame in 1962, in his first year of eligibility.

Before Feller pitched his next game against the Giants, Hub pitched in Shawnee, Oklahoma, to a gathering of 5,000, many from his nearby hometown of Meeker. Despite Oklahoma's famous dust storms, Hub dazzled his admirers, even though it was not his turn to pitch. He struck out four in three innings but did give up a home run to Hal Trosky. The Giants won 8-7.

Hubbell and Feller faced each other again, this time in New Orleans, where each pitched five innings of shutout baseball to the delight of an overflow crowd of 13,000. All the Giants could manage off of Feller's fastball were four walks, as he fanned six. Feller's wildness kept him in trouble in several innings, but his escape mechanism was the ability to throw the fastball by hitters. Hub, as usual, gave up a few hits but was never in trouble. Cleveland won 2-1.

On April 8, Feller, now called the "mound marvel" by the press, held the Giants hitless for three innings again. This time he walked three and struck out four. In the three games he pitched against New York, which totaled 11 innings, the farm boy has yet to give up a hit. The Giants won 9-2 behind Schumacher's excellent seven innings of pitching.

Well, it appears Cleveland manager, Steve O'Neill, went to the well once too often when he selected Feller to face the Giants for the fourth time. To put it bluntly, the 18-year-old was hammered. He gave up eight hits, five runs, capped by Mancuso's home run with a man on. Despite Feller's poor performance, the Indians still won the game, 8-6. The Giant's newest addition to the rotation, Cliff Melton, was even worse than the celebrated youngster.

The final game of the 18-game series was played at the Polo Grounds. It featured Cleveland's inexperienced star in the making against the Giants' veteran magician, Carl Hubbell. The anticipated meeting of Feller and Hubbell drew 31,486 fans. It was the largest ever at the Polo Grounds to witness a pre-season exhibition game. The fans got their monies worth . . . and more.

After eight innings trailing 4-1, Hubbell left the game on a three-run homer by Moose Solters. In the last of the eighth, the Giants scored a run off the youngster, the result of three walks, cutting the Cleveland lead to 4-2. That was all for Feller. Ironically, the Giants scored three in the ninth to win the game 5-4 on a hit by Moore. The thrilling ending was a bonus for the New York fans, but the main attraction was the once-in-a-lifetime match-up of two Hall of Famers, one soon to be out of baseball, the other an emerging super-star. Against the Giants, Bob Feller pitched extremely well, considering his age and inexperience. In five games against the National League champions, he pitched 27 innings and struck out 37 batters. Not bad for a kid of 18.

After 18 games between the two teams, traveling "randomly across the map," it ended in both clubs winning nine games each. It was still a great success, regardless of Hubbell's belief the training session was too long. "It was also reported that New York's training season had been the most financially successful ever by a team. Counting the games in Havana and Florida, before hooking up with Cleveland, the Giants drew a total of approximately 175,000 paying customers."[6]

The 1937 season finally began with a great deal of interest focused on Hubbell's 16-game winning streak. Hub didn't pitch opening day, so Giant fans would have to be patient. Terry chose Schumacher, who beat Brooklyn 4-3 in the usual rowdy atmosphere these two clubs generated among fans. Hubbell pitched the following day, at the Polo Grounds, blanking the Boston Bees 3-0 on three singles. His consecutive game winning streak was now at 17.

Before a Ladies Day crowd of 14,512 at the Polo Grounds, King Carl yawned through his second victory of the season, beating Brooklyn 11-2. Some of the more faint-hearted in the stands were upset and possibly scared in the first inning when Brooklyn scored two runs on Heinie Manush's home run with a runner on and two out. But that's all Hub would yield for the next eight innings. In the meantime, by the fourth inning, the Giants exploded for nine runs led by Ripple's grand slam. From that point on, Hubbell coasted to his second win of the early season. His consecutive game winning streak was now at 18.

On May 4, King Carl won his third game of the season, beating Cincinnati and Paul Derringer at the Polo Grounds, 7-6. Hub needed help, and he received it big time from Harry Gumbert for his marvelous clutch relief effort. The game began as a laugher. By the end of five innings, the Giants and Hub were ahead 7-0. Most of the damage was done in the third inning when the Giants scored six runs, led by Bartell's two-run homer. It looked like Hub would sleepwalk the rest of the way as this was his usual practice with big leads. Then the fifth inning arrived. It turned out to be an inning in which he wasn't fooling anyone. In lightning speed, the Reds scored four runs on a triple, walk, three singles, and an error by Chiozza! The score was now 7-4 as Hubbell entered the top of the seventh. He weakened once more, allowing two runs before Terry called for Gumbert to get the final out. In the next two innings, Gumbert slammed the door shut on Cincinnati, not allowing a batter to reach first and preserving Hubbell's winning streak at 19.

This victory brought out the record books showing Hubbell had tied Rube Marquard's record of 1912 and Tim Keefe in 1888. Both played for the Giants and accomplished the streak in one season. Since then, Roy Face of the Pittsburgh Pirates ran off 22 consecutive victories in 1958-1959.

Four days later, Hubbell carved out a new record before a large and enthusiastic crowd of 36,529 at the Polo Grounds. He waltzed through a 4-1 victory over the Chicago Cubs, defeating his nemesis from last year, Bill Lee. The Giants scored two in the seventh and two in the eighth on Bartell's homer with a runner on. Hub had the Cubs shutout until the ninth when Frank Demaree homered. It was Hubbell's 20th straight victory. His record this season is 4-0.

On May 13, Hubbell and the Giants beat first-place Pittsburgh 5-2, maintaining his perfect 5-0 record. It was also his 21st consecutive victory. Again, King Carl controlled the game allowing six hits, two runs, and zero free passes. If not for Arky Vaughan, who hit a pair of homers, the Meeker marvel would have blanked the Pirates. The victory put the Giants four games back of the league leaders.

Hubbell would next pitch on the road as the Giants embarked on their first western swing, meeting the St. Louis Cardinals in a three-game series. The Giants lost the first game, 4-3, setting up one of the great pitching match-ups of the 1930s, Carl Hubbell versus Dizzy Dean. So, on May 19, when the two best pitchers in the National League met, they drew an unusually large weekday crowd of 26,399. The unsuspecting fans were privy to two events for the price of one. The game began innocently enough, with Hub giving up a second-inning home run to the Cardinals Ducky Medwick for a 1-0 lead. For the next three innings, the shaky lead held up, and the fans settled in for the pitching excellence they anticipated. In the top of the sixth inning, the Giants scored three runs off Dizzy. Here's how it happened. Whitehead led off with a single and was sacrificed to second by Hubbell. Up next was Bartell. Dean half turned to second from the stretch, checking Whitehead, and then threw home to Bartell, who flied to left. At least, that's what appeared to happen. But umpire George Barr saw the play differently. ". . . Barr ruled out the play and called a balk on Dean for failing to pause a full second in his delivery, as prescribed by the rules."[7]

After Dean and the Cards objected vociferously, Bartell went back to home plate, and Whitehead moved to third. On the next pitch, Bartell lined a pitch to right field where Pepper Martin dropped the ball, allowing Whitehead to score. Singles by Chiozza and Moore plated two more runs as the Giants took a 3-1 lead.

Dean, known to be strong-willed, hot-headed, and an emotional individual, was angry and frustrated. In retaliation, he began employing "chin music" and the "brush back" pitch on almost every Giant batter as they ducked and twisted in self-defense. It all came to a head in the ninth inning when Ripple hit the dirt as a Dean pitch narrowly missed him. As Ripple got up and dusted himself off, he glanced into the Giant dugout and nodded as if giving his teammates a signal. The next pitch, "Ripple sent a rather sharp bunt just inside the first baseline. The ball bounded to second baseman Jimmy Brown who prepared to throw it to Jack [Johnny] Mize. But Dean, who apparently no longer had any business in the play, also was at first, determinedly blocking Ripple's path to the bag."[8]

What happened next, one could easily predict. Dean and Ripple crashed into each other, and fists began to fly. Both benches emptied, and fights broke out all over. Off to the side, Mancuso and Mickey Owen had their own private bout. The melee was so out of control, the umpires called in the St. Louis Police to regain authority. The umpires ruled Dean and Ripple were allowed to stay in the game, a very strange decision. However, Mancuso and Owen were ejected and fined the next day by the league president, Ford Frick, another weird decision. The game ended with the Giants winning 4-1. Hubbell's record was now 6-0. His consecutive game winning streak was 22.

The Terrymen continued their western swing to Chicago, splitting the two-game series. Schumacher lost the first contest, and Castleman won the second game, 3-2. Ott accounted for all the runs with a three-run homer in the first inning. The victory began a timely eight-game winning streak as New York moved into Pittsburgh, where they swept the two-game series. Hubbell won the second game, 4-3, but came much too close to blowing a 4-1 lead entering the bottom of the eighth inning.

The hero of the day was right-hander Dick Coffman, who faced one batter and saved Hub's winning streak. In the eighth, the Pirates roughed up Hub for two runs on a single, triple, single, to cut the Giants' lead to 4-3. In the ninth, Hubbell ran into trouble once more. With two out and Pirates on first and third, Terry decided Hub had enough and called on his rookie, 6'5" Cliff Melton, to get one out. However, the man standing at the plate was Paul "Big Poison" Waner, a .354 hitter in 1937. Perhaps Melton was nervous. If he wasn't, he should have been. Anyway, Melton walked Waner. Now the Pirates had the tying and winning runs on third and second, respectively. Terry walked to the mound and removed Melton, and called on Coffman to face Johnny Dickshot. Coffman struck him out on a sweeping curveball. It was Coffman's first save of the season and probably the most important of his career. Hubbell's record was now 7-0, and his winning streak at 23.

From Pittsburgh, the Giants traveled to Cincinnati, the last stop before heading back East. New York swept the three-game series, making it six in a row, with Hub winning the last game, 3-2. Schumacher started the game and was given a one-run lead when Bartell doubled in Whitehead in the third. The Reds scored two in the sixth to take a 2-1 lead.

Coffman, the hero of the Pirates game, held the Reds scoreless in the seventh until a pinch-hitter replaced him in the eighth. Whitehead and Bartell teamed up again, both doubling, tying the game at 2-2. Hub entered in the eighth and held the Reds scoreless. Ott blasted his seventh homer in the ninth, a "towering" drive that landed in the bleachers, over 400 feet from home plate. That was the game as Hub mowed down Cincinnati in the ninth. Hubbell's record was now an awesome 8-0. His two-year consecutive game winning streak reached its pinnacle at 24.

Carl Hubbell's now-famous record-breaking 24 consecutive game winning streak came to a screeching halt on May 31, in the first game of a Memorial Day doubleheader between New York and Brooklyn. A disappointed crowd of 61,756, the second-largest in Polo Grounds history, watched King Carl get hammered. There were no heroic relievers patiently waiting in the bullpen this afternoon. The game was decided early on when the Dodgers scored two runs in the first, two in the third, and another in the fourth off Hub before Terry realized there must be an impostor on the mound and yanked him in favor of Coffman. But there was no stopping the Dodgers. Gabler followed Coffman and gave up three runs. Fitz finished the last inning with the Dodgers winning 10-3. Hub's stat line read: seven hits, five runs in three and a third innings. His record was now 8-1 and his 24-game winning streak over, which proudly still stands today.

Moments after the game ended, ". . . he [Hubbell] was presented with the award as the National League's Most Valuable Player for the 1936 season. The presenter was a 'round and very portly gentleman in a snappy tan suit,' Babe Ruth."[9] Now that the streak was over, attention was focused back on the pennant race. The Giants trailed Pittsburgh by only 1½ games.

After his winning streak ended, Hubbell's first game came against the Cubs at the Polo Grounds. In hindsight, Hub should have won the game, although he didn't pitch like the '36 MVP. He was relieved in the eighth by Coffman after three singles accounted for another run but was still leading 5-3. Coffman gave up a hit as the Cubs narrowed the lead to 5-4. He was immediately replaced by rookie Melton (3-4), who, by his record, was having a rough beginning. Melton gave up a run in the ninth and another in the 11th to lose the game, 6-5. With solid relief pitching, Hub could have had another victory but came away with a no-decision. His record remained at 8-1.

A day later, Terry called on Hubbell to finish an important game against the Pirates. Schumacher started and was given a comfortable lead with Mancuso's three-run homer and two RBIs each by Ripple and Kiddo Davis. It appeared the weather was more of a problem for Schumacher than Pittsburgh batters, although he did give up eight hits and five runs. The weather was atrocious, with dark, ominous clouds and periodically heavy rains. Schumacher entered the ninth with a 9-5 lead. After two walks and an out, the downpour came, delaying the game thirty-five minutes. When the rain slowed, the umpires ordered the game to resume. Terry called in Hub, who efficiently retired Lloyd Waner on a popup and struck out Woody Jensen. The victory put the Giants into first place by a full game over Pittsburgh. It was their 13th win in the last 17 games. It was Hubbell's first save of the season as his record remained 8-1.

The St. Louis Cardinals arrived at the Polo Grounds for only one day to play a doubleheader. Over 55,000-weekday fans (a Polo Grounds record) fully expected to see a priceless matchup between Hubbell and Dean. Sadly, the crowd was disappointed. There is no other way to explain the game. Hubbell was simply outpitched. He allowed 13 hits and seven runs in eight innings, while Dizzy, going the distance, yielded three hits and one run. Hubbell's record was now 8-2. The Giants won the nightcap 3-2, behind the relief pitching of Melton, and are now one game ahead of the Cubs as the Pirates slipped to third, two games back, in this tightly contested race.

Two days later, on June 11, Giant fans were shocked to discover Freddie Fitzsimmons was traded, and to of all teams, the hated Brooklyn Dodgers. In return, the Giants received 24-year-old right-hander Tom Baker who, the previous year with Brooklyn, had a 1-8 record with a 4.72 earned run average. To be sure, Giant fans were pulling their hair out, trying to understand Terry's thinking. Granted, Fitz at 35, and with New York for 13 seasons, wasn't the same pitcher as he was in his mid-twenties. Although Giant fans were upset over losing the popular Fitz, Terry accessed information not available to everyone. "He had been told by Fitzsimmons' doctor that his arm was going bad—that, in effect, the pitcher was through. Terry thought he was putting one over on Grimes [Dodger manager] . . . He was wrong, of course. Fitzsimmons took his arm into the shop, had it worked on, and pitched successfully in Brooklyn for seven more years, once leading the league in winning percentage with .889 [16-2 record]. He didn't quit until 1943, two years after Terry had left as the Giants' manager."[10]

The Terrymen didn't stay in first place long. In their first game, beginning the second western trip, the Pirates routed Hubbell at Forbes Field early, with a four-run barrage in less than two innings. Since his magnificent streak ended, King Carl lost three in a row. In the first inning, with two out and two runners on, Pittsburgh's Gus Suhr smacked a home run. In the next inning, Hub managed to get the first two Pirates, only to allow three consecutive singles for another run, ending his short appearance. Despite Ott's two-run homer in the ninth, the Giants lost 7-5. Regrettably, Hubbell's slump would get worse before it got better. His record was now 8-3. Also, the Giants now trailed first-place Chicago by a half-game.

The loss to Pittsburgh might have prompted Terry to add more batting punch to his lineup. It was announced just before the trading deadline the Giants sent their young right-hander, Frank Gabler, to the Boston Bees for power-hitting Wally Berger and a reported $25,000 (some sources claimed $35,000). The veteran outfielder came with a resume as a .300 hitter with power. In 1935, he led the league with 34 home runs and 130 runs batted in. Berger played in 59 games for Terry and batted .291 with 12 home runs and 43 RBIs, a respectable showing. However, the following season, Terry wasn't thrilled with Berger's early performance. After 16 games and a .188 batting average, he traded Berger to the Cincinnati Reds for infielder Alex Kampouris.

The Giants moved on to Cincinnati, where they lost two of three games. Hubbell, now mired in an ugly slump, lost to the Reds, 5-3. Again, Hub couldn't complete three innings. The key blows came in the second when the Reds scored four runs. Regrettably, this happened after his teammates gave Hub a three-run lead in the first inning. Hubbell's pathetic stat line was: four hits, five runs, and an unbelievable three walks in less than three innings. Clearly, Terry was concerned about his star pitcher. Hubbell has lost four consecutive games, and, equally alarming, he had failed to complete a game in his last six starts. The Giants were now a full game back of Chicago. Since their eight-game winning streak in late May, the Terrymen have been playing mediocre baseball.

Happy to get out of Cincinnati, the Giants headed to Chicago for three games with the league leaders and lost two of three. But there was a welcome sign coming out of the series. Hubbell won his first game since the streak ended, beating the Cubs, 8-4. Hub wasn't back with a vengeance, but with the help of the Giants' bats, he pitched a complete game. Home runs by Berger, Ott, and Leslie helped give Hub a comfortable 8-0 lead. But entering the eighth, Chicago roughed up King Carl for four runs, topped by Augie Galan's two-run homer. Overall, Hubbell gave up 12 hits but scattered them and was tough in the clutch. On a more positive note, he didn't walk a batter. Hub's record was now 9-4.

Hubbell's victory happened to fall on Frank Chance Day, the peerless leader who had died years before, was being honored with a bronze memorial plaque. Among a host of other old-time Chicago ballplayers were Chance's immortal double-play partners, Joe Tinker and Johnny Evers. Noted columnist Franklin Pearce Adams wrote a famous poem about the three titled "Baseball's Sad Lexicon." This author has taken the liberty to include his poem about the three, taken from his book, *Baseball Memories A Collection of 101 Poems Celebrating Immortal Players, Classic Games, and Wacky Events of the National Pastime* (p. 73). Here it is.

The Immortalized Three

The Chicago Cubs boasted the best double play combo
From 1902 to 1912 . . . a very, very long time ago
They won four National League pennants during this time frame
And two World Series few other teams could claim

And what made them a sensation?
Their solid double-play combination
Created by way of happenstance
Tinker to Evans to Chance

Joe Tinker was a third baseman before Chicago
Moved to short and in the position would grow
Johnny Evers, originally a shortstop, moved to second base
When Cubs manager Frank Selee explained face to face

Frank Chance was a catcher who moved to first
Initially objected but was finally coerced
Their talent made the Cubs a great winning team
While other owners could only envision and dream

Adams' 8-line poem, *Baseball's Sad Lexicon*
Popularized the trio enabling their names to live on
Three out of position Cubs was the circumstance
Which created and immortalized Tinker to Evers to Chance

The Giants ended their road trip on a positive note, taking two of three from the Cardinals. After losing the first game, Melton (6-4) beat the Cards 5-3 to begin a much-needed six-game winning streak. Hubbell kept it going with one of his typical "grand masterpieces" before an overflowing crowd of 38,719. Hub was in total control and narrowly missed a shutout when the Cardinals scored a run in the ninth with two out, making the final score 8-1. His mound opponent, of course, was Dean (11-6), who was chased after six innings. He allowed 10 hits and six runs, not a good day for the Diz. It appeared the Meal Ticket was back, allowing six hits, one run, and no free passes. The pennant race in the National League was now closer than Siamese Twins. Hub's record was now 10-4.

Here are the Standings as of June 27

TEAM	W	L	PCT.	GB
Chicago	36	24	.600	–
St. Louis	35	24	.593	½
New York	36	25	.590	½

Back at the friendly confines of the Polo Grounds, the Giants continued their mini winning streak by sweeping the Phillies and now faced the red-hot Boston Bees, winners of six straight. New York was also sporting a five-game streak, so something had to give when Hubbell took the mound. King Carl stopped the Bees cold, 6-2, despite four walks, an unusually high number for the master of control. It was Hub's third straight victory since his slump ended in Cincinnati. His record was now 11-4.

The bottom of the Giants' order, Chiozza and Mancuso, were responsible for most of the offense. Between the two, they were six for eight with five RBIs—not too shabby for your seventh and eighth hitters.

By the time Hubbell was to pitch again, the Giant streak had ended. In a strange scheduling situation, the Giants were facing the Dodgers for one game. In fact, the game was as strange as the scheduling. After six innings, Brooklyn was leading 5-0. Brooklyn's Cookie Lavagetto had accounted for three of the runs with two homers off of Slick Castleman. It looked like an easy victory for Mungo until the seventh when the Giants scored two runs. Then the wild eighth, when the Giants finally got to Mungo and scored four runs. With the bases loaded, Moore doubled, scoring two. Manager Burleigh Grimes quickly relieved a stunned Mungo with Luke Hamlin. The right-hander was greeted by Ripple with a single, scoring two more runs, as the Giants took the lead 6-5. Immediately, Terry called on his Meal Ticket, who finished off Brooklyn in the ninth. Coffman, who had relieved Castleman, picked up the win and Hubbell the save, his second of the season. His record remained at 11-4.

Hubbell would pitch next at the July 7 All-Star Game. It was Bill Terry's second chance to manage a group of National League All-Stars, the first in 1934 when the fans chose the players, and the game was more a fun event. So, Terry tried to play everyone and not be overly concerned about the outcome. This time, however, the players were chosen by their respective managers, Terry and McCarthy. This changed Terry's attitude and strategy. Except for pitchers, limited to three innings, Terry could manage his All-Stars as he saw fit and implement strategic moves. Dick Bartell was the only starter from the New York Giants. However, Whitehead, Mancuso, Moore, Ott, and Hubbell were selected too.

The two best pitchers in the National League, Dean and Hubbell, were sub-par. Diz looked good until the third inning when DiMaggio singled, and Gehrig took him deep for a 2-0 lead. The National League got one run back in the top of the fourth. Hubbell came on in the bottom of the fourth and was hit hard. Bill Dickey walked, Sam West singled, and then Red Rolfe tripled, scoring two. Charlie Gehringer singled, sending Rolfe home for the third run of the inning. Cy Blanton relieved Hubbell to get the final out. The National League continued to peck away with single runs in the fifth and sixth but was no match for the American League sluggers. The final score was American League 8 National League 3. As author Williams noted in his book, "Not surprisingly, most of the damage was done by Yankee players. After the game, Red Sox catcher Moe Berg suggested that Terry would have been justified in demanding that

McCarthy use no more than one Yankee player at a time. Otherwise, he said, the whole matter should be referred to the Crime Prevention Society."[11]

Three days after the beating Hubbell took at the All-Star Game, he faced the Brooklyn Dodgers at Ebbets Field. As if to say, "I'm back," King Carl hurled a brilliant three-hit shutout, winning 4-0. This was the same club that ended Hubbell's marvelous winning streak on May 31. It would not be surprising if the sparse Dodger crowd were shaking their befuddled heads trying to figure out this game of baseball.

Recently traded and long-time Giant stalwart, Freddie Fitzsimmons, was on the mound for Brooklyn. Fitz pitched a decent game but had the misfortune of facing Hub at his best. The Giants scored single runs in the fourth and fifth innings to give Hubbell the lead, but in the eighth, Berger launched a home run into the left field stands with Moore aboard. With a 4-0 lead, Hub breezed through the next two innings. It was his fourth straight victory. His record was now 12-4.

Four days later, the Giants opened their third homestand of the season, beginning with the Pittsburgh Pirates. Now on a hot streak with his tantalizing screwball, King Carl tamed the Pirates, 4-2. The left-hander was staked to an early two-run lead in the first inning when Pirates right-fielder, Paul Waner, crashed into second baseman Lee Handley with runners on first and second. One run scored and the second on a sacrifice fly. Pittsburgh scored in the second, making it 2-1, but Bartell's homer (13th) in the third and Ott's (18th) in the sixth upped the lead to 4-1. Pittsburgh added an unearned run in the seventh, which ended the scoring. This was Hubbell's fifth straight win. His record is now 13-4.

After the Pirates left, the St. Louis Cardinals arrived for four games, with the Giants winning three. Hubbell pitched the first game of a doubleheader, which attracted over 51,000 fans. Hubbell outlasted three Cardinal pitchers to win a topsy-turvy game. Not quite up to his recent sparkling victories, the master of the screwball hung on to a 6-5 win with plenty of help from his teammates. Moore, who was having a solid season, drove in the winning run in the bottom of the seventh. Homers by Ott and Chiozza also helped to deflate the Gas House Gang. Hubbell gave up nine hits, five runs, and one free pass to record his 14th victory against four losses. New York still trailed league-leading Chicago by three percentage points.

Cincinnati arrived next at the Polo Grounds. The Giants continued their winning ways by beating the cellar-dwelling Reds two out of three games. They were important victories as the Giants faced the Cubs in a critical series, now one full game back.

In the first game of the Cub series, with Hubbell on the mound, the 25,000 Ladies Day crowd was excited as the Giants jumped all over pitcher Curt Davis for two runs before the first inning was over. Veteran Charlie Root was brought in to stop the bleeding. He did just that and more. The right-hander pitched the rest of the game, allowing only a solo home run by Moore in the third inning. In the meantime, Hubbell was pounded for 13 hits and seven runs before Terry took him out, trailing 7-3. If there was any chance of a miracle comeback, Baker, who relieved Hub, was not the man for the job. He allowed five hits and four runs to complete the 11-3 debacle and drop the Giants two games back of the Cubs. Hubbell's record was now 14-5.

The Giants split the next two games with the Cubs, leaving them still in second place, two back before they were on the road again for twelve games. They would manage to lose seven of the 12 before heading back to the Polo Grounds, now trailing the Cubs by six!

Hubbell pitched the first road game against the St. Louis Cardinals at Sportsman's Park. If Giant fans were stunned when Hubbell was hammered his last outing against the Cubs, then they must have been mortified when they discovered what happened in the fourth inning. Hubbell was working smoothly for the first three innings, leading 1-0, when he took the mound in inning four.

The *Times* described Hubbell's meltdown. "Don Gutteridge singled, and Jack [Johnny] Mize hit for the circuit over the right-field pavilion. Then followed five more hits, including a pair of doubles by Don Padgett and Terry Moore, and before Dick Coffman was able to quell the disturbance, Frankie Frisch's Gas House Gang had scored eight runs."[12]

The score was 8-1, but the Giants showed some spunk and, believe it or not, fought back to tie the game in the eighth, 8-8. Looking back, it would have been easier to accept an 8-1 loss rather than the heartbreaking home run by Medwick (21st) in the ninth. The walk-off was given up by Smith, who took the loss. Hubbell was lucky to get away with a no-decision. His record remained at 14-5.

The following day, Cliff Melton struggled early against the Cardinals, giving up three runs in the first inning but held on to win 8-4 as the Giants erupted for five runs in the top of the eighth. The rookie sensation was now 11-5.

Cliff Melton was born on January 3, 1912, in Brevard, North Carolina. His father, Charles, was a farmer, and his mother, Callie, a homemaker. He had an older brother, William. The Melton's moved to Black Mountain, North Carolina, when Cliff was almost eight years old. For a tall youngster, he was quite athletic, playing both basketball and baseball during his formative years. By the time he entered Black Mountain High School, he was 6'5" and was offered several basketball scholarships. He preferred baseball and began his professional career in 1931 at age 19, with the Asheville Tourists of the Piedmont League (Class A). The tall left-hander had a 5-5 record, pitching in 100 innings, for a club that finished fourth with a 66-67 mark.

The following year Melton moved up to the Baltimore Orioles of the International League (Class AA). He struggled at the higher classification with a 0-4 mark and an inflated 6.45 ERA in 60 innings. One of his teammates was Harry Gumbert, who he would meet up with years later as a New York Giant. During his poor showing with Baltimore, the New York Yankees grabbed Melton for their club in the Central League (Class B). They were called the Erie Sailors. At this level, Melton showed great promise compiling a 6-2 record with a minuscule 1.33 ERA in 61 innings.

In 1933 and 1934, Melton was back with Baltimore. In '33, he had an outstanding season. He pitched in 258 innings, the most of his short career, and posted a 16-10 record with a 4.08 earned run average. The club finished in sixth place with an 84-80 record. Melton returned in '34 and had the misfortune to be part of a last-place club. Three managers: Guy Sturdy, Beauty McGowan, and Joe Judge, couldn't get the club on a winning track. They finished last with a 53-99 record, with Melton contributing to the demise. He led the club with a 6-20 record and the second-worst ERA at 6.80. He also pitched the most innings, 209.

Melton's career hit another snag in 1935, which turned out to be a horrible experience. According to Jack Zerby, author of Melton's biography for the SABR project, Cliff signed with the Yankees for $2,400. At spring training, he was tagged with the nickname "Mickey Mouse" by Cubs catcher Gabby Hartnett. Let's be honest. The gangling southpaw had large, floppy ears. The name seemed to fit, and the bench jockeying began. Melton couldn't handle the tormenting, so the Yankees sent him to their Binghamton (Class A) farm team, where he was 3-1 in 27 innings. In the meantime, the Yankees "exercised their right to return Melton to Baltimore." According to *Baseball-Reference*, in Baltimore, pitching in 216 innings, Melton posted a 10-16 record, which doesn't account for his stay in Binghamton.

Years later, Melton compared the Giants with his short stay with the Yankees. "When I was with the Yankees, they never had a pre-game meeting. They don't use their brains. They get up and swing. If they connect—o.k., they win. If they don't, they're licked. What kind of sport is that?"[13]

Melton was feeling his oats and on a role in his interview with sportswriter Harry Forbes. "With the Giants, it's different. We mix up every batter. We pitch with our brains. Before each game, Terry goes over every hitter. We all chime in."[14]

Melton in 1936 had a breakout season, leading the Baltimore club with a 20-14 record in 271 innings under manager Guy Sturdy. He led the club to the International League playoffs, where the Buffalo Bisons defeated them for the Governor's Cup. Although Baltimore lost the playoffs, something beneficial emerged, during the season, a lesson in fighting back.

According to Christopher Tompkins, writing for *Baseball Magazine*, Melton was given unconventional advice to handle bench jockeying. In a playoff game against Rochester, John Ogden, business manager for Baltimore, was upset over the names the opposition was calling Melton. The 6'5" skinny giant with large floppy ears was an easy target for taunts and humiliation. The most hurtful of the nicknames was Mickey Mouse. Ogden told Melton to fight back, but the young lad had no idea what to do. At that point, "Ogden thought briefly, then took out his pocketbook and extracted a crisp $100 bill. 'I'll tell you what to do,' he said and thrust the money into the staring young southpaw's horny hand. 'You hustle out to the Rochester dugout and punch Ray Blades (manager) right in the nose for calling you Mickey Mouse yesterday—and keep the change.'"[15] And that's exactly what the southpaw did. He also nailed Ray Schalk, Buffalo manager, in another playoff game. $200 was a lot of money for a kid from Black Mountain. However accurate or embellished this story might be, it is interesting and noteworthy.

"Mountain Music," another of Melton's sobriquets, was growing up quickly, both emotionally and professionally. Apparently, the Giants liked what they saw and signed Melton on July 27. He didn't report to the Giants until 1937 . . . and what a season it would be.

Melton posted a record of 20-9 with an excellent 2.61 earned run average, the lowest of the Giant pitching staff. The southpaw also led the rotation with a WHIP of 1.093, better than Hubbell's 1.208. He also led the league with seven saves. During the tight pennant race, Melton, among others, was a key factor in the Giants narrowly beating out Chicago. During September, Melton was 6-0 as the Giants finished three games ahead of the Cubs.

In an interview with sportswriter Joe King, Melton gave credit to Hubbell for his success. King Carl suggested he grip the ball across the stitches. Melton explained, "After Carl talked to me . . . I could get the screwball to break at four different speeds—the change of pace I badly needed—and I now slow down even the curve occasionally."[16]

Babe Ruth, retired since 1935 and before the beginning of the Giants and Yankees World Series, believed Melton would "prove the toughest on the mound." Ruth reasoned the young southpaw had the tools and finally found himself this year. When Melton was with the Yankees, he believed he was inexperienced and didn't know how to use his stuff. Ruth might have overestimated Melton's ability or underestimated Joe McCarthy's Yankees.

In the '37 World Series against the New York Yankees, Melton was 0-2 as the Giants lost in five games. Melton started game two and lasted only four innings, giving up six hits and two runs as the Yankees beat the Giants 8-1. Despite this poor showing, Terry showed confidence in his young rookie when he sent him to the mound in crucial game five, down three games to one. Melton left the game after five, trailing the Yankees 4-2, which turned out to be the final score. Perhaps it was his inexperience, or the Yankee hitters were just too good.

In 1938, Melton didn't let his poor showing in the World Series affect his early pitching. By May 11, his record was 6-0. Bill Terry was still high on the youngster, promising 25 victories from the lanky hurler. Before August, however, the Giants' pitching staff had fallen apart, including the promising Melton. Cliff would end the season with a 14-14 record and a 3.89 ERA, a far cry from '37. The Giants finished in third place with an 83-67 record, five games back of the first-place Cubs.

After a disappointing '38 season, Cliff remained with the Giants for another six, for a total of eight. His final record was 86-80 with a 3.42 earned run average. He never came close to winning 20 games again.

From '39 on, Melton's pitching is best described as erratic. At times he would display the brilliance of 1937, and at other moments he would be hit hard. He was, to put it mildly, inconsistent. According to former catcher Gabby Hartnett, Melton's pitching problem was pacing. "He has beautiful stuff, Gabby used to explain, but he blows up come the sixth or seventh inning because he does not know how to ease up and bear down only when he has to."[17]

Apparently, Terry agreed with Hartnett and turned the problem over to the veteran catcher. Gabby tried everything as sportswriter Joe King reported. "Gabby, who bulldozed, cajoled, kidded, and finally begged Melton for results but had to give up. Come the sixth or seventh inning and boom-boom went the ball game on the home run ball."[18]

Irrespective of Hartnett's comments and tutoring, Melton knew he had a problem, so in 1940 he began developing a change of pace to accompany his fastball. He gave credit to Jersey City southpaw Roy Joiner for teaching him the pitch. It is delivered the same way as the screwball but only gripped lightly, slowing the ball to the plate but does break as sharply. Apparently, it worked for Joiner, who won 21 games the previous season with Jersey City. In 1940, Melton's record was 10-11 with a 4.91, the highest of his career. He completed only four games, so much for the new pitch.

The following year, Melton was not much better, with an 8-11 record but an improved ERA of 3.01. He did complete nine games, more than double the '40 season. Once again, Melton began the '41 season showing great promise. By late May, he was 4-2, raising the hopes of Terry only to be disappointed as the season developed. Sadly, Melton finished badly. During his last 20 appearances, Terry watched Melton salvage only four wins and nine losses.

Then in 1942, Melton looked like he was on his way to a repeat of his rookie season (20-9). By July 4, Melton's record was 11-5 with a 2.63 ERA in over 143 innings. He also completed 12 of 17 starts and was selected to the All-Star team but did not pitch, as the American League beat the National League, 3-1.

Why was Melton having such a marvelous season, at least up to this point? Was it Hartnett's instructions? Was it the change of pace pitch he adopted from Joiner? Was it a gradual maturing? Was it the new manager, Mel Ott? Or was it a combination of all of the above? Melton admitted in the spring he was "experimenting" with his "pitching variety." In an interview with King, Melton confessed, " The main thing I had to learn was Hubbell's screwball, which I practiced day after day. I think I have it under control now. It is an easy pitch for me to throw, and I used it quite a bit against the Cubs. That is the big difference in my pitching from last year."[19]

Suddenly, after the July 4 game, Melton complained to manager Mel Ott of pain in his left elbow. Melton stopped pitching for a month, hoping rest and treatment would help the pain. It didn't. So, Melton went off to John Hopkins in Baltimore for an examination. The exam revealed several bone chips in the elbow socket. An infection also developed, which had to be cleared up before surgery. With that bad news, Ott sent Melton home. His promising season was over.

The surgery was a success, and Melton reported to New Jersey in 1943 to begin spring training. The Giants, under the direction of Ott, were preparing for the new season at Lakewood, New Jersey. Commissioner Landis had imposed travel restrictions during World War II because gas and oil were scarce, and trains constantly moved troops across the country.

Melton's arm didn't respond favorably to the cold weather in New Jersey. After one game, Slim experienced swelling in the elbow area. Ott, however, was reassured it was to be expected. Despite press reports that Melton's arm was fine and ready to pick up where he left off in '42, his performance did not reflect the optimism. His record was 9-13 with a 3.19 earned run average. He completed only six of 28 starts. He was the workhorse and best of the miserable rotation, which tells you why the Giants finished last, 49½ games behind the pennant-winning St. Louis Cardinals.

In 1944, as Ott desperately tried to get the New York Giants out of the basement and back to respectability, Melton struggled. However, before the season began, Melton received some interesting news. The Baltimore draft board had declared the southpaw 4-F. The reason was the surgical procedure he had in 1942, which he explained shortened his arm "by three inches," therefore, not meeting military requirements.

Shortened arm or not, Slim did not pitch well for the Giants with a 2-2 record and a high 4.06 ERA in a little over 64 innings. Clearly, Melton was suffering arm problems. So late in June, Ott had no choice but to send Melton to the Giants' minor league (Class AA) club in Jersey City, hoping he could regain the excellence he once possessed. It quickly became obvious at Jersey City; Melton was not impressing Ott. In 45 innings, pitching sporadically, Melton won three and lost four.

In 1945, Melton sat out the entire season as he refused to take a salary cut. On December 29, 1945, the gangling Giant was sold to the San Francisco Seals of the Pacific Coast League (Class AAA). Melton pitched five years for the Seals, 1946-1950, and apprised himself very well. In his first three years, he compiled a solid record of 50-33 but then slipped the next two at 5-6 and 11-18.

It came as no surprise; in 1951, the Seals sold his contract to Kansas City of the American Association (AAA). From that point on, Melton bounced around the minor leagues until the end of 1954, when the southpaw retired at 42.

After baseball, Melton worked for the Lou Grasmick Lumber Company as a truck driver. He met Grasmick in 1950 when both were hurling for the Seals. Interestingly, Grasmick spent five years in the minor leagues with nine different teams before landing with the Philadelphia Phillies for the proverbial cup of coffee. Then back to the minors for two more seasons before he called it quits at age 25. As luck would have it, Melton met Grasmick during his second tour in the minors. He drove for Grasmick for over 20 years before he retired. Cliff Melton died of cancer on July 28, 1986, at St. Joseph's Hospital in Baltimore. He was 74 years old.

Now back to the hot pennant race. After Melton beat the Cardinals for his 11th win, the Giants lost the following day to St. Louis, this time 5-2. It was an untimely loss putting the Giants three games back of Chicago as they headed for the Windy City and this important series. After Gumbert lost the first game, 5-3, Hubbell pitched the next day. King Carl didn't fare much better as the Cubs, led by Hartnett, who drove in four runs to lead his club to a 7-1 victory. Hub was roughed up for 12 hits and seven runs in eight innings. He fanned seven but issued four walks, a rare lack of control, one of his strengths. Hub's record was now 14-6.

The following day the Cubs swept the series beating Melton 5-4 in 11 innings. The Giants were now six games back of Chicago and prompted Terry to shake up the lineup. Beginning with the opening game of the upcoming Cincinnati series, he brought in Mel Ott to play third base, replacing Chiozza. This move would free up Ripple for more playing time in the outfield. The other change was to replace McCarthy at first base with Leslie. "Most experts considered the successful switch of Ott to third base, which permitted the potent Ripple to play regularly, and Melton's strong season as the keys to the Giants' pennant win."[20]

Hubbell missed the Cincinnati series as the Giants won two of three from the Reds. Despite August beginning poorly for the Giants, it turned out well. The club would finish the month, winning 17 of 24 games. During August, Hubbell won three games, lost none, and saved two to help bring New York to within one game of the Chicago Cubs.

Hub opened the Pittsburgh series, winning 6-3. The game was tied 2-2 entering the 8th when the Giants exploded for four runs to ice the game. Hub was steady throughout, allowing nine hits but walking only one batter. His record was now 15-6.

The Giants split the next two games with the Pirates, winning 10-2 behind young Melton, who pitched a solid game as his record went to 12-6. Blondy Ryan drove in three runs, and Ott hit his 23rd homer to lead the offensive attack. The next day, the Pirates Jim Weaver blanked the Giants on three hits as New York headed back home where they lost both games to the Bees.

The following day Hub stopped the bleeding by handcuffing Philadelphia 5-0. It was his third shutout, and the pitching line almost perfect. The Meal Ticket allowed six hits, no walks, and nine strikeouts. Hub's record was now 16-6. Equally important, the victory was the beginning of a five-game Giant winning streak.

Five days later, Hub beat Boston 9-1, dominating the Bees, giving up seven hits, walking two, and fanning six, another well-pitched game. Hub's record improved to 17-6.

With only one day's rest Terry, in an unusual move, called on Hubbell in a relief role with the Giants leading comfortably, 8-5. Apparently, Terry was taking no chances of blowing the game against Philadelphia. In hindsight (always 20-20), it wasn't a smart move. Hub could have used the rest. He wound up pitching 3 1/3 innings, allowing five hits, one run, while fanning three. And the Giants scored five runs in the ninth, led by Ott's 25th home run with two on! The Giants won 13-6. Hub picked up save number three.

Beginning August 25, the Giants were ready and waiting for the western clubs' arrivals, beginning with Chicago. The Cubs' visit to the Polo Grounds was a case of odd scheduling, a doubleheader. The Giants won both games, 8-7 and 4-2, and now trailed the Cubs by only two games. Hub started the first game and didn't have much on the ball as he was replaced after seven innings, trailing 6-2. Chicago tacked on another run off Schumacher in the top of the ninth, making the score 7-2. But the Giants came roaring back, scoring five, led by Ripple's three-run homer in the ninth, sending the game into extra innings, which the Giants won in the 11th, 8-7. A sure loss turned into a win for the Giants and a no-decision for Hubbell.

After losing the first game to Pittsburgh, the Giants swept the next three. Hub started the third game and was handed a 4-0 lead. Normally, this would be enough for Hub, and he would coast the rest of the game. Not so on this day. Hub gave up two runs in the fifth and another two in the seventh before Terry called on Coffman to stop the Pirates. Once again, the Giants scored late in the game; three runs in the seventh and two more in the eighth, compliments of Mel Ott's 27th home run, a two-run blast. It was another no-decision for Hub, which should have been a win.

Before August ended, Hubbell picked up his fourth and final save of the season against Cincinnati. He relieved Coffman, who had replaced starter Melton, as the Giants won 4-3. Hub pitched 2 2/3 innings, fanning three and walking none, while Melton's record went to 14-8.

The Giants continued their winning ways, taking two of three from the visiting St. Louis Cardinals as the calendar turned over to September. Brooklyn followed St. Louis for two games, winning the first but losing the second 3-0, as the Meeker Marvel was at the top of his game on this day. He scattered six singles, didn't issue a free pass, and struck out eight. It was his fourth shutout and last of the season as his record climbed to 18-6. This victory put the Giants in first place by one full game.

Entering September, the National League was now engaged in a tight pennant race among New York, Chicago, and Pittsburgh. It would be determined by the club that could put together a few substantial winning streaks. So, it was obvious Terry was focused on winning every game, and with the talent he had from the beginning of the season. It is safe to assume Terry spent little time concerning himself with what was happening in the American League.

The New York Yankees started the season slowly but by early June had a 4½ game lead over their chief rival, Detroit. From this modest lead, the Yankees began steamrolling the rest of the AL clubs. By September 1, the Yankees boasted an 11-game lead and soon after would clinch the pennant.

Author Koppett summed up the Tigers demise when he wrote, "Whatever competition the Tigers might have given the Yankees disappeared May 25, when a Hadley pitch fractured Cochrane's skull. He survived and returned to managing late in the year, but his career was over. Since Rowe was also out all year with a bad arm, Greenberg's 40 homers and Gehringer's .371 batting title didn't matter."[21]

After Hubbell notched his 18th victory, the staff's workhorse found himself stuck in a pitching stalemate. For the next four outings, he would lose one, win one, lose won, and win one. Mediocrity began against, of all teams Brooklyn, the club he shutout five days ago. And it began in the very first inning when Babe Phelps smacked a three-run homer. The Dodgers tacked on two more runs in the fifth as Hub was replaced after seven innings by Coffman in the 5-1 defeat. Hub's record was now 18-7.

Hubbell bounced back in his next start, a laugher against Pittsburgh, which the Giants won 12-2. It began in the first inning when the Giants handed Hub four runs, thanks to Ott and Leiber, hitting two-run homers off Ed Brandt. In the sixth, New York added eight more runs, seven off right-handed reliever Mace Brown. Surprisingly, with the game over by the sixth, Terry would have given Hubbell some well-deserved rest, but he didn't, so his tired lefty went the full nine, allowing ten hits and two walks. Hub's record was now 19-7.

Hubbell's next start was against Cincinnati at Crosley Field. Aiming for the coveted 20th victory, King Carl had to wait another day. He was nicked for three runs in the third and left the game after pitching five innings, trailing 3-1. Jumbo Brown, in relief, gave up a run in the eighth while the Giants scored a run in the ninth but came up short. Cincinnati won 4-3 as Hub's record went to 19-8.

Two days later, rookie Melton was on the mound against St. Louis before a small crowd of 6,000 at Sportsman's Park, a reflection of the fact the Cardinals trailed the league-leading Giants by 12½ games. It was a strange game in several ways. Melton was handed a five-run lead in the first inning. The lefty gave three back and left the game after one out! Brown relieved and did a credible job but left after the second inning. The Giants scored two more in the top of the third and led 7-3. In a bizarre move, Terry brought in Hubbell, who pitched seven innings of shutout baseball. He allowed four hits, walked one, and struck out six for his 20th victory against eight losses. The final score was New York 10 St. Louis 3.

The Giants left St. Louis and headed for Chicago for a critical three-game series with the second-place Cubs. The Giants were sporting a 2½ game lead, but a sweep by the Cubs could send New York reeling. Chicago won the first game 7-5 and had the Giants back on their heels, but then lost the next two. The Giants had increased their lead to 3 1/2. In game two, young Melton tossed a clutch six hit (all singles) shutout before almost 42,000 fans at hostile Wrigley Field. The following day the Giants won 8-7, with Hub picking up the victory in relief of Schumacher. Frankly, Hubbell did not pitch well, allowing three hits and three runs in only two innings. Timely hitting by Ott, McCarthy, and Danning gave Hub the win. His record was now 21-8, and his last two victories came in relief.

After beating Chicago twice, the Giants beat Brooklyn 7-3 and 4-3 at the Polo Grounds. After Brooklyn, the Giants whipped the Boston Bees in a doubleheader 5-4 and 3-1, extending their winning streak to six straight. Hubbell started and pitched well in the first game of the twin bill, giving up three hits and three runs in seven innings. The big blow was Tony Cuccinello's three-run blast in the fourth inning. But the Giants fought back, led by Moore's two-run homer in the seventh to eventually win for Brown, 5-4. Hubbell was credited with a no-decision.

Three days later, on September 30, Bill Terry called on his ace of the rotation to clinch the National League pennant for the New York Giants . . . and the Meal Ticket delivered. In the first game of a doubleheader against Philadelphia, he pitched a sparkling game, dominating the Phillies over nine innings, 2-1 on five hits, one of them Dolf Camilli's 27th home run in the bottom of the ninth. He also struck out nine, an unusually high number for him. It was a masterful performance from King Carl, who notched his 22nd victory versus eight losses . . . and nailed the National League pennant for the Giants.

The clubhouse was a mixed scene and nowhere like today's pennant winners screaming and yelling in a flood of champagne. Author Williams described the somewhat confused and dazed mood. "The picture of the clubhouse celebration shows a bunch of men who seem to feel they are supposed to demonstrate elation. It looks like everybody had been told to face the camera. True, Bartell is grinning, but he was never as much a Giant as the others. Mancuso looks embarrassed. The photographer has evidently asked Melton and Hubbell to wave their caps, and they are obliging, though they look stiff and neither can manage an authentic smile."[22]

Perhaps the lack of enthusiasm from the Giants' players had to do with the mood caused by the terrible Depression. It could have been that players found it difficult to show excitement and cheerfulness over a kid's game, while millions of people lost jobs and homes and were forced to stand on bread lines. Whatever the reason, Terry and the Giants were the National League champs and deservedly so.

Hubbell, as he did the previous four years, had another marvelous season. He led the league with 22 victories and a .733 winning percentage along with a surprising 159 strikeouts, a first for him. He was the workhorse of the Giants' rotation, pitching in over 261 innings, the most on the staff but the lowest of his fabulous five seasons. He made the All-Star team for the fifth time and, despite Melton's (20-9, 2.61 ERA) wonderful rookie season, was still the ace of the rotation. And the Giants would need both left-handers in the upcoming World Series against the powerful New York Yankees.

In 1937 those baseball fans who were closely following pennant races in both the National and American Leagues expected the New York Yankees to be the overwhelming favorite to defeat the New York Giants. It was not a denigration of the Terrymen but more of a realistic assessment of an incredible club, managed by Joe McCarthy, who guided them during a relatively easy season. The Yankees finished with a record of 102-52, 13 games ahead of the Detroit Tigers.

Poetically, you could say the Yankees waltzed to the AL pennant while the Giants scrambled for every victory and finished with a hard-earned record of

95-57, three games ahead of the pesky Cubs, finally clinching the NL pennant with four games remaining in the season. In addition, the following chart gives a clearer picture of the Yankees' dominance, assuming the abilities of both leagues were equal or close.

	NY YANKEES	NY GIANTS
Earned Run Average	3.65 (1)	3.43 (2)
Shutouts	15 (1)	11 (3)
Home Runs	174 (1)	111 (1)
Batting Average	.283 (3)	.278 (4)
Runs Scored	979 (1)	732 (3)
Fielding	.972 (3)	.974 (3)

( ) indicates league position

It is clear from the above stats why the Yankees were favored to win the World Series. Their power numbers, home runs, and runs scored, are significantly higher than the Giants. However, the Giants have a slight edge in pitching (ERA) while the fielding is about equal. The Giants' pitching advantage might be deceiving for this reason: the Yankees featured two 20-game winners in Lefty Gomez (21-11), Red Ruffing (20-7), along with relief specialist Johnny Murphy (13-4). However, the Giants have two 20-game winners also, Hubbell (22-8) and Melton (20-9). The rookie, however, is a wildcard since he has not been tested under the pressure of a World Series. Beyond these two lefties, Terry's rotation is mediocre.

Once you get to the offense, the picture changes dramatically. The Yankees' powerful lineup featured three key players: Joe DiMaggio, Lou Gehrig, and Bill Dickey. DiMaggio batted .346 and led the league with 46 home runs proving his rookie season was no fluke. He also drove in a team-leading 167 runs and hitting streaks of 19, 21, and 22. Gehrig batted .351 with 37 home runs while knocking in 158. It would be his last great season. While catching 140 games, the less-heralded Dickey managed to hit .332 with 29 homers and 133 RBIs. The rest of the lineup wasn't too shabby either.

Conversely, the Giants' power is focused on one player, Mel Ott. Master Melvin hit .294 and led the team with 31 home runs and 95 runs batted in. It was a solid season for most players but an off-year for Ott. The last season he drove in less than100 runs was in 1928 at age 19. After Ott, Terry will have to pray for plenty of singles, doubles, and timely hitting. But as the saying goes, the game is played on the field, not on paper. World Series history is sprinkled with upsets; the White Sox defeat of the Cubs in 1906; the Giants beating the Indians in 1954; and the Pirates beating the Yankees in 1960, to name a few.

Terry also had to contend with a very shrewd manager in McCarthy. Author Alan H. Levy in his wonderful biography, *Joe McCarthy Architect of the Yankee Dynasty,* wrote the following. "McCarthy was taking no chances. After the Yankees had wrapped up the pennant, he left the team in the hands of Art Fletcher for a series in Washington and stayed in New York, scouting the Giants. McCarthy decided that left-handers would start against Carl Hubbell. He figured Hubbell's screwball was more like a right-hander's curveball. The move proved wise."[23] And now on to the World Series, and a rematch of two great New York teams.

Game 1, October 6, 1937, at Yankee Stadium

As anticipated, Terry chose Hubbell to start against Gomez before over 60,000 boisterous fans. Nothing but goose eggs for the first four innings until the Giants scored in the top of the fifth. The lead didn't last long. The Yankees exploded for seven runs on five hits and two costly errors in the bottom of the seventh. And that was the game as Gumbert replaced Hub. Oddly, the power bats of the Yankees did not get an extra-base hit during the outburst. The five hits were all singles! The final score was Yankees 8 Giants 1.

According to author Levy, the victory played into the psychology of the game. Gehrig claimed McCarthy predicted Hubbell would walk the first batter in the seventh inning, and that's when the Yankees would have a big inning. And that's exactly what happened. "The game and, more important, the mental edge belonged to the Yankees. The Yankees had ground up Hubbell and the Giants in the very way no National League team would have dared even to attempt."[24]

Game 2, October 7, 1937, at Yankee Stadium

As expected, the pitching matchup featured another two 20-game winners, Yankee veteran Red Ruffing, and rookie sensation Cliff Melton. The youngster was determined and particularly not fond of the Yankees dating back to his minor league days with the organization. Another large crowd of 57,000 watched almost a rematch of the first game. The Giants scored a first-inning run. After Moore struck out, Bartell doubled and scored on Ott's clutch single, and just like that, the Giants were ahead 1-0. Melton made the slim lead hold up for four innings . . . and then came the fatal fifth. A double my Myril Hoag and three consecutive singles by Selkirk, Lazzeri, and Ruffing, and Melton was replaced by Gumbert. That's all the runs Ruffing needed as the Yankees went on to win by the same score as the previous day, 8-1.

Game 3, October 8, 1937, at Polo Grounds
Game 3 moved across the Harlem River to the Polo Grounds as the Giant fans were understandably nervous, down 2-0 in the Series. Terry, left with little choice, selected right-hander Schumacher to stop the Yankee juggernaut. Perhaps Terry remembered last year's Series when Schumacher pitched a gutsy game beating the Yankees 5-4 in 10 innings. At the time, the Giants were behind three games to one.

McCarthy selected right-hander Monte Pearson, who finished the regular season with a record of 9-3 and a 3.17 ERA. The previous year, he won 19 games, plus a World Series victory in Game Four, when he outpitched Hubbell in a 5-2 Yankees win.

The Yankees scored early, beginning in the second inning, with a single run. By the end of the fifth, they led the Giants 5-0. In the meantime, Pearson didn't allow a hit until the bottom of the fifth when Chiozza laid down a bunt single. The Giants picked up their first and only run in the seventh.

In the bottom of the ninth, the Giants gave the crowd, of over 37,000, something to cheer about. A single and two walks loaded the bases with two out. McCarthy taking no chances, called on his star reliever Johnny Murphy. The Fireman, as he was called, induced Danning to fly out to center field, ending the game at 5-1.

Game 4, October 9, 1937, at Polo Grounds
The Giants were now in serious trouble beginning Game 4. They were on the brink of elimination, down three games to none. The Yankees have outscored them 21-3, and Terry had no choice but to call on Hubbell with two day's rest. A well-rested Bump Hadley was his opponent. Although Hadley won 11 games during the season, he must have had a lot of run support because his ERA was a bloated 5.30.

Behind 1-0, the Giants bats finally came alive in the second inning, when they exploded for six runs on seven hits, all singles. Hub gave up another run in the third, making the score 6-2 in favor of the Giants. The Terrymen scored again in the seventh when Danning doubled to right, chasing Leiber home.

After the third inning, Hubbell handcuffed the Yankees until Gehrig homered to deep right field, making the final score 7-3 Giants. Once again, the man called the Meal Ticket proved he was a big-game pitcher. Interestingly, his World Series record is further proof he was a star on the big stage. In six World Series games, Hub won four and lost two with a phenomenal 1.79 ERA. Also, the New York Yankees lost only three World Series games during their incredible streak, from 1936 to 1939, under McCarthy. Carl Hubbell won two of those games!

Game 5, October 10, 1937, at Polo Grounds
Terry gave Melton a second chance to beat the Yankees and extend the Series. But it was not to be. Melton pitched a credible game. However, Gomez pitched an incredible game. The Yankees jumped to an early 1-0 lead when Hoag homered to right field in the second inning. The following inning DiMaggio homered to deep left field, 2-0 Yankees. Ott gave Giant fans something to cheer about at the bottom of the third, blasting a home run to right, scoring Bartell to tie the game at 2-2.

The game remained tied until the fifth when the Yankees scored two runs. Gomez and Gehrig each drove in a run to take a 4-2 lead. And that's the way the game and the Series ended. The Yankees and Giants wouldn't meet again in a Fall Classic until 1951. Sadly, for Giant fans, they would lose again, this time in six games.

After Ott's homer in the third, Gomez blanked the Giants over the next six innings allowing five singles and one walk. However, the unflappable lefty once more lived up to his nickname, "El Goofy," and nearly drove McCarthy over the edge in the seventh. Author Williams explains. "This was also the famous game in which the unpredictable Gomez did something that combined the showboating of Dean and the nonchalance of Hubbell. In the seventh inning, with one Giant on base and the tying run at the plate, he stopped pitching for quite some time to gawk at a plane that was circulating overhead."[25]

It was bizarre enough to send McCarthy scampering to the mound. There are two versions of what happened next. McCarthy snapped at Gomez, reminding him of where he was and its importance. The other, McCarthy jokingly asked what was going on. Take your pick, but keep in mind McCarthy was noted to be all business when it came to baseball and not much of a jokester; thus, the first version seems more likely.

Before the World Series, several well-known and respected sportswriters were claiming Hubbell was finished, all washed-up. These opinions were offered despite his excellent season and a key victory against the Yankees, a win that avoided an embarrassing sweep. Perhaps these writers knew something in 1937 other knowledgeable baseball people did not . . . or were not saying publicly. Apparently, there was more going on with Hub's arm from the many years of throwing the screwball. Years later, he admitted his "elbow had been troubling him for some time." So, it is not surprising this calm, reticent man of few words would ever complain about pain. It was troubling, but he worked through it, he said.

Although Hub pitched six more years, 1938-1943, King Carl was no longer King or the Meal Ticket. These years were his sad farewell. But as the saying goes, "as one door closes, another opens," and Carl Hubbell would happily walk through that door and begin a new career.

12

Farewell and a New Career

". . . THE MOST IMPORTANT THING ABOUT THE
HANDLING OF YOUNG PLAYERS IS TO SEE THAT
THEY GET OFF ON THE RIGHT TRACK."

In 1938 and for the next six years, Carl Hubbell and the New York Giants would wallow in mediocrity. Over this span, Hubbell posted a record of 61-52, a far, far cry from his fabulous five seasons when he won 115 and lost 50, and the Giants won three pennants and a World Series.

The Giants during this time frame and beyond would not win a National League pennant until 1951, under the leadership of Leo Durocher, and took Bobby Thompson to hit an unbelievable, and now, legendary home run. However, focusing simply on the six years Hubbell was no longer the dominating and elite pitcher, the Giants could do no better than third place. The club finished dead last in 1943, 49½ games back of the St. Louis Cardinals. Clearly, there was a connection between Hubbell's demise and that of the Giants. Of course, many other factors led to the Giants' downfall.

Hubbell's trouble began, innocently enough, during the 1938 season. The Giants won the season opener 13-1 behind Melton but lost the next day with Schumacher on the hill, 6-4. Then New York ran off 11 straight wins, with Hub picking up two of the victories as New York enjoyed an early 3½ game lead over the Cubs.

After beating Chicago 4-1 on June 8, Hub's record was a nifty 7-2. Aside from some minor arm soreness, it appeared Hub was headed for another 20-game season. Also, it was King Carl's 199th victory. It took a while to record his 200th win as he went into a slump after the Chicago victory, losing three straight as the early pennant race tightened up. Ironically, the Meal Ticket finally notched number 200 on June 26 at the hands of; you guessed it, the Chicago Cubs, 5-1. He gave up 11 hits but was tough in the clutch. The fact he didn't walk a batter contributed mightily to the notable achievement. Hub's record was now 8-5.

During July, Hub won four and lost two games, bringing his record to 12-7. Once again, Terry selected him for the July 6 All-Star Game. The Meal Ticket didn't play but contributed to the National League victory. But first, some vital background information to this important win for Terry. Since 1933 Terry was unhappy with the New York writers he claimed were "treating him with a bias." Over the years, it got to Terry, and he fired back. He was also not thrilled with losing two consecutive World Series to McCarthy and the Yankees. So, at the All-Star Game, both Terry and McCarthy kept most of their starters in for most of the game. "In effect, Terry used what he felt was his best team for the entire game. In the top of the fourth inning, when the Cubs' Bill Lee walked the first man he faced, Terry got Hubbell up and throwing in the bullpen; Hubbell never made it into the game, but Terry knew the mere sight of him out there would be discomfiting. The final score was 4-1 in favor of the National League, which, like Terry himself, had finally gained a little pride."[1]

Then came August, and the month turned into a disaster for Hubbell and the Giants. On August 2, at the Polo Grounds, against the Cubs, Hubbell was hit hard. He gave up ten hits and seven runs in 6 1/3 innings, losing 7-0. Four days later, against Pittsburgh, King Carl was whacked around even harder. He allowed 10 hits and an unheard of 10 runs in only 6 1/3 innings as the Pirates won 13-3.

Terry, recognizing his Meal Ticket was struggling, gave him additional rest between starts. Apparently, it had some effect on his next start on August 13. Hub showed signs of his greatness when he defeated the Phillies 11-1. Granted, Philadelphia was not much of a challenge, but they were still a major league team that could do damage. Hub allowed four hits and walked only one batter going the distance. His record was now 13-9.

Five days later, Carl Hubbell's season came to a surprising and screeching halt as his nemesis, the Brooklyn Dodgers, beat him 5-3. He lasted five innings, giving up all five runs on five hits and three walks. Hubbell's arm was bothering him, so the next day, he went to Terry. "Hubbell took Bill Terry's advice and went to Memphis, Tennessee, to consult a bone specialist, Dr. J. Spencer Speed. It didn't take Dr. Speed long to discover that Carl's pitching elbow was afflicted by loose bone chips, which were jamming the elbow and causing all the pain. On August 22, the doctor operated and removed the chips. With his arm in a sling, Hub quit baseball for the year. He knew there was nothing for him to do except try to prepare himself for the 1939 season."[2]

Hubbell's stats for '38 were not up to the high standard he set during the fabulous five seasons, but most major leaguers, just beginning a pitching career, would be quite pleased. Hub won 13 lost 10 with a decent 3.07 era in 179 innings. Not too shabby when it was later discovered Hub was pitching in pain most of the time.

The loss of Hubbell was a huge blow to the Giants. In addition, the rest of the rotation was struggling, but Terry never gave up. The Giants kept fighting, but it was in a losing cause. Moreover, Terry worked with an unsettled infield, particularly at second, with Alex Kampouris and Lou Chiozza sharing playing time. Not surprisingly, the Giants finished third, 83-67; five games back of the pennant-winning Chicago Cubs.

Over the winter of 1938-1939, speculation was rampant among the sportswriters on how effective Hubbell would be during the coming baseball season. Most writers were not optimistic as to Hub's future. So, Hub stopped listening to the depressing chatter and took matters into his own hands. "Carl tried to do something constructive by bathing the stiff arm in water heated to 135 degrees. Then coating the arm with paraffin to keep in the heat. He repeated this procedure three times a day, and by the time spring training began, he felt as though he had a chance."[3]

Besides, Hubbell played a lot of golf and admitted the swinging didn't bother him at all. He also confessed the real test would come during a game when he had to cut loose with a pitch.

Terry wisely used his now-former Meal Ticket sparingly during the early part of the new season. He wanted to build his arm strength before letting him start and pitch nine innings. Hub's first appearance came May 8, against Chicago, at the Polo Grounds. A small crowd attended; a little over 6,000 fans. Hub entered in the eighth inning with the Giants trailing 4-2 and did a marvelous job. He threw two perfect innings, not allowing a hit or walk while fanning two Cubs. It was to no avail, as the Giants failed to score the last two innings.

Terry liked what he saw but was still being cautious with the ace of the rotation. Six days later, on May 14, Terry named Hubbell to start against the weak-hitting Philadelphia Phillies. Hub pitched extremely well, and as fate would have it, the game was tied after nine, 1-1. Hub was back on the mound in the 10th and retired the side. The Giants scored in the bottom of the 10th on pinch hitter Ken O'Dea's home run. It was a timely homer in more ways than one. This was O'Dea's first season with the Giants. He was picked up in a trade with Chicago in early December. O'Dea was not a power hitter. The gift to Hubbell was one of three homers O'Dea would hit all season.

From this point on, Hubbell had his good and bad days throughout the rest of the '39 season. For example, from May 21 to June 4, Hub lost all four starts, the last one a real disaster. Against Cincinnati, Hubbell failed to retire a batter in the first inning, giving up two hits, a walk, and two runs. That's when Terry came to his rescue.

But then there was the July 25 game against the St. Louis Cardinals at Sportsman's Park. The Hubbell from his fabulous five seasons (1933-'37) showed up to pitch. And pitch he did. Entering the 13th inning, the score was 3-3. That's when the Giants exploded for three runs, led by Frank Demaree's two-run homer and Otts solo shot. Hub's pitching line read: 10 hits, three runs (two earned), two walks, and three strikeouts.

To prove the Cardinal victory wasn't a fluke, Hub whipped the Cubs at Wrigley Field 3-1 on July 30. It was a typical King Carl performance. He allowed 10 hits but didn't walk a Cub and was tough in the clutch. At the time, his record was 4-5.

It was an up-and-down season for Hubbell. To his credit, he did finish strong with a record of 11-9, and an impressive 2.75 earned run average. Hub's 11 victories were the lowest compared to the Giants' four other starters, and it paled when stacked up against his 26 wins in 1936. But his 2.75 ERA was, by far, the best on the club and second to the National League leader, Cincinnati's Bucky Walters with 2.29.

Without their ace and poor seasons from Schumacher, Melton, and Bill Lohrman, Terry had a major challenge keeping the Giants competitive. The pitching staff finished sixth, in an eight-team league, with a 4.07 ERA and last with 1,319 innings pitched. It came as no surprise the pitching was the major reason the Giants finished fifth with a 77-74 record, an embarrassing 18½ games back of the first-place Cincinnati Reds.

To a certain degree, 1939 established the pattern for Hubbell and the New York Giants for the next several years. No longer was Hubbell the staff ace, the Meal Ticket, or King Carl. He was now a mediocre, aging left-hander, holding on until the end of his career. Granted, Hubbell didn't view his aging and loss of effectiveness as did the sportswriters and Giant fans. In an interview with Rod

Roberts, he said, ". . . as long as I could win 10 to 12, 13 ball games, I probably would stay around."[4]

Sportswriter Fitzgerald explains Hubbell's dilemma quite pointedly. ". . . the Meal Ticket had reached an age [37] when he simply wasn't able to take a regular turn anymore. Hub became a spot pitcher, thrown into the breach every so often, and counted on to win the big ball games with the top clubs. For four years in a row from 1939 through 1942, he won exactly 11 games a season. Not a disgraceful showing, by any means, but a far cry from the Hubbell of old."[5]

Spot pitcher or not, every so often, Hubbell would display glimpses of his past heroics. One such moment came on May 30, 1940. Of all places, it was at Ebbets Field. It was the first game of a Memorial Day doubleheader. It was a sellout crowd of almost 34,000, and Hub met the challenge, and then some. King Carl wore his crown proudly that day, dominating the Dodgers 7-0. He allowed one scratch hit by Johnny Hudson, who was quickly erased by a double play. Over the nine unbelievable innings, Hub allowed only that one hit, walked none, and struck out six. "To make the occasion even more cheerful, Carl had the satisfaction of knocking the Dodgers clear out of first place."[6]

By the end of the 1940 season, Hubbell's stats were still wanting, as were the Giants. Hub finished with an 11-12 mark and a 3.65 ERA. The best of the five starters was Schumacher, with a record of 13-13. No wonder the Giants finished sixth with a 72-80 record, 27½ games back of Cincinnati.

In 1941, Hubbell was named to the All-Star team for the eighth time. Hubbell didn't play as the American League beat the Nationals 7-5. The American League won the game in the bottom of the ninth after trailing 5-3. Ted Williams hit a three-run homer to cap a four-run rally with two out. The walk-off was one of the most exciting home runs in All-Star Game history.

As he did in previous years, Hubbell showed signs of the young Meal Ticket when he beat Bill Lee and the Chicago Cubs, 2-0. Although he did allow eight hits and walked one batter, it still brought back fond memories to Giant fans of Hub's fabulous five seasons. Also, it was Hubbell's last shutout of his career, number 36. He finished the season with a mark of 11-9 and a 3.57 earned run average in 164 innings. Looking back over the glory years, when he pitched over 300 innings, it was a clear indication Hubbell was on his way out. In addition, Terry and the Giants were having their problems. The Giants finished fifth, 25½ back of Brooklyn.

In 1942, as the baseball season rolled around, the United States found itself in the early stages of World War II. Although the war affected every American institution, including baseball, President Roosevelt gave the "green light" to proceed as usual. Nowhere near as devastating as the war, manager Bill Terry announced his resignation. His replacement was none other than Mel Ott, soon to be the former roommate of Hubbell. Regardless of who was managing the Giants in 1942, Hub's arm was still the problem, whether starting a game or in relief, as he admitted. "The screwball isn't what it used to be. It just couldn't be because I no longer can put the snap on it that I used to. The old arm has twisted around too much for that. And, of course, I can't throw as hard as I used to, either."[7]

By season's end, the results were the same for Hubbell and the New York Giants, not good. Hub's record was 11-8 with a 3.95 ERA in 157 1/3 innings. In his first year as manager, Ott brought the Giants back to third place with a credible record of 85-67. The acquisition of Johnny Mize from the Cardinals helped the offense as the big first baseman batted .305 with 26 home runs and a team-high 110 RBI's. At least that's the way it looked at first glance. But a closer examination reveals the Giants were never seriously in the race. They finished 20 games back of St. Louis, which took the shine off the third-place finish.

As in previous seasons since his surgery, Hub pitched some noteworthy games in 1942. One of those games was on May 17 when he stymied the World Champion St. Louis Cardinals 7-1. Hub scattered eight hits to pick up his first win of the season. The Giants scored four runs in the first inning off Ernie White, and that's all Hub needed, reminding fans of the old days.

On July 11, after a string of losses and a record of 1-6, he beat the World Champs again, this time 8-3. He pitched the full nine innings, giving up nine hits but issuing only one walk. The victory was the start of a personal eight-game winning streak. Although it was welcome and joyful, Hub knew in his heart, if not his arm, his days were numbered as one of the elite pitchers in baseball. Inevitably, Hub's streak ended August 25 as Cincinnati beat him 3-1.

Even with the tainted third-place finish, Giant fans were hoping it was a steppingstone, and Ott could revitalize the Giants for the 1943 season. It did not happen and, in fact, was just the opposite. As author Hynd so boldly points out, "The 1943 season was one of the worst in the history of the New York Giants."[8] Mize, Danning, Dave Koslo, and Schumacher left for military duty, which meant the Giants were without a first baseman, catcher, and a diminished pitching staff. In addition, Commissioner Landis asked all major league teams to train in the North. The Giants trained at Lakewood, New Jersey, on a wooded estate owned by the Rockefeller family. "The practice diamonds were gently carved out of a golf course where the old monopolist himself had once handed out dime tips to caddies who'd earned his favor. The players stayed in a mansion that had also once been the residence of John D. the First. It featured private rooms for the players, a jukebox, and, most importantly, heat. When spring began, the edge of the golf course was blanketed with snow."[9]

It appears from Hynd's description, the accommodations for the Giants were more than satisfactory. However, New Jersey was not conducive to a spring training camp. It was noted for its unpredictable spring weather, mostly cold, damp days, and not unusual to have rain and snow. Hot or even warm days were rare. Clearly, New Jersey weather was not good for Hubbell, who at age 40 lacked the arm strength and stamina he showed since the bone chips were removed from his left elbow.

As expected, Hubbell was not ready to pitch when the season opened. His first start came May 13 at the Polo Grounds against the Chicago Cubs. He left in the seventh trailing 4-1. But the Giants scored six in the bottom of the ninth, led by Bartell's three-run homer to win the game for the Giants.

The next game Hub pitched was on May 23 against St. Louis, and his performance was even worse than against Chicago. In three innings, he gave up eight hits and four runs before Ott yanked him. Bill Sayles came on in relief and was not up to the task. The Giants lost 6-5 as Sayles was charged with the loss.

It was quite evident, the so-called spring training in Lakewood did little preparing Hub for the '43 season. By June 5, however, the real Carl Hubbell showed up at Forbes Field and brought back wonderful memories of the fabulous five seasons. Hub went the distance and almost pitched a no-hitter. If it weren't for the Pirates Elbie Fletcher's seventh-inning solo shot, he would have. It was Hub's 250th major league victory, a milestone for the great lefty.

After his noteworthy victory, Hub went on to beat Philadelphia 6-2 on June 13 in another complete game. Six days later, still pitching with finesse and guile, he beat Boston 5-3 but needed relief help after seven innings. His record was 3-0. However, the seven-inning stint against Boston might have been the tell-tale sign the end of a legendary career was near.

For Hub lost his next four starts with plenty of rest between each. In two of the losses, one against Boston, the other St. Louis, he didn't go beyond the sixth inning. Against Chicago, he lasted three innings and Pittsburgh four and a third. His record was now 3-4.

After a long rest and the four defeats behind him, Hubbell pitched his last game as a starter. The date was August 18. He beat Pittsburgh 3-2. He allowed nine hits and walked three, evening his record at 4-4. It was his 253rd and final victory as a major league pitcher. In hindsight, this should have been the perfect time to call it a career. It was a positive moment. He won the game. What could he have been thinking? Was he waiting for one more victory? Those questions and others were never asked, as history shows.

Hubbell's final game was six days later, on August 24. The game was at the Polo Grounds against the Chicago Cubs. Ott was ill, so coach Adolfo Luque took over. For some strange reason, Hubbell entered the game in the eighth and pitched to two batters, Bill Nicholson and Ival Goodman. Biographer Blaisdell continues the story from here. "Each batter swung at Hubbell's first pitch and singled sharply. Carl thereupon left the engagement, the pitch to Goodman the last one he ever threw in his major and minor league career. In this ignominious fashion, his pitching days drew to a close. Hubbell deserved a celebratory departure commensurate with his greatness as a hurler. Wartime conditions, of course, precluded it. As it actually ended, he departed as unheralded as he had come."[10]

While Hubbell was struggling during the 1943 season and finally calling it quits, the Giants and manager Ott had their troubles too. As most teams did, the Giants lost many good players to the war. Those clubs that had depth were in much better shape than the Giants, who didn't. So, Ott picked up catcher Ernie Lombardi from the Braves, pitcher Ken Chase from the Red Sox, and Ducky Medwick to help in the outfield.

In late July, Ott pulled off a "blockbuster," sending Bill Sayles, Bill Lohrman, and Joe Orengo to Brooklyn for pitcher Johnny Allen and first baseman Dolf Camilli. All this activity was to no avail. In addition, one could argue the pressure of winning that faced Ott, with lesser talent, affected his season. The Giants finished last 55-98 and an ugly 45½ games back of St. Louis. Ott batted .234, the lowest in 18 years, and walloped 18 home runs. The last season he hit 18 was in 1928. His RBI total of 47 was the lowest since 1927.

The Giants' last-place finish wasn't the reason Hubbell retired, but it certainly didn't help. He told Ott he couldn't help him anymore. Ott agreed, and Hub resigned. Hub admitted years later, in an interview with Ed Fitzgerald, his arm was the problem. "My arm was never the same after the operation. It never came back. It didn't hurt, I could throw, but I just couldn't get any stuff on the ball. Funny."[11]

Carl Hubbell wasn't retired very long. In December 1943, Giant president Horace Stoneham announced to the press the naming of King Carl as the "Field Director of Minor League Clubs." It couldn't have come at a better time. The Giants were desperate to build up their farm system like Branch Rickey was doing in St. Louis. At the time, New York owned two clubs: Jersey City in the International League (Double A) and Bristol in the Appalachian League (Class D). Hubbell was 40 years old, too young to sit home in a rocking chair, so it was the perfect fit.

The Giants counted heavily on Hub to build the farm system, working with nine scouts throughout the country. They were also counting on his fame and personality to help in his success. Hubbell didn't disappoint Stoneham or Ott as he took to the job immediately and didn't mind the extensive traveling. One of his first moves was to hook up with Springfield of the Ohio State League and Erie of the Pony League. Both clubs were considered Class D. By 1946, Hubbell had built the farm system to the point he was rewarded with a five-year contract at $20,000 per year. As reported in the press, "Hubbell is director of a chain that embraces eleven minor league clubs and includes more than a dozen scouts in different sections of the country. Eight farm clubs operate under working agreements, three the Giants own outright."[12]

The three teams the Giants own are: Jersey City in the International League, Trenton in the Interstate League, and Fort Smith in the Western League. Early on, Hubbell was a hands-on director, going down on the field with the young kids, showing them what they were doing wrong. Hub preferred this approach rather than sitting in the stands and observing. He strongly believed this was the best way to help the youngsters.

While Hubbell was kept busy with his duties overseeing the Giants' growing farm system, he received exciting news from Cooperstown. On January 21, 1947, Carl Hubbell was elected to baseball's Hall of Fame. But Hub wasn't alone. His three associates elected at the same time were Frankie Frisch, Mickey Cochrane, and Lefty Grove . . . the class of '47. What a foursome. All you can say is WOW!

During Hubbell's long tenure as farm director, the Giants won three pennants in 1951, 1954, and 1962. The club also won the World Series in 1954. This was the Series in which the Cleveland Indians were heavily favored to win. Shockingly, the Giants swept the Indians in four. Some of the most famous baseball names came up through the Giant farm system run by Hubbell—Bobby

Thomson, Bobby Bonds, and Juan Marichal are just a few. The most celebrated, of course, is Willie Mays.

Then in 1957, the New York Giants and Brooklyn Dodgers moved to California—the Giants to San Francisco and the Dodgers to Los Angeles. Hubbell stayed the course and moved with the Giants organization. However, as Hubbell aged, his influence appeared to dwindle over the next two decades.

According to biographer Buckallew, "Hubbell turned sixty the summer after the Giants won their 1962 pennant, and it would certainly not be unusual for a sexagenarian to find that his ideas and methods were beginning to be discounted."[13]

By 1973 it appeared Hubbell's influence was diminishing as he was moved to the "minor league department" as the director of player development. He was 70 years old and not in the best of health. Then in 1977, he suffered a severe stroke. He was in a coma for weeks but finally recovered to the point he could walk with the aid of a cane. Years later, in an interview with Roberts, he explained the after effect. "I had no balance whatsoever, and I crippled my leg. I have hardly enough life in my leg to stand up or bend. It affected nearly every faculty I had. I can drive my car now, and I can get to the ball games,"[14]

In the meantime, Stoneham sold the club to Bob Lurie and employed Spec Richardson as the general manager. Richardson wasted no time and moved Hubbell into semi-retirement. According to Blaisdell, "Lurie provided him with a small yearly pension. In return, Hubbell was to do occasional college and high school scouting on behalf of his old team."[15]

Hubbell was now living in Mesa, Arizona, in an apartment by himself and financially not well off. His wife, former (Sue) Herrington, had died in 1967. They had two boys: Carl Jr. and James. Both lived out of state. Also, it is unclear whether Hubbell remarried after Sue's death to Julia Stanfield.

On the surface, it appeared to be a lonely life, but Hub still managed to get out once in a while. Sadly, on the morning of November 18, 1988, Hubbell was out driving near his Mesa home, lost control of his car, and the vehicle struck a metal pole. He was taken to the Scottsdale Memorial Hospital-Osborn in Scottsdale, Arizona. Two days later, on November 21, Hubbell died from "head and chest injuries." Doctors speculated the cause of the accident could have been another stroke.

On November 28, a week later, the Memorial Service was held at 2:00 pm at the Meeker, Oklahoma, High School Gym. Presiding over the ceremony was Vernon Markwell, president of the Carl Hubbell Museum in Meeker and longtime friend. Markwell did a marvelous job in presenting the eulogy. He traced Hub's baseball career from the time he "began to throw rocks and a worn-out baseball on the side of the barn" to his election to the Hall of Fame. Markwell also spoke about Hubbell, the man, and the wonderful qualities he possessed, attested to over the years by many celebrities.

"And that brings me to remembering some of the other characteristics of Carl Hubbell . . . for through all of these years and all of these outstanding achievements, even to becoming famous, Carl was and remained a humble man, a kind man, a modest man, and a quiet man."[16]

Those few lines by Vernon spoke volumes about Carl Hubbell, the man.

Appendix A

Carl Hubbell's 1933 45 1/3
Consecutive Scoreless Innings

DATE	OPPONENT	LOCATION	SCORE	INNINGS	CUMMU-LATIVE	HOW ACHIEVED	WINNER
July 13	St. Louis	Away	3-2	3	3	Started	Giants/Hubbell
July 16	Cincinnati	Away	1-0	9	12	Started	Giants/Hubbell
July 19	Pittsburgh	Away	7-3	8 1/3	20 1/3	Relief	Giants/Hubbell
July 22	Pittsburgh	Away	1-0	9	29 1/3	Started	Giants/Hubbell
July 27	Brooklyn	Home	2-0	9	38 1/3	Started	Giants/Hubbell
July 30	Boston	Home	5-3	2	40 1/3	Relief*	Boston/Cantwell
August 1	Boston	Home	3-1	5	45 1/3	Started**	Boston/Betts

*Hubbell received a no-decision. Schumacher lost.
**Hubbell lost. Record at the time was 16-7.

Source: Baseball Almanac, *1933 New York Times*

Appendix B

Carl Hubbell's 1933
Shutout Record

DATE	OPPONENT	LOCATION	SCORE	INNINGS	HITS	WALKS	STRIKE-OUTS
April 20	Boston	Home	1-0	9	4	2	13
April 24	Brooklyn	Home	4-0	9	4	3	6
May 7	Cincinnati	Home	1-0	9	5	1	5
June 22	Cincinnati	Home	4-0	9	5	2	0
July 2	St. Louis	Home	1-0	18	6	0	12
July 16	Cincinnati	Away	1-0	9	8	0	2
July 22	Pittsburgh	Away	1-0	9	6	0	4
July 27	Brooklyn	Home	2-0	9	4	3	3
August 29	St. Louis	Home	3-0	9	5	1	12
Sept 1	Boston	Away	2-0	10	4	1	6

Source: *Baseball Almanac*, 1933 *New York Times*

Appendix C

Carl Hubbell's 1933
Won/Lost Record (23-12)

DATE	OPPONENT	LOCATION	SCORE	WON	LOST	CUMMU-LATIVE	REMARKS
April 20	Boston	Home	1-0	x		1-0	Shutout #1
April 24	Brooklyn	Home	4-0	x		2-0	Shutout #2
April 27	Philadelphia	Home	5-2	x		3-0	Won in relief
April 30	Boston	Away	3-0		x	3-1	
May 7	Cincinnati	Home	1-0	x		4-1	Shutout #3
May 11	Pittsburgh	Home	7-6		x	4-2	
May 16	Chicago	Away	4-1	x		5-2	
May 21	St. Louis	Away	2-1		x	5-3	
May 28	Brooklyn	Away	5-4		x	5-4	
June 2	Philadelphia	Away	11-3	x		6-4	
June 6	Brooklyn	Away	7-2	x		7-4	
June 8	Philadelphia	Home	7-6	x		8-4	Won in relief
June 13	Boston	Home	6-3	x		9-4	
June 22	Cincinnati	Home	4-0	x		10-4	Shutout #4
June 28	Pittsburgh	Home	5-2		x	10-5	
July 2	St. Louis	Home	1-0	x		11-5	18 innings; Shutout #5
July 9	Chicago	Away	4-0		x	11-6	
July 13	St. Louis	Away	3-2	x		12-6	
July 16	Cincinnati	Away	1-0	x		13-6	Shutout #6
July 19	Pittsburgh	Away	7-3	x		14-6	Won in relief
July 22	Pittsburgh	Away	1-0	x		15-6	Shutout #7
July 27	Brooklyn	Home	2-0	x		16-6	Shutout #8
August 1	Boston	Home	3-1		x	16-7	
August 6	Brooklyn	Away	6-3		x	16-8	
August 13	Philadelphia	Home	2-1		x	16-9	
August 19	Chicago	Home	8-4	x		17-9	
August 26	Pittsburgh	Home	2-1	x		18-9	
August 29	St. Louis	Home	3-0	x		19-9	Shutout #9
Sept 1	Boston	Away	2-0	x		20-9	10 innings; Shutout #10
Sept 5	Pittsburgh	Away	6-1		x	20-10	
Sept 8	Pittsburgh	Away	2-1	x		21-10	
Sept 13	Chicago	Away	2-0		x	21-11	
Sept 16	Chicago	Away	2-1	x		22-11	
Sept 18	St. Louis	Away	4-3		x	22-12	Lost in relief
Sept 27	Philadelphia	Home	3-1	x		23-12	

Source: Baseball Almanac, *1933 New York Times*

Appendix D

Carl Hubbell's 1934
Won/Loss Record (21-12)

DATE	OPPONENT	LOCATION	SCORE	WON	LOST	CUMMU-LATIVE	REMARKS
April 17	Philadelphia	Home	6-1	x		1-0	
April 21	Boston	Home	2-0	x		2-0	Shutout #1
April 28	Boston	Away	4-1	x		3-0	
May 4	Pittsburgh	Away	4-3		x	3-1	
May 7	Cincinnati	Away	3-2	x		4-1	
May 11	St. Louis	Away	3-2		x	4-2	10 innings
May 15	Chicago	Away	10-3	x		5-2	
May 20	St. Louis	Home	9-5		x	5-3	
May 24	Chicago	Home	7-1	x		6-3	
May 28	Pittsburgh	Home	1-0	x		7-3	Shutout #2
June 6	Boston	Home	6-2	x		8-3	
June 10	Philadelphia	Away	18-7	x		9-3	
June 16	Pittsburgh	Away	5-2	x		10-3	
June 21	Chicago	Away	4-0		x	10-4	
June 25	St. Louis	Away	10-7	x		11-4	
June 30	Brooklyn	Home	8-4		x	11-5	
July 4	Boston	Home	15-0	x		12-5	Shutout #3
July 12	Pittsburgh	Home	11-1	x		13-5	
July 17	Chicago	Home	2-1		x	13-6	
July 21	Cincinnati	Home	3-2		x	13-7	
July 26	St. Louis	Home	7-2		x	13-8	
July 29	Philadelphia	Home	2-0	x		14-8	Shutout #4
August 3	Philadelphia	Away	2-0	x		15-8	Shutout #5
August 7	Brooklyn	Home	6-4	x		16-8	Won in relief
August 10	Boston	Home	6-3	x		17-8	
August 14	Pittsburgh	Away	3-2		x	17-9	
August 17	Pittsburgh	Away	8-3	x		18-9	
August 29	Chicago	Away	1-0		x	18-10	
Sept 4	Philadelphia	Away	3-2	x		19-10	
Sept 7	Chicago	Home	4-2		x	19-11	
Sept 12	Pittsburgh	Home	3-2	x		20-11	
Sept 16	St. Louis	Home	3-1		x	20-12	11 innings
Sept 20	Cincinnati	Home	4-3	x		21-12	

Source: Baseball Almanac, *1934 New York Times*

Appendix E

Carl Hubbell's 1935
Won/Lost Record (23-12)

DATE	OPPONENT	LOCATION	SCORE	WON	LOST	CUMMU-LATIVE	REMARKS
April 16	Boston	Away	4-2		x	0-1	
April 20	Philadelphia	Away	6-4	x		101	Won in relief
April 22	Philadelphia	Away	8-1	x		2-1	
April 26	Philadelphia	Home	5-5			2-1	13 innings
May 3	Cincinnati	Home	9-2	x		3-1	
May 9	Pittsburgh	Home	3-1	x		4-1	
May 13	St. Louis	Home	3-2		x	4-2	10 innings
May 20	Pittsburgh	Away	11-4		x	4-3	
May 25	Chicago	Away	3-2	x		5-3	
May 31	Boston	Away	4-2	x		6-3	
June 5	Philadelphia	Away	7-4	x		7-3	
June 12	Cincinnati	Home	10-4	x		8-3	
June 16	St. Louis	Home	7-3	x		9-3	
June 29	Brooklyn	Away	3-2		x	9-4	Lost in relief
July 3	Philadelphia	Home	4-3		x	9-5	10 innings
July 7	Brooklyn	Home	9-2	x		10-5	
July 13	Pittsburgh	Away	7-6	x		11-5	
July 17	Cincinnati	Away	6-3	x		12-5	
July 21	Chicago	Away	5-4		x	12-6	
July 24	St. Louis	Away	4-2	x		13-6	
July 28	Brooklyn	Away	6-0	x		14-6	Shutout #1
July 31	Philadelphia	Home	5-3		x	14-7	
August 4	Boston	Home	3-1	x		15-7	
August 8	Philadelphia	Away	6-3		x	15-8	
August 14	St. Louis	Home	6-4	x		16-8	
August 18	Cincinnati	Home	8-4	x		17-8	
August 20	Cincinnati	Home	6-5	x		18-8	Won in relief
August 24	Chicago	Home	9-4	x		19-8	Won in relief
August 28	Pittsburgh	Home	6-1		x	19-9	
Sept 4	Cincinnati	Away	6-4	x		20-9	
Sept 8	Pittsburgh	Away	3-1	x		21-9	
Sept 12	St. Louis	Away	5-2		x	21-10	
Sept 15	St. Louis	Away	7-3	x		22-10	
Sept 19	Chicago	Away	6-1		x	22-11	
Sept 23	Boston	Home	3-2	x		23-11	
Sept 27	Boston	Away	6-4		x	23-12	

Source: Baseball Almanac, *1935 New York Times*

Appendix F

Carl Hubbell's 1936
Won/Lost Record (26-6)

DATE	OPPONENT	LOCATION	SCORE	WON	LOST	CUMMU-LATIVE	REMARKS
April 17	Boston	Away	6-4	x		1-0	
April 22	Philadelphia	Home	7-2	x		2-0	
April 29	St. Louis	Away	2-1		x	2-1	16 1/3 innings
May 4	Cincinnati	Away	1-0		x	2-2	
May 9	Philadelphia	Away	5-3		x	2-3	
May 14	Chicago	Home	5-0	x		3-3	Shutout #1
May 18	Pittsburgh	Home	4-2	x		4-3	
May 23	Philadelphia	Home	9-0	x		5-3	Shutout #2
May 27	Brooklyn	Home	5-4	x		6-3	12 innings
June 6	St. Louis	Away	4-3	x		7-3	
June 12	Pittsburgh	Away	3-2		x	7-4	
June 16	Cincinnati	Home	5-2	x		8-4	
June 20	St. Louis	Home	7-6	x		9-4	
June 24	Pittsburgh	Home	4-3	x		10-4	
June 28	Chicago	Home	3-0		x	10-5	
July 13	Chicago	Away	1-0		x	10-6	
July 17	Pittsburgh	Away	6-0	x		11-6	Shutout #3; Start of streak (24)
July 19	Cincinnati	Away	4-3	x		12-6	Won in relief
July 21	St. Louis	Home	2-1	x		13-6	10 innings
July 30	Chicago	Home	3-1	x		14-6	
August 2	Pittsburgh	Home	3-2	x		15-6	
August 8	Philadelphia	Away	3-2	x		16-6	
August 15	Philadelphia	Home	4-1	x		17-6	
August 19	Brooklyn	Home	3-2	x		18-6	
August 26	Cincinnati	Away	6-5	x		19-6	
August 30	Chicago	Away	6-1	x		20-6	
Sept 3	St. Louis	Away	2-1	x		21-6	
Sept 7	Philadelphia	Away	6-2	x		22-6	
Sept 11	Chicago	Home	5-1	x		23-6	
Sept 14	St. Louis	Home	7-5	x		24-6	Won in relief
Sept 19	Brooklyn	Away	9-1	x		25-6	
Sept 23	Philadelphia	Away	5-4	x		26-6	

Source: Baseball Almanac, *1936 New York Times*

Appendix G

Carl Hubbell's 1937
Won/Lost Record (22-8)

DATE	OPPONENT	LOCATION	SCORE	WON	LOST	CUMMU-LATIVE	REMARKS
April 23	Boston	Home	3-0	x		1-0	Shutout #1
April 30	Brooklyn	Home	11-2	x		2-0	
May 4	Cincinnati	Home	7-6	x		3-0	
May 9	Chicago	Home	4-1	x		4-0	
May 13	Pittsburgh	Home	5-2	x		5-0	
May 19	St. Louis	Away	4-1	x		6-0	
May 24	Pittsburgh	Away	4-3	x		7-0	
May 27	Cincinnati	Away	3-2	x		8-0	Won in relief
May 31	Brooklyn	Home	10-3		x	8-1	End of streak
June 9	St. Louis	Home	8-1		x	8-2	
June 15	Pittsburgh	Away	7-5		x	8-3	
June 18	Cincinnati	Away	5-3		x	8-4	
June 23	Chicago	Away	8-4	x		9-4	
June 27	St. Louis	Away	8-1	x		10-4	
July 2	Boston	Home	6-2	x		11-4	
July 10	Brooklyn	Away	4-0	x		12-4	Shutout #2
July 14	Pittsburgh	Home	4-2	x		13-4	
July 18	St. Louis	Home	6-5	x		14-4	
July 23	Chicago	Home	11-3		x	14-5	
July 31	Chicago	Away	7-1		x	14-6	
August 6	Pittsburgh	Away	6-3	x		15-6	
August 13	Philadelphia	Home	5-0	x		16-6	Shutout #3
August 18	Boston	Away	9-1	x		17-6	
Sept 4	Brooklyn	Home	3-0	x		18-6	Shutout #4
Sept 9	Brooklyn	Away	5-1		x	18-7	
Sept 14	Pittsburgh	Away	12-2	x		19-7	
Sept 18	Cincinnati	Away	4-3		x	19-8	
Sept 20	St. Louis	Away	10-3	x		20-8	Won in relief
Sept 23	Chicago	Away	8-7	x		21-8	Won in relief
Sept 30	Philadelphia	Away	2-1	x		22-8	

Source: Baseball Almanac, *1937 New York Times*

Appendix H

Carl Hubbell's 24 Consecutive Game Winning Streak (1936-1937)

1936

DATE	OPPONENT	LOCATION	SCORE	INNINGS PITCHED	CUMMULA-TIVE WINS	REMARKS
July 17	Pittsburgh	Away	6-0	9	1	Shutout #3
July 19	Cincinnati	Away	4-3	2 2/3	2	Won in relief
July 21	St. Louis	Home	2-1	10	3	
July 30	Chicago	Home	3-1	9	4	
August 2	Pittsburgh	Home	3-2	9	5	
August 8	Philadelphia	Away	3-2	9	6	
August 15	Philadelphia	Home	4-1	9	7	
August 19	Brooklyn	Home	3-2	9	8	
August 26	Cincinnati	Away	6-5	9	9	
August 30	Chicago	Away	6-1	9	10	
Sept 3	St. Louis	Away	2-1	9	11	
Sept 7	Philadelphia	Away	6-2	9	12	
Sept 11	Chicago	Home	5-1	9	13	
Sept 14	St. Louis	Home	7-5	5	14	Won in relief
Sept 19	Brooklyn	Away	9-1	9	15	
Sept 23	Philadelphia	Away	5-4	9	16	

1937

DATE	OPPONENT	LOCATION	SCORE	INNINGS PITCHED	CUMMULA-TIVE WINS	REMARKS
April 23	Boston	Home	3-0	9	17	Shutout #1
April 30	Brooklyn	Home	11-2	9	18	
May 4	Cincinnati	Home	7-6	6 2/3	19	
May 9	Chicago	Home	4-1	9	20	
May 13	Pittsburgh	Home	5-2	9	21	
May 19	St. Louis	Away	4-1	9	22	
May 24	Pittsburgh	Away	4-3	8 2/3	23	
May 27	Cincinnati	Away	3-2	2	24	Won in relief

Source: Baseball Almanac, *1936-1937 New York Times*

Appendix I

Carl Hubbell Quotes

"I learned that even the best hitters in the major leagues couldn't hit the screwball."

"When I get two strikes and no balls on a fellow, I never come right back with a third strike."

"I was learning by my own experience that the best ball I had was the screwball."

"If I'm playing cards for pennies, I want to win."

"Control is everything. Next comes a knowledge of each batsman's weak points."

"Hitters always have one thing in mind—they have to protect themselves against the fastball."

"You can't get by in this league on one pitch."

"I never forgot what McGraw told me about getting the ball over the plate."

"I came out of a small town in Oklahoma, and suddenly, I was playing for John McGraw."

"I could always come through with the screwball if I was in a spot."

"I think a fellow pitches with his legs and wind as much as with his arm."

"I didn't even know what a screwball was."

"What I really needed was a curve [later on]."

"Personally, I think I have several more years left as a player."

"My arm was never the same after the operation."

"When I first pitched, there wasn't a trainer anywhere who knew the first thing about an arm—not a doctor who knew anything about treating one."

"It probably was the greatest game [18 innings] I ever pitched."

"Once you get to the big leagues and become an established player, your next big ambition is to get into a World Series."

"I didn't care to become a manager. I never thought I had the right disposition for it."

"Unless you're awfully fast, and not many are, a pitcher hasn't got too much of a chance with a very lively ball."

"Baseball had been played for many years before I tried it [screwball], but I did develop it in the 1920s after watching a left-hander throw a sinking fastball in the minors."

"It was the screwball which struck out Babe Ruth, Lou Gehrig, Jimmy Foxx, Al Simmons and Joe Cronin, top hitters in the American League, in that All-Star game at the Polo Grounds in 1934. That feat took twenty-three pitches and gained me more recognition than many a longer and harder afternoon's work."

"I've tried never to let pitching success turn my head; but it has twisted my arm."

"One of the first lessons I learned in the big leagues was never to spurn the weakling."

"I can throw a fastball because I know how to throw it—not because I am fast."

"I noted it [screwball] became a semi-slow ball and dropped away from right-handed batters, and curved in on the left-handers. The batters seemed to have difficulty hitting it solidly. When I used the fast one or the wide curve, they'd whack it high and far."

". . . when a pitcher is going good, he must guard against complacency. It can set in unconsciously. I know I had to look out for it."

"I know I couldn't have won those games [24 consecutive] without the help of the other seven members behind me and the man behind the plate. They deserve the credit."

"If you can change speeds, that's a plus."

"I never felt the pressure of those 24 straight victories . . ."

"What made it [screwball] work for me was I threw it with the same overhand motion as my fastball and curveball. It served as my change of pace too."

"I like to remember baseball at that time [when he played]. There was a fondness for the game. They played it because they loved it. It wasn't a business for us."

"I always felt like the underdog. When I did finally get to the big leagues, I still felt like an underdog."

"I was never really a strikeout pitcher, I always preferred to throw one pitch and get a ground ball."

"In the 1930s, we had the Depression, and you sure as hell didn't want anybody to get your job. There were millions of people in breadlines, and you didn't want to go back to that."

"Like all pitchers, I had a fastball and a curve. But I noticed that every pitcher who eventually made the big show had a little bit more than the standard equipment."

"It's a fast game, but you have to slow down to play."

"The toughest job of all was not winning the 24 games [consecutive streak] but living up to the expectations."

"I never tried to set any streaks or go for any kind of record. It just happened."

"Nobody makes an error on purpose. All you can do is bear down harder and resist the temptation to blame the other fellow."

"You can pitch with a sore elbow, but not with a bad shoulder."

"But I was able to do both starting and relieving. You know some pitchers cannot."

"Oh, I got him [Gabby Hartnett] out my share of times, but he always scared me, just standing there, twisting sawdust out of a bat with his bare hands."

"But, thanks to that All-Star game [1934], people think about me at least once a year."

(Source: Multiple)

Appendix J

Quotes about Carl Hubbell

"Hub was the best left-hander of my time . . ." —FREDDIE FITZSIMMONS

"Such control in a left-hander is incredible. There must be a skeleton in Hubbell's closet somewhere, perhaps a right-handed maternal grandmother."
—HEYWOOD BROWN

"I find the best way to bat against him is to go up there, say a little prayer, close your eyes, and swing. If you're lucky, you may connect." —GABBY HARTNETT

"No team in the world can beat Hub twice in a row." —BILL TERRY

"When Hubbell is right, he has more than any pitcher I ever saw."
—DOLLY STARK, UMPIRE

"The source of his skill is his matchless control in using his curveball to set up his screwball. Emotions, if he has any, never affect him." —WAITE HOYT

"Trying to lift Carl Hubbell's screwball was like a guy trying to hit fungoes out of a well." —BASEBALL DIGEST

"Carl, I believe, had many characteristics, and one of the greatest was the determination to be the very best that he could be in what he did."
—VERNON MARKWELL, PRESIDENT OF THE CARL HUBBELL MUSEUM

"Carl wasn't argumentative. He wasn't a very talkative person, but he was a wonderful fella. He never caused a fuss when I was officiating a game."
—JOCKO CONLON, UMPIRE

"Carl was a humble sort who talked about himself only after every other subject was exhausted." —VERNON MARKWELL

"Shoot, I knew Carl was about to run out of stuff after 18 innings, so I decided to come home and score the run to end the game." —JO-JO MOORE

"I never saw a pitch [screwball] quite like it." —LOU GEHRIG

"He's a great pitcher, no doubt about that. I'd say he's the best there is . . ."
—JOE MCCARTHY

"He could throw strikes at midnight." —BILLY HERMAN

"I could play second base fifteen more years behind that guy. He doesn't need any help. He does it all by himself." —FRANKIE FRISCH

"He could close his eyes and throw strikes; his control was that perfect."
—BILLY HERMAN

"One of the best pitchers of all time. Give him a one-run lead, and that's all he needed to win." —JO-JO MOORE

"Listen, this Hubbell is twice the pitcher Dean is . . ."
—JIM COLLINS, HALL OF FAME

(Source: Multiple)

Notes

Preface

1. Kevin Kerrane, *The Hurlers* (Virginia: Redefinition, 1989), 39.

Chapter One: A Bumpy Road to the Major Leagues

1. Fritz A. Buckallew, *A Pitcher's Moment Carl Hubbell and the Quest for Baseball Immortality* (Oklahoma City: Forty Sixth Star Press, 2010), 8.
2. Rod Roberts interview with Carl Hubbell. Date unknown. Hubbell's Hall of Fame player file, 2.
3. Sid C. Keener, "Carl Hubbell Reveals His Secrets," a clipping in Hubbell's Hall of Fame player file.
4. Fritz A. Buckallew, *A Pitcher's Moment Carl Hubbell and the Quest for Baseball Immortality*, 12.
5. Rod Roberts interview with Carl Hubbell, 3.
6. Sid C. Keener, "Carl Hubbell Reveals His Secrets," a clipping in Hubbell's Hall of Fame player file.
7. Ibid.
8. Lowell L. Blaisdell, *Carl Hubbell A Biography of the Screwball King* (NC: McFarland & Company, Inc., Publishers, 2011), 9.
9. Rod Roberts interview with Carl Hubbell, 6–7.
10. Peter Levine, ed., *Baseball History 2* (Connecticut: Meckler Books, 1989), 79.
11. Ibid., 81.
12. David Wencer, "Historicist: Hats off to Howley and his Hustling Horde," October 10, 2015, https://torontoist.com/2015/10/historicist-hats-off-to-howley-and-his-hustling-horde/.

Chapter Two: An Eye-Opening Rookie Season

1. Fred Stein, *Under Coogan's Bluff* (Maryland: Automated Graphic Systems, 1978), 1.
2. CBS News Website.
3. Fritz A. Buckallew, *A Pitcher's Moment: Carl Hubbell and the Quest for Baseball Immortality* (Oklahoma City: Forty-Sixth Star Press, 2010), 32–33.
4. Ed Fitzgerald, "King Carl the Meal Ticket," a clipping in Hubbell's Hall of Fame player file.
5. Nathan Salant, *Superstars, Stars, and Just Plain Heroes* (New York: Stein and Day, 1982), 176–177.
6. Ibid., 177.
7. Joseph Wallace, *The Autobiography of Baseball* (New York: Harry N. Abrams, Inc., 1998), 27.
8. "Travis Jackson, 84 Played Baseball for New York Giants," a clipping in Jackson's Hall of Fame player file.
9. Greg Erion, Travis Jackson (SABR.ORG).
10. "Travis Jackson, 84 Played Baseball for New York Giants," a clipping in Jackson's Hall of Fame player file.
11. *The New York Times*, September 21, 1928, 22.
12. *The New York Times,* October 1, 1928, 18.

Chapter Three: Eighteen Wins . . . And a No-Hitter

1. Ray Schalk, Baseball Hall of Fame website.
2. *The New York Times,* December 14, 1928, 32.
3. *The New York Times,* January 6, 1929, Sports 3.
4. *The New York Times,* May 9, 1929, 23.
5. Ed Fitzgerald, "King Carl the Meal Ticket," a clipping in Hubbell's Hall of Fame player file.

6. Noel Hynd, *The Giants of the Polo Grounds* (New York: Doubleday, 1988), 276.
7. Noel Hynd, "Shanty at the Plate," a clipping in Shanty Hogan's Hall of Fame player file, 12.
8. Ibid.

Chapter Four: Almost a Second No-Hitter
1. *The New York Times,* May 22, 1930, 21.
2. Donald Honig, *The October Heroes* (New York: Simon and Schuster, 1979), 258–259.
3. Ibid., 255.
4. Ibid., 266–267.
5. John Bowman, "With Memories of the Hitters of Baseball Fame Comes Fred Lindstrom—Who Hit with the Best," a clipping in Lindstrom's Hall of Fame player file.
6. "Lindstrom's kin view induction," a clipping in Lindstrom's Hall of Fame player file.
7. Leonard Koppett, *Koppett's Concise History of Major League Baseball* (Philadelphia: Temple University Press, 1998), 179.

Chapter Five: Pitched Well but Lacked Support
1. *The New York Times*, February 4, 1931, 28.
2. *The New York Times*, March 3, 1931, 37.
3. *The Sporting News*, February 26, 1966, 9.
4. Noel Hynd, *The Giants of the Polo Grounds*, 263.
5. Ibid., 287.
6. Ibid., 305.
7. Red Barber, "Fat Freddie," a clipping in Fitzsimmons's Hall of Fame player file.

Chapter Six: Becoming the Ace
1. *The New York Times*, April 11, 1932, 20.
2. Fred Stein, *Under Coogan's Bluff,* 11.
3. Noel Hynd, *The Giants of the Polo Grounds,* 273.
4. *The New York Times*, June 4, 1932, 10.
5. Joseph Durso, *The Days of Mr. McGraw* (New Jersey: Prentice Hall, Inc., 1969), 215.
6. Anthony J. Conner, *Baseball for The Love of It* (New York: Macmillan Publishing Co. Inc., 1982), 165.
7. *The Sporting News,* September 19, 1935, 2.
8. An unidentified clipping in Mel Ott's Hall of Fame player file.
9. Cullen Cain, "Ott, Wonder Boy," a clipping in Ott's Hall of Fame player file.
10. Dan Parker, "Mr. Meek Takes the Reins," a clipping in Ott's Hall of Fame player file.
11. *The New York Times*, December 3, 1941, 34.
12. Mike Shatzkin, ed., *The Ballplayers* (New York: Arbor House, 1990), 834.

Chapter Seven: Most Wins, Lowest ERA, MVP
1. Fred Stein, *Under Coogan's Bluff,* 17.
2. Noel Hynd, *The Giants of the Polo Grounds,* 279.
3. *The New York Times*, April 11, 1933, 24.
4. Ibid.
5. Fred Fitzsimmons, "Did the Best Teams Get in The Series?" a clipping in Fitzsimmons Hall of fame player file.
6. *The New York Times*, May 17, 1933, 20.
7. Rod Roberts interview with Carl Hubbell, 9–10.
8. Nathan Salant, *Superstars, Stars and Just Plain Heroes*, 177.
9. *The New York Times*, June 23, 1933, 22.
10. Peter Williams, *When the Giants Were Giants* (North Carolina: Algonquin Books of Chapel Hill, 1994), 127.

11. Noel Hynd, *The Giants of the Polo Grounds*, 283–284.
12. Mike Shatzkin, ed., *The Ballplayers,* 771.
13. *The Sporting News,* August 10, 1933, 1.
14. *The New York Times*, September 2, 1933, 7.
15. Fred Stein, *Under Coogan's Bluff*, 22.
16. Peter Williams, *When the Giants Were Giants*, 153.
17. *The Sporting News,* September 7, 1933, 1.
18. *The New York Times*, October 3, 1933, 29.
19. Ibid.
20. Peter Williams, *When the Giants Were Giants,* 158.
21. Ibid., 159.
22. Ibid., 161.

Chapter Eight: Lowest ERA, Most Saves

1. "Mancuso Suffers Mild Typhoid Case," a clipping in Gus Mancuso's Hall of Fame player file.
2. Fred Stein, *Under Coogan's Bluff*, 33.
3. Ibid.
4. *The New York Times*, February 26, 1934, 23.
5. Fred Stein, *Under Coogan's Bluff*, 34.
6. Mike Shatzkin, ed., *The Ballplayers*, 909–910.
7. "Mancuso's Pluck Won Fight for Major League Career," a clipping in Mancuso's Hall of Fame player file.
8. Ibid.
9. Warren Corbett, Gus Mancuso (SABR.ORG).
10. "Mancuso's Pluck Won Fight for Major League Career," a clipping in Mancuso's Hall of Fame player file.
11. Will Wedge, "Mancuso Proves His Mettle," a clipping in Mancuso's Hall of Fame player file.
12. Harold Parrott, "Player's Life Begins at Thirty, Says Mancuso," a clipping in Mancuso's Hall of Fame player file.
13. Edward T. Murphy, "Setting the Pace," a clipping in Mancuso's Hall of Fame player file.
14. "At Last the Secret's Out! Old Gus Taking 'Em Too," a clipping in Mancuso's Hall of Fame player file.
15. An unidentified clipping in Mancuso's Hall of Fame player file.
16. *The New York Times*, May 25, 1934, 27.
17. Noel Hynd, *The Giants of the Polo Grounds*, 294.
18. *The New York Times,* June 15, 1934, 27.
19. Peter Williams, *When the Giants Were Giants*, 173–174.
20. "Hubbell's Screwball Baffles American League Sluggers," a clipping in Hubbell's Hall of Fame player file.
21. *The New York Times,* July 30, 1934, 16.
22. Jack Kavanagh and Norman Mach, *Uncle Robbie* (Cleveland: The Society for American Baseball Research, 1999), 186.
23. *The New York Times,* August 10, 1934, 22.
24. *The New York Times,* September 13, 1934, 28.
25. Noel Hynd, *The Giants of the Polo Grounds*, 296.
26. *The New York Times*, October 1, 1934, 1.

Chapter Nine: Third Consecutive 20-Plus Season

1. *The New York Times,* October 30, 1934, 25.
2. Noel Hynd, *The Giants of the Polo Grounds,* 297.
3. Peter Williams, *When the Giants Were Giants*, 181.
4. *The New York Times*, November 3, 1934, Sports 9.
5. *The New York Times,* April 15, 1935, 23.
6. *The New York Times,* April 17, 1935, 30.
7. The Official Licensing Website of Amelia Earhart.
8. *The New York Times*, June 6, 1935, 26.
9. Ibid.

10. Peter Williams, *When the Giants Were Giants,* 187.
11. *The New York Times,* July 22, 1935, 10.
12. Leonard Koppett, *Koppett's Concise History of Major League Baseball,* 198.
13. Joe Moore, "I Learned About Baseball," a clipping in Jo-Jo Moore's Hall of Fame player file.
14. Jim Sargent, "Joe Moore," a clipping in Moore's Hall of Fame player file.
15. *The Sporting News,* July 31, 1930, 3.
16. Peter Williams, *When the Giants Were Giants,* 135.
17. Ibid., 136–137.
18. Mike Shatzkin, ed., *The Ballplayers,* 757.
19. Bill McCullough, "Jo-Jo Moore, Thin Man of Giants, Is Stout in All-Around Ability," a clipping in Moore's Hall of Fame player file.
20. Brent Kelley, "Joe Moore: New York's Consummate Team Player," a clipping in Moore's Hall of Fame player file.
21. Richard Goldstein, "Jo-Jo Moore, All-Star Outfielder In 1930s, Is Dead At 92," a clipping in Moore's Hall of Fame player file.
22. *The New York Times,* September 5, 1935, 27.
23. Peter Williams, *When the Giants Were Giants*, 188–189.

Chapter Ten: Most Wins, Highest WP, Lowest ERA, MVP

1. Fred Stein, *Under Coogan's Bluff,* 45.
2. *The New York Times,* January 7, 1936, 21.
3. *The New York Times,* April 13, 1936, 21.
4. Fred Stein, *Under Coogan's Bluff,* 46.
5. P.R. White, "Cardinals Grooming Whitehead on Farm as Eventual Successor to Frankie Frisch," a clipping in Burgess Whitehead's Hall of Fame player file.
6. An unidentified clipping in Whitehead's Hall of Fame player file.
7. Peter Williams, *When the Giants Were Giants,* 251.
8. Joe King, "Whitehead Giant Star in Comeback," a clipping in Whitehead's Hall of Fame player file.
9. C. Paul Rogers, Burgess Whitehead (SABR.ORG).
10. baseballinwartime.com Burgess Whitehead.
11. Bob Broeg, "Whitehead a Keystone Gazelle," a clipping in Whitehead's Hall of Fame player file.
12. Ibid.
13. Peter Williams, *When the Giants Were Giants,* 196.
14. *The New York Times,* July 3, 1936, 12.
15. *The New York Times,* July 10, 1936, 22.
16. Roger Gregory, *Diz* (New York: Viking, 1992), 293.
17. Ibid.
18. Ibid., 296.
19. *The New York Times,* August 14, 1936, 23.
20. Ibid.
21. *The New York Times,* September 4, 1936, 12.
22. *The New York Times,* September 24, 1936, 30.
23. Noel Hynd, *The Giants of the Polo Grounds,* 303.
24. *The Sporting News,* September 24, 1936, 1.
25. *The New York Times,* October 6, 1936, 31.

Chapter Eleven: Most Wins, Highest WP, Most Strikeouts

1. *The Sporting News,* April 8, 1937, 1.
2. Mike Shatzkin, ed., *The Ballplayers,* 187.
3. Peter Williams, *When the Giants Were Giants,* 224.
4. *The New York Times,* March 10, 1937, 30.
5. Ibid.
6. Peter Williams, *When the Giants Were Giants,* 229.

7. *The New York Times,* May 20, 1937, 25.
8. Ibid.
9. Peter Williams, *When the Giants Were Giants,* 231.
10. Ibid., 232.
11. Ibid., 233.
12. *The New York Times,* July 28, 1937, 23.
13. Harry Forbes, "The Slim Man," a clipping in Cliff Melton's Hall of Fame player file.
14. Ibid.
15. Christopher Tompkins, "The Giants' Twenty-Game Freshman," a clipping in Melton's Hall of Fame player file.
16. Joe King, "Melton's Rise Traced to New Pitching Grip," a clipping in Melton's Hall of Fame player file.
17. Joe King, "Melton Hero in Giant Drive," a clipping in Melton's Hall of Fame player file.
18. Ibid.
19. Joe King, "New Delivery Key to Rise of Melton," a clipping in Melton's Hall of Fame player file.
20. Fred Stein, *Under Coogan's Bluff,* 60.
21. Leonard Koppett, *Koppett's Concise History of Major League Baseball,* 200.
22. Peter Williams, *When the Giants Were Giants,* 237.
23. Alan H. Levy. *Joe McCarthy Architect of the Yankee Dynasty* (North Carolina: McFarland & Company, Inc., Publishers, 2005), 224.
24. Ibid., 225.
25. Peter Williams, *When the Giants Were Giants,* 242.

Chapter Twelve: Farewell and a New Career

1. Peter Williams, *When the Giants Were Giants,* 252–253.
2. Ed Fitzgerald, "King Carl the Meal Ticket," a clipping in Hubbell's Hall of Fame player file.
3. Ibid.
4. Rod Roberts interview with Carl Hubbell, 30.
5. Ed Fitzgerald, "King Carl the Meal Ticket," a clipping in Hubbell's Hall of Fame player file.
6. Ibid.
7. *The New York Times,* March 14, 1942, 20.
8. Noel Hynd, *The Giants of the Polo Grounds,* 326.
9. Ibid., 327.
10. Lowell L. Blaisdell, *Carl Hubbell A Biography of a Screwball King,* 175.
11. Ed Fitzgerald, "King Carl the Meal Ticket," a clipping in Hubbell's Hall of Fame player file.
12. James P. Dawson, "Hubbell Received 5-Year Contract," a clipping in Hubbell's Hall of Fame player file.
13. Fritz A. Buckallew, *A Pitcher's Moment Carl Hubbell and the Quest for Baseball Immortality,* 164.
14. Rod Roberts interview with Carl Hubbell, 42.
15. Lowell L. Blaisdell, *Carl Hubbell A Biography of a Screwball King,* 187.
16. Vernon Markwell, Eulogy in Hubbell's Hall of Fame player file.

Bibliography

Books

Appel, Marty. *Casey Stengel: Baseball's Greatest Character.* New York: Doubleday, 2017.

Astor, Gerald. *The Baseball Hall of Fame 50th Anniversary Book.* New York: Prentice-Hall Press, 1988.

Bak, Richard. *Peach: Ty Cobb in His Time and Ours.* Michigan: Sports Media Group, 2005.

Blaisdell, Lowell L. *Carl Hubbell: A Biography of the Screwball King.* North Carolina: McFarland & Company, Inc., Publishers, 2011.

Buckallew, Fritz A. *A Pitcher's Moment: Carl Hubbell and the Quest for Baseball Immortality.* Oklahoma City: Forty-Sixth Star Press, 2010.

Connor, Anthony T. *Baseball for The Love of It.* New York: Macmillan Publishing Co., Inc., 1982.

Curran, William. *Strikeout: A Celebration of the Art of Pitching.* New York: Crown Publishers, Inc., 1995.

Gregory, Robert. *Diz.* New York: Viking Penguin, 1992.

Grimm, Charlie and Ed Prell. *Jolly Cholly's Story: Baseball I Love You!* Chicago: Henry Regnery Company, 1968.

Hirshberg, Dan. *Phil Rizzuto: A Yankee Tradition.* Illinois: Sagamore Publishing, 1993.

Honig, Donald. *The October Heroes.* New York: Simon and Schuster, 1979.

Hynd, Noel. *The Giants of the Polo Grounds.* New York: Doubleday, 1988.

Kavanagh, Jack and Norman Macht. *Uncle Robbie.* Ohio: The Society for American Baseball Research (SABR), 1999.

Kerrane, Kevin. *The Hurlers.* Virginia: Redefinition, 1989.

Koppett, Leonard. *Koppett's Concise History of Major League Baseball.* Philadelphia: Temple University Press, 1998.

Levine, Peter, ed. *Baseball History 2.* Connecticut: Meckler Books, 1989.

Levy, Alan H. *Joe McCarthy Architect of the Yankee Dynasty.* North Carolina: McFarland & Company, Inc., Publishers, 2005.

Mayer Ronald A. *The 1923 New York Yankees: A History of their First Championship Season.* North Carolina: McFarland & Company, Inc., Publishers, 2010.

———. *Baseball Memories: A Collection of 101 Poems Celebrating Immortal Players Classic Games and Wacky Events of the National Pastime.* Pennsylvania: Sunbury Press, Inc., 2020.

Porter, David L., ed. *Biographical Dictionary of American Sports: Baseball.* Connecticut: Greenwood Press, 1987.

Reidenbaugh, Lowell. *Cooperstown: Where the Legends Live Forever.* New York: Gramercy Books, 1999.

Ritter, Lawrence and Donald Honig. *The Image of Their Greatness.* New York: Crown Publishers, Inc., 1984.

Salant, Nathan. *Superstars, Stars, and Just Plain Heroes.* New York: Stein and Day, 1982.

Shatzkin, Mike, ed. *The Ballplayers.* New York: Arbor House, 1990.

Stein, Fred. *Under Coogan's Bluff.* Maryland: Automated Graphic Systems, 1978.

Stump, Al. *Cobb: The Life and Times of the Meanest Man Who Ever Played Baseball.* North Carolina: Algonquin Books of Chapel Hill, 1994.

Sullivan, Neil. *The Minors.* New York: St. Martin's Press, 1990.

Wallace, Joseph. *The Autobiography of Baseball.* New York: Harry N. Abrams, Inc., Publishers, 1998.

Williams, Peter. *When the Giants Were Giants.* North Carolina: Algonquin Books of Chapel Hill, 1994.

Newspapers
The Brooklyn Daily Eagle, September 24, 1930.
The Brooklyn Daily Eagle, January 4, 1931.
Chicago Tribune, August 10, 1976.
Daily News, January 18, 1939.
The Daily Northwestern, May 25, 2018.
The New York Times, September-December 1928.
The New York Times, May-December 1929.
The New York Times, May 1930.
The New York Times, February-March 1931.
The New York Times, April-June 1932.
The New York Times, April-October 1933.
The New York Times, February-November 1934.
The New York Times, April-October 1935.
The New York Times, January-October 1936.
The New York Times, April-November 1937.
The New York Times, December 1941.
The Sporting News, May 2, 1970.
The Sporting News, August 21, 1930.
The Sporting News, August 14, 1930.
The Sporting News, February 26, 1966.
Torontoist, October 10, 2018.

Internet Resources
Ballparks of baseball.com
Baseball in Wartime
Baseball Universe
Bioproject (SABR.org)

CBS News website
Clem's Baseball Blog
Dave Bancroft Baseball Hall of Fame website
D.C. Baseball History
From Deep Right Field
MLB Trade Tracker
MyHeritage website
RetroSimba
Stats Crew
Vintage Detroit Collection

Articles and Periodicals

Fitzsimmons, Fred as told to Stanley Frank. "Did the Best Teams Get in the Series." *The Saturday Evening Post.* The story is in Fitzsimmons's Hall of Fame player file.

Index

Numbers in *bold italics* indicate pages with photographs.

About the Author

Ronald A. Mayer is an author of baseball history books. He's written about immortal players, single-season sagas, and even a collection of poems called *Baseball Memories* that celebrates America's favorite pastime in its biggest and smallest moments. He is a diehard New York Yankees fan through the good and not-so-good years, and he is an avid appreciator of the two greatest screwball pitchers of all time, Christy Mathewson and Carl Hubbell.

His love for the sport comes from his father, who in his later years, would intrigue him with stories of Babe Ruth, Lou Gehrig, Earle Combs, and Bill Dickey. As many boys did, he played the game as a youth and through his college days at Montclair State University. He gave up the dream of playing major league baseball, like so many others, when pitchers began throwing that dastardly curve ball. The same curve scientists once claimed was an optical illusion.

He is a former member of the Society for American Baseball Research (SABR) and a life-long resident of New Jersey. He currently resides in East Hanover with his wife Arlene.

Made in the USA
Las Vegas, NV
26 October 2024

10493693R00163